Dear Faye,

I hope you receive as much understanding, guidance and inspiration as I have from <u>studying</u> this book.

Love,
Phil

Why we need a life centered on God & Christ & how we attain it

To Sandra and our dear children
Cynthia
Maria
Stephen
Sean
David
Catherine
Colleen
Jenny
Joshua
each so satisfying and fulfilling to me

THE
DIVINE
CENTER

STEPHEN R. COVEY

BOOKCRAFT
Salt Lake City, Utah

Library of Congress Catalog Card Number: 82-73496
ISBN 0-88494-471-9

7th Printing, 1987

Lithographed in the United States of America
PUBLISHERS PRESS
Salt Lake City, Utah

Preface

For many years I have felt and seen the need for an organizing principle in life, a principle that would enable us to get a handle on things—unravel confusion, clarify relationships, get to the bottom line fast. The principle would have to be simple but not simplistic. It must also be capable of serving as the directing or controling center of a person's life.

This book is about that principle. I excitedly wrote the first draft over five years ago. Since then many synchronistic learning experiences have spurred considerable rewriting and reworking of the material. My central purpose is to invite readers to examine their faith and lives from a fresh perspective or angle, and consequently to deepen their commitment to the gospel of Jesus Christ. The approach is essentially inductive, that is, it starts with the specific (the problems) and moves to the general (suggested solutions).

As far as content is concerned, while I am fully responsible for what is written here, I acknowledge with a deep sense of gratitude and reverence the influence, encouragement, inspiration, and help of many individuals—truly too many to mention by name. These include family and friends, missionaries from the Irish Mission and elsewhere, Church leaders, mission and stake leaders, students, counselees, managers, professional colleagues, secretaries, editors, publishers, and good people in and out of the Church all over the world.

As to the manuscript and the book design, I must mention with appreciation and respect three people by name: Shirley Smith, for her loyal and able second-mile secretarial / managerial services; Michael Graves, for his splendid artistic sense and touch; and George Bickerstaff, senior editor at Bookcraft, for his unique talents, superb editorial assistance, and complete integrity.

Contents

The Perceived World *Chapter 1*

*For with thee is the fountain of life: in thy
light shall we see light. (Psalm 36:9.)*

This is a book about attaining the one perspective that puts
everything else in proper perspective. In recommending this
perspective I advocate a specific spiritual approach to life and its
problems, an approach which combines solid gospel principles
and practices with some of our modern understandings about
human motivations and relationships. The primary focus of the
book is behavior rather than doctrine. I suggest ways to achieve
the perspective and indicate the transcendent benefits to be ex-
pected from it.

Before I can attempt to do this, however, I must be sure that
you understand a major concept that leads up to it. And by
understand, as I have just used the word, I am not speaking
merely of an intellectual appreciation. For this reason I am inviting you—urging you, in fact—to have an experience. Have this
experience right now, before you get any further into this book.

This experience is a very simple one. It will take only a few
minutes but it is vitally important if you are really to understand
the essential approach to the message of this book.

Now, if you choose to keep on reading rather than to have
this experience, you will still come to understand *intellectually*
the point being made, but you won't understand it *emotionally*
as well. If you "feel" the point, however, you will not forget it,
and this could have a significant impact for good upon you as
you read the book—and perhaps for your entire life. So I once
more encourage you to make the small effort required to have
this important learning experience.

Here is the experience:

Step 1: Turn to page 49 of this book and look at it for a few
seconds.

Step 2: Ask someone else to take the book and turn to page 85 and look at it for a few seconds. Don't look at that page yourself and don't let the other person look at page 49.

Step 3: Now together turn to page 244 and look at that.

Step 4: Each of you try to convince the other person about what you see. Don't ask questions, just try to persuade the other person how right you are in this matter.

Step 5: Still looking only at page 244, continue your discussion with each other, and if you haven't by this time come to see each other's point of view, try to do so. Each of you shift your purpose from selling or persuading to one of understanding. Continue to communicate until both of you can see each other's point of view.

Last step: Now that you have seen each other's point of view, briefly discuss what happened and why. Then both of you look at pages 49 and 85 to understand the initial experience which essentially conditioned or programmed your respective minds.

Now, it may be that by chance you had already seen one or more of these pictures or had had this experience. If so, give the experience to two others to whom it is new, having them proceed carefully through the outlined steps. Do this too if the initial programming picture didn't take with you (and inexplicably it doesn't with about 10 percent of those who saw the old woman on page 85 and 5 percent of those who saw the young girl on page 49.)

EXPERIENCE DETERMINES PERCEPTION

Whether you have the experience yourself or observe others having it, you will get the point: *prior experiences have great impact on present perceptions, and these perceptions significantly affect or even determine our feelings, our communication, and our behavior.*

You may think the lesson of this simple experience is completely self-evident. Whether it is or not, I suggest that its implications are staggeringly profound and far-reaching.

I first had the experience in the fall of 1955, in an administrative practices class at the Harvard Graduate School of Business. It impressed me then, but the point the instructor made about perception focused primarily on the importance of communicating in such a way as to understand other people's points of view. In effect, I compartmentalized the experience, limited it primarily to that application. For the next twenty years I used these pictures scores of times in various contexts all over the world, through this experience teaching people important and fairly obvious lessons in interpersonal communication.

PERCEPTION GOVERNS MEANINGS

Several years ago I began to realize that there was an intrapersonal (within self) dimension also to this concept. I saw that the effects of our experience-induced perception do not stop at our communication with others. That area is, so to speak, the tip of the iceberg. Much more importantly, I came to realize that *our perception governs our beliefs, our attitudes, and our behaviors.*

How, then, do we see? Most of us think we see the world as it is, but I believe this is not the case. We each see not with the eye but with the soul. Each person sees the world not as *it* is but as *he* or *she* is. When he opens his mouth to describe what he sees, he in effect describes himself, that is, his perception.

This does not mean that there are no facts. Going back to the picture experience again, two individuals who initially have been influenced by different pictures look at the third picture together. They are now both looking at the same identical facts—black lines, white spaces, and so on—and they both would acknowledge these as facts. But each person's interpretation of these facts represents his prior experiences, and *the facts have no meaning whatsoever apart from this interpretation.* We are constantly looking for meaning. The interpretation or the explanation or the meaning which we place upon the facts represents the revelation of self, the self which has been formed by previous experiences.

As another example, if an American who knew no French were sitting with a Frenchman listening to a broadcast of a speech in French, both the listeners would have the same identical facts—that is, noise available to them. To the Frenchman, the speech would have meaning. He would understand it. To the American, it would be simply noise or gibberish, and he would need a translator to make sense out of it.

Consider another case. If someone criticized ordinances of the gospel, say, temple ordinances, calling them archaic social rituals, would you not immediately think that that person was revealing himself rather than the temple?

BEHAVIOR

PERCEPTION

A SELF-FULFILLING PROPHECY

ATTITUDE

EXPERIENCES

Now let's go a little closer to home. When you describe to another person your spouse or your child or your friend or a Church leader, are you conscious that you are revealing yourself? That is, that you are relating your perceptions rather than describing the person?

PERCEPTION DIRECTS BEHAVIOR

Since we do not see the world as it is, and our interpretations are not accurate and complete, another question arises: Can a person act with integrity outside of his perceptions? The answer to this is no.

I have seen this demonstrated countless times in my old woman/young lady presentations. I ask a person who sees either the old lady or the girl if he could act outside his perception and be honest about it. Invariably he can't. For instance, I sometimes set up a role-playing situation in which the person who sees the young girl is trying to "line up" his young unmarried friend with this "lovely young sister-in-law" of his. There is no difficulty about this, but when I ask the other person, the one who can see only the old woman, if he could do the same thing and maintain his integrity, the answer is always no. We simply cannot act contrary to our perceptions—and stay honest.

There is an apparent or seeming exception to this rule, and that is when our perception of the recommending person, based on past experiences, gives us such confidence in the recommendation that we are willing to subordinate our own perception to his. This was Adam's situation when he first offered sacrifices to the Lord. When the angel questioned him why he was doing so, Adam responded, "I know not, save the Lord commanded me" (Moses 5:6). In other words, because of prior experiences with the Lord, Adam had such faith and confidence in His omniscience and omnipotence, such trust in Him, that he was willing to act accordingly. This is often called "blind faith." In fact, it is a highly intelligent faith.

In my presentations I sometimes set up a role-playing experience in which the boss, who sees the young girl, recommends to his subordinate, who sees the old woman, that the subordinate hire this person to be the receptionist in his office, a position in which she will greet the public. Since they both think they see the woman as she is instead of as each of them is—that is, as their perceptions are—a fairly pleasant disagreement takes place. When it becomes evident that the cause of the difficulty is the difference in their perceptions, the boss will perhaps try to resolve the issue by traditional methods such as telling the other person to try harder or to think positively or to go along for the sake of cooperation. The futility of these methods is demonstrated by the fact that the subordinate simply cannot do so with integrity. Sometimes the boss borrows strength from position power and threatens his subordinate—he must "hire the woman or else." But none of these approaches are solutions, because they do not change perception. The other person may "go along in order to get along," but in a real-life situation there would be several negative consequences later on.

TWO BASIC COMMUNICATION PROBLEMS: PERCEPTION AND CREDIBILITY

This whole problem is greatly compounded if either party, having had the prior conditioning experience, just "happens" to run on to the third picture. He then is absolutely convinced that he sees that picture as it is, not as *he* is. At that time I have those people who have seen different initial pictures interact with each other regarding the third picture in various role-playing situations. Invariably the first reaction is that each simply believes that the other person is "putting him on." Here a credibility problem develops that only serves to reinforce the perception difference, because both parties begin to assert their position, in effect investing their ego in their perception. This will often result in a "fight or flight" reaction or in borrowing strength and power from position or rank.

There are two broad categories of communication problems. One is *perception*. In that case, based on their prior experiences,

I believe that if you trace to its genesis almost any credibility problem, personality conflict, or communication breakdown, you will find a perception problem.

different individuals are placing different interpretations on the same facts. The other is *credibility*. In that situation, one or both of the persons is questioning the sincerity, the integrity, the competence, or perhaps the sanity, of the other. Semantics, or word definition problems, would fall under the perception category. I am convinced that most credibility problems originate in a perception difference, but because most of us think we see the world as it is, not as the perceiver himself is, we won't acknowledge this. So instead of making a communication effort to solve the perception difference, each of us, seeking to justify himself, immediately begins to judge the other person as insincere, dishonest, uninformed, or whatever. Alternatively, if a person's self-confidence is low, he may seek to justify the other and condemn himself. These credibility problems may ultimately result in what we call "personality conflicts" or "communication breakdowns."

Credibility problems are far more difficult to solve than perception problems, primarily because each of the individuals involved thinks he sees the world as it is rather than as he is. Therefore, if B disagrees with A, in A's eyes B is automatically wrong, simply because A is sure he himself is right. He is simply unaware of the effect of his own perception and thinks it to be a fact instead. I believe that if you trace to its genesis almost any credibility problem, personality conflict, or communication breakdown, you will find a perception problem.

Perception problems are relatively easy to solve, because the individuals involved are aware that they are seeing the world as they are—that is, as their *perceptions* are—rather than as *it* is. This tends to lead them to adopt the three following attitudes: First, awareness of a genuine perception difference (they are not questioning each other's sincerity). Second, a caring response about the other person and about the subject at hand; each will desire to understand the other's perception or point of view. Third, consequently each has an open mind. These three attitudes will lead to three behaviors or practices. First, the individuals will listen to understand; second, they will speak to be understood; third, they will find a common referent point or point of agreement at which they can begin their communication with each other. For instance, one will point a finger and ask the other, "What does that mean to you?" and will later tell the other what it means to him.

When these three attitudes and three behaviors are followed, almost any perception problem can be solved. So can most credibility problems, if one or both of the parties involved will realize that, at root, it is a perception problem and will adopt these attitudes and behaviors.

THE SELF-FULFILLING PROPHECY

Our perceptions can bring about the self-fulfilling prophecy too. The term *self-fulfilling prophecy* refers to a situation in which a person sees his world in a certain way; that perception affects his behavior; and his behavior in turn produces the "evidence" which supports the perception. As an example, if I see a person as being disagreeable, I will perhaps react to that person in terms of that perception; the other person may perceive my behavior as unjustified and unfair; he will then in consequence make aggressive or defensive reactions, thus "confirming" my perception or prophecy.

The self-fulfilling prophecy concept has been validated countless times in scientific, experimentally designed studies, but a classic instance took place by accident in England some years ago. Two groups of students were mistakenly labeled the opposite of their test scores. That is, those who tested to be very bright were called the less bright group, and those who were tested to be less bright were called the very bright group. The mistake was not discovered for several months, during which time the teachers acted on the incorrect perceptions. When they discovered the mistake they immediately tested the students again, only to find that the group wrongly labeled extra bright had increased their test scores significantly, while those wrongly labeled less bright had decreased their test scores significantly.

Without question, one of the most powerful forces influencing people's behavior is the perception or expectation that significant others surrounding them have of them. When we come to realize this, the implication and significance of the self-fulfilling prophecy to a parent, a leader, a teacher, a missionary, is simply staggering.

Admittedly there are many factors at play in the self-fulfilling prophecy situation, but a central one is the effect of our perception on our behavior. Generally speaking, the way we see the world leads us to behave in ways that produce the evidence to confirm our perceptions. Thus we fulfill our own prophecy.

Once one of my sons failed to fulfill his commitment to do a particular job, and I asked (told!) him, "Son, why are you so irresponsible?" He answered, "Dad, that's how irresponsible people act."

To express the concept directly and personally, *your head creates your world.* The obvious implication is that the best way to change the world is to change your head, that is, your thinking, your perceptions. Remember, you see the world as *you* are, not as *it* is. You are the map of your world.

THE MAP IS NOT THE TERRITORY

A nother way semanticists put this is that "the map is not the territory." If you had an inaccurate map of a city and you were looking for a certain location, you would be both lost and frustrated. If someone counseled you to try harder and you doubled your speed, you would merely be lost twice as fast. If the person sensed how discouraged you were and counseled you to think positively rather than negatively, you would still be lost but perhaps you wouldn't care about it as much. Even though your lack of progress, your "doing nothing," had produced both frustration and discouragement, perhaps superficially suggesting laziness and/or a negative approach, the problem really would have nothing to do with either diligence or attitude. The real problem would be an inaccurate map.

The history of science is that of a constantly developing, increasingly accurate map of the territory. All true scientists know this and are hesitant to speak as if the latest theoretical explanation is a fact. It is merely the best map that has been developed to that point. It has higher predictive and explanatory value than its predecessors. Thus Einsteinian physics eclipsed Newtonian physics essentially because it had higher explanatory and predictive value. Brilliant as it is, it is a more accurate map of the territory rather than a proven fact in every detail and implication. It is still a theory, an explanation of observed facts and phenomena, not yet disconfirmed or eclipsed by a better map. Throughout the history of scientific thought most laymen have been so anxious for certainty and have had such low tolerance for ambiguity and change that they have been eager to say that a theory is a fact—in other words, that the map is complete and accurate. A true scientist knows better and maintains a posture of humility, constant curiosity, inquiry, and experimentation in order to develop more advanced maps, more correct and more detailed representations of the territory.

The map may suffer distortion too through the very humanness of the scientists themselves. Stephen Jay Gould, a leading evolutionary biologist who teaches at Harvard University, made this comment:

> In evaluating these and other arguments by scientists, it is important that people be wary of the claim that science stands apart from other human institutions because its methodology leads to objective knowledge. People need to realize that scientists are human beings like everybody else and that their pronouncements may arise from their social prejudices, as any of our pronouncements might. The public should avoid being snowed by the

scientist's line: "Don't think about this for yourself, because it's all too complicated."

I wish scientists scrutinized more rigidly the sources of justification for their beliefs. If they did, they might realize that some of their findings do not derive from a direct investigation of nature but are rooted in assumptions growing out of experience and beliefs.

But don't draw from what I have said the negative implication that science is a pack of lies—that it's merely social prejudice. On the one hand, science is embedded in society, and scientists reflect the social prejudices of their own lives and those of their class and culture. On the other hand, I believe that there are correct answers to questions, and science, in its own bumbling, socially conditioned manner, stumbles toward those answers. (*U. S. News & World Report*, March 1, 1982, page 62.)

Continuing with the map / territory analogy, let's modify it slightly to make it more a part of the individual rather than some external piece of paper we look at. Let's say it's the lens through which we see the world. It represents the pair of glasses we wear. After wearing them for a while, we fail to realize that the lens is affecting our interpretation or explanation of everything we see; we simply come to conclude that we are seeing the world objectively, as it is, that our map is accurate. In fact, though, we have become completely subjective, unaware that the lens interprets the world and reveals it as we are rather than as the world is. We become unaware that we think; we simply think.

CHANGED CIRCUMSTANCES CHANGE MAPS

We have all had experiences from time to time that changed our pair of glasses—not the physical pair but the mental pair. That is, we changed our frame of reference or the map through which we viewed the territory, the so-called "objective world," "the facts." When this happened we found that our behavior changed to reflect that new frame of reference.

I am convinced that the fastest way to change a person's behavior is to change his map or frame of reference by calling him a different name, giving him a different role responsibility, or placing him in a different situation. Think of how the frame of reference changes when you get married, when you are called on a mission, when you have your first child; or when you are called to teach in Sunday School, or to be a bishop or a stake president.

Think of the frame of reference change that would take place if suddenly a terrible accident occurred that paralyzed you or took the life of a dear one, or if you were informed that you or someone you loved had a terminal illness. Almost anything in life is seen differently through the lens of such an experience. Apart from the big change, the facts are all the same as before. But the interpretation or explanation or importance of those facts may well be dramatically changed by the different frame of reference now used to examine them.

One of my favorite stories, which my wife and I like reading every year or so, is called *Precious Jeopardy*. (It is by Lloyd C. Douglas, the author who wrote the best-seller *Magnificent Obsession*.) It tells the story of a businessman who is distraught over yesterday's losses and tomorrow's threat. Suddenly he meets with an accident that places his life in constant jeopardy. He is in full possession of his physical and mental powers, yet he knows that his life may come to an end at any moment. He is required to live on the possibilities of the present hour, borrowing nothing from the future either of promise or of menace. He learns for the first time how to live fully, richly, and happily. His whole frame of reference changes; his map of the world changes; he has on a different pair of glasses. He now has a different mental/emotional set. As compared with the past, he sees everything differently, he interprets everything differently, he ascribes a different meaning to all his experiences.

MOST BREAKTHROUGHS ARE BREAKWITHS

In the world of science, these changes in perceptions or frames of reference, these new perspectives, are called *paradigm shifts* (pronounced par-a-dime). The science historian and philosopher Thomas Coon, in his landmark book *The Structure of Scientific Revolutions* (1962), introduced the term *paradigm shift* to represent change in the framework of thought, change in one's scheme for understanding and explaining reality. The paradigm shift is a distinctly new way of thinking about old problems. As briefly touched on above, Einstein's special theory of relativity eclipsed or superseded Newton's physics. With it our understanding of nature shifted from a clockwork paradigm to an uncertainty paradigm, from the absolute to the relative. Similarly almost every true scientific breakthrough is a break with well-established, traditional paradigms.

In life generally, people who work with the old view tend to become emotionally and intellectually attached to it and to go to the grave with their faith unshaken. Even when they are confronted with overwhelming evidence, they stubbornly stick with the wrong but familiar. But whenever a person has a new world view or a new paradigm, he feels both exhilarated and humbled by it. He feels that the former view was not so much wrong as partial, as if he had been observing with restricted vision. He is exhilarated because in making the shift *he has gained not simply more knowledge but a whole new way of knowing.* He is humbled because he knows that improvements in his world view still will and must take place.

THE CORRECT MAP

You've often heard the expression, "I'll believe it when I see it," which implies that seeing is believing. In fact, the opposite is the case. As we will see throughout the rest of this book, *Believing is seeing.* Believing in the Creator of the territory as one who has complete integrity, power, and love opens up to us the most accurate map of the territory, enabling us to see and understand it better.

In modern revelation, the Lord defines truth as "knowledge of things as they are, and as they were, and as they are to come" (D&C 93:24). Notice very carefully the words used to describe

In modern revelation, the Lord defines truth as "knowledge of things as they are, and as they were, and as they are to come." Truth is a knowledge of things. In other words, it is an internal mental understanding or grasping of the way things really are. This revealed definition suggests that truth is in the mind; it is an internal rather than an external thing.

truth. Truth is a *knowledge* of things. In other words, it is an internal mental understanding or grasping of the way things really are; it is the subjective accurately reflecting the objective, the personal correctly reflecting the real, the map truly reflecting the territory. This revealed definition suggests truth is in the mind; it is an internal rather than an external thing.

The correct map, of course, has been made available at various points in history. It was given in connection with dispensations of the gospel—through Adam, Enoch, Noah, Abraham, Moses, and the Savior himself. Not always was the map complete at all times, but as revealed from heaven it was accurate to the level of detail communicated.

But each time, as the years passed, the map gradually became polluted, smeared; parts were torn off through disuse or misuse, essential routes obliterated by encrusted dirt or redrawn by ignorant or self-serving pens. Each time the true map had to be restored through a prophet. Each time, since the old map had become totally unreliable, the restoration brought about a tremendous "paradigm shift."

The nineteenth century would see the last of the restorations of the true map. The situation that then obtained in the world in general is portrayed in the scriptures: "And the whole world lieth in sin, and groaneth under darkness and under the bondage of sin. And by this you may know they are under the bondage of sin, because they come not unto me. For whoso cometh not unto me is under the bondage of sin." (D&C 84:49-51.)

Viewing in this light some of the solutions offered by modern advocates, we see their futility in terms of finding the true map. Prior to the restoration of the gospel, it would have made no difference how diligent a person was, for example, nor how far he was into Positive Mental Attitude, Yoga, meditation, reformation activities, or whatever. The whole world was under the bondage of sin. Not that everyone necessarily was knowingly sinning, for many were good people who were faithful to the light they had. But they believed incorrect creeds or maps which did not reflect things as they really are, and they acted accordingly; hence no amount of counsel based on a reading of the existing maps could direct them to the proper destination. The whole world still is under the bondage of sin, of incorrect maps, but now there is a difference; for to the degree that people will be true to whatever light they have been given, they will receive more light until eventually they will be led to the true map of the covenant gospel and receive its fulness. (See D&C 84:46-48.) Then there will be no limitations on the full development of their capacities and potential.

Doctrine and Covenants 93:39 is perhaps pinpointing what it means to be under the bondage of sin. There we read: "And that wicked one cometh and taketh away light and truth, through disobedience, from the children of men, and because of the tradition of their fathers."

From this we learn that Satan comes and takes light and knowledge from the children of men in two basic ways: first, through disobedience (personal apostasy), and second, through "the tradition of their fathers." Tradition essentially means incorrect maps, false maps, false ideas in the form of beliefs or doctrines or creeds. These creeds become an abomination in the sight of God, as the Lord told the Prophet Joseph Smith in the Sacred Grove (Joseph Smith—History 1:19). This is because they limit and distort the growth and the happiness of his children.

The story of the restoration of the gospel is an excellent illustration of how the Lord is attempting to bring to the world a correct understanding, a correct map, if you will, of the territory, of things as they really are. Joseph Smith was an honest, spiritually minded young man and he earnestly sought to know the truth. Torn and confused by the many different maps being put into his mind by others, he placed his faith in the promise of James (1:5) that if he would ask of God his prayer would be answered. As a result our Heavenly Father and his Beloved Son, Jesus Christ, appeared to Joseph Smith, officially rejected all the existing maps, and commenced the reintroduction of the correct map.

When the fourteen-year-old Joseph Smith left the Sacred Grove he had in his mind a correct idea or map of the Father, of the Son, and of himself. That was essentially it. At that point he was given no additional powers or talents or capacities, and the map he received, though correct, was incomplete. Little by little, as Daniel prophesied (Daniel 2:31-45), that correct plan or map is rolling forth, and it will eventually fill the entire earth. Every person who has ever lived will be influenced by it.

As of this writing, over five million people have covenanted in the waters of baptism to govern their lives by this map. The gospel is being taken to every nation of the world that will permit the missionaries to enter, as well as to the spirit world for all of our Heavenly Father's disembodied children to hear. This map tells us who we are, who we *really* are. It tells us where we came from, what our purpose in life is, and what our eventual destiny may be. It tells us the laws upon which our happiness and growth are based. "We believe all that God has revealed, all that He does now reveal, and we believe that He will yet reveal many great and important things pertaining to the Kingdom of God." (Ninth article of faith.) Since the early days of the Restoration, more and more of the complete map has been revealed, till we have sufficient today to exalt any individual and family in the celestial kingdom of our Heavenly Father as long as they govern themselves by this map.

On the other hand, incorrect maps still flourish. Joseph Smith wrote, "For there are many yet on the earth among all sects, parties, and denominations, who are blinded by the subtle craftiness of men, whereby they lie in wait to deceive" (D&C 123:12). In the mission field I have personally witnessed the disastrous effects when active Church members have been drawn into believing false doctrine. Observing the apostate effect they had on others, I became convinced that even open behavioral transgression would have had less negative impact all around. How the adversary must rejoice at his ability to distort the maps in people's minds through either disobedience or tradition! He almost gets a stranglehold on them, simply because most people never question their maps. They assume that's the way it is. They don't hold viewpoints; their viewpoints hold them.

No wonder Joseph Smith under inspiration identified the "creeds of the fathers" as "the very mainspring of all corruption." No wonder he affirmed that "the whole earth groans under the weight of its iniquity. It is an iron yoke, it is a strong band; they are the very handcuffs, and chains, and shackles, and fetters of hell." (D&C 123:7-8.)

For this reason I am persuaded that intellectual pride is more basic and serious than either social or material pride. We know we can lose our prestige or our possessions. They are external. But when the problem lies in our very thinking and we are unaware of that fact, what then? The internal root produces the external fruit. "For every thousand hacking at the leaves of evil there is one striking at the root" (Henry David Thoreau).

Furthermore, extending the above reasoning, I am persuaded that the intellectual leaders (map designers), such as Augustine, Aquinas, Copernicus, Darwin, Freud, Marx, and Dewey, have greater impact on the world, for good or for evil, than all the political, social, military, or aesthetic leaders put together. Paradigms control. Hence the importance of our having and understanding the Lord's map. For only the Creator of the territory can offer the correct map—only he and those to whom he entrusts part of it.

THE PROPER FOCUS

Now we may carry the map/territory metaphor a little further. The correct map is on the earth and is made available to all to whatever extent the Church's programs can do so. Many accept it when it is presented to them. Many do not, and these continue to pursue their lives "in the bondage of sin." Why the different responses?

The key is faith in the Lord Jesus Christ. That faith is not only the first principle of the gospel, fundamental and basic as that makes it. It is *the principle through which all other gospel principles are understood.* Faith in the Lord Jesus Christ, if you will, is more than part of the correct map. It is the means of focusing properly onto the correct map or frame of reference. When the map is brought into correct focus by this means, it gives a correct understanding, interpretation, and explanation about everything else in life. To borrow and adapt a metaphor from the Christian writer the late C. S. Lewis, contained in his book *Miracles*, we can say that we believe in Christ as we believe in the sun at noonday; not that we can see it, but that by it we can see everything else.

It is clear, then, that unwittingly we for the most part surrender to our perceptions, our mental frame of reference, our map. This governs us, controls us. It interprets life for us and thus guides us and directs our paths. Based on the accuracy and our understanding of this map, of this center in the individual's life, all our capacities and powers may be released to bring us increasingly to that joy which is a major purpose of life here and hereafter.

A question remains: If the gospel is the correct map, and faith in Jesus Christ is the means of focusing on it with understanding, why is it that there are such divergent levels of understanding and devotion among Latter-day Saints who profess that faith? How could this situation be righted?

Possible answers to these questions will emerge as you read on.

The Typical Distortions   *Chapter 2*

A double minded man is unstable in all his ways. (James 1:8.)

I hope I established to your satisfaction in chapter 1 that normally each person sees himself and the world through the lens of his past experiences. These glasses, his frame of reference, become the center through which he sees and interprets and explains everything else.

I suggest too that whatever lies at the center of a person's life, whatever pair of glasses he looks through, becomes *the primary source of his life-support system.* In large measure, I believe, that system is represented by four fundamental dimensions of personality and life which substantially embrace all the others. These four are security, guidance, wisdom, and power. Let's first define and explain each of these in turn.

FOUR FUNDAMENTAL DIMENSIONS

Security represents a person's sense of worth, his identity, his emotional anchorage, his self-esteem, his basic personal strength or lack of it. Security is not an all-or-nothing matter. Rather it lies somewhere on a line or continuum between a deep sense of high intrinsic worth and personal security on one end and, on the other end, extreme insecurity wherein a person's life is buffeted by all the fickle forces that play upon it. The extremes of this continuum might be represented by the Savior's words on the mount:

> Therefore whosoever heareth these sayings of mine, and doeth them, I will liken him unto a wise man, which built his house upon a rock:
> And the rain descended, and the floods came, and the winds blew, and beat upon that house; and it fell not: for it was founded upon a rock.

> And every one that heareth these sayings of mine, and doeth them not, shall be likened unto a foolish man, which built his house upon the sand:
>
> And the rain descended, and the floods came, and the winds blew, and beat upon that house; and it fell: and great was the fall of it. (Matthew 7:24-27.)

Guidance means direction one receives in life. Encompassed by our map, our internal frame of reference that interprets for each of us what is happening out there, are standards or principles or criteria that govern decision making and doing. Over a period of time, this internal monitor becomes our source of guidance. It serves as a conscience. This conscience may have very little to do with the divine voice or divine conscience given to every man that comes into the world, which we call the Spirit of Jesus Christ (John 1:9; D&C 84:46), or it may have a great deal to do with it, depending on what is at the center of a person's life.

If we represent guidance on a continuum, the lower end will signify the strong satanic conscience, which has been indoctrinated and conditioned by the person's centering on selfish living and evil ends until for practical purposes he has lost the Spirit of Christ entirely and has become a puppet of the adversary. A position toward the middle of the continuum would represent development of the social conscience, the conscience which has been educated and cultivated by centering on human institutions, traditions, and relationships. Such a social conscience may have effectively subordinated or eclipsed the still, small voice of the spiritual conscience. The other end of the continuum would symbolize the spiritual conscience, the spirit of Jesus Christ (and the Holy Ghost, in the case of Church members), wherein a person's guidance comes from the Lord's servants or his principles, or from the Lord when we seek such aid—as, for example, when some of the elders sought it early in this dispensation. "Hearken, O ye elders of my church, and give ear to the voice of the living God; and attend to the words of wisdom which shall be given unto you, according as ye have asked and are agreed. . . ." (D&C 50:1.)

Wisdom indicates perspective on life, a sense of balance, an understanding of how the various parts and principles apply and relate to each other. It embraces judgment, discernment, comprehension. It is a gestalt or oneness, an integrated wholeness. The lower end of the wisdom continuum would be represented by a completely inaccurate map, so that the person's actions and thinking are based on distorted, discordant principles. In his confused thinking he is likely even to find the Lord at fault:

> I command and men obey not; I revoke and they receive not the blessing.
> Then they say in their hearts: This is not the work of the Lord, for his promises are not fulfilled. But wo unto such, for their reward lurketh beneath, and not from above. (D&C 58:32-33.)

The upper end of the wisdom continuum would represent an absolutely perfect, accurate, and complete map of life wherein all the parts and principles are properly related to each other. In moving toward that end there is a clear sense of increasing idealism and purpose (things as they should be) as well as a sensitive, practical approach to realities (things as they are).

Power is the faculty or the capacity to act.

> Verily I say, men should be anxiously engaged in a good cause, and do many things of their own free will, and bring to pass much righteousness;
> For the power is in them, wherein they are agents unto themselves. And inasmuch as men do good they shall in nowise lose their reward. (D&C 58:27-28.)

Power is the strength and potency to accomplish something. It is the vital energy to make choices and decisions. It also represents human and divine capacity to overcome deeply embedded habits and to cultivate higher, more effective, even godly habits; the capacity to change one's nature and to become, as Peter puts it, a partaker of the divine nature (2 Peter 1:3-8). Such power includes the wisdom to discern pure joy and happiness as distinct from temporary pleasure. Perhaps most importantly, it includes the facility to draw down the powers of heaven in the service of our Heavenly Father's other children.

Security, guidance, wisdom, and power are interlocking and interdependent. Security and well-founded guidance bring true wisdom; wisdom becomes the spark or catalyst to release and direct power, both human and divine, in the person.

At the lower end of the power continuum would be the person who is essentially powerless. He is insecure and completely a product of what happens or has happened to him. He is a dependent person — dependent on circumstances and on others. He may be a total reflection of other people's opinions and directions. He finds himself repenting of the same sins over and over again but unable to repent of sinning. He has no real comprehension of what true joy and happiness is.

At the upper end of the continuum is the person who possesses greatly developed powers — one with a high level of self-discipline whose life is a functional product of his decisions rather than of external conditions. Such a person causes things to happen. He is proactive rather than reactive; that is, he chooses his response to any given situation based upon principles, standards, or criteria which he has made an integral part of himself. He takes responsibility not only for his *response* to what happens to him but in a large measure for what happens to him. He ultimately takes responsibility for his feelings and moods and attitudes as well as his thoughts and actions. Such a person becomes a conduit for powers from above in doing the Lord's work.

The four factors defined above — security, guidance, wisdom, and power — are interlocking and interdependent. Security and well-founded guidance bring true wisdom, and wisdom becomes the spark or catalyst to release and direct power, both human and divine, in the person. When these four factors are present together, harmonized and enlivened by each other, they create the great force of a noble personality, a balanced character, a beautifully integrated individual.

Now let's look at several possible life centers, maps, or frames of reference and see how they measure up as promoters or otherwise of these four fundamental dimensions of personality.

SPOUSE-CENTEREDNESS

First, *the spouse.* The core of a family is the husband-and-wife relationship. Eventually the children will leave home, get married, and have their own children, who in due course will likewise leave home, get married, and have their own children. The one intimate relationship that will persist on a continuous basis in time and in eternity is the marriage relationship. Marriage is a divine institution; it is a growth-producing and sanctifying institution and is meant to provide a continuous, unending source of satisfaction and fulfillment which will ride through many ups and downs in the family and in life generally. Since marriage has this high status in the Lord's kingdom, it could seem a natural and proper course to become centered on one's husband or wife.

EMOTIONAL DEPENDENCE

But experience and observation tell a different story. Over the years, I have been involved in working with many marriages — not professionally, but in relation to my Church, teaching, and family stewardships — and I have observed a certain thread weaving itself through almost every spouse-centered relationship I have encountered. That thread is strong emotional dependence. And I observe that when a person's sense of emotional worth comes primarily from the marriage relationship, then he or she becomes highly dependent upon that relationship. That makes him or her extremely vulnerable to the moods and feelings, the behavior and treatment, of the partner, or to any external event which may impinge on the relationship — a new child, in-laws, economic setbacks, social successes, and so forth.

To a greater or lesser extent each husband and wife has come from dissimilar backgrounds which stretch back through generations, and deeply embedded tendencies have therefore been transmitted into the character of each spouse. When stresses and pressures are made upon the marriage, when enlarged responsibilities and demands emerge, these tendencies are stirred again. Dissimilar ways of handling financial, child discipline, or in-law issues come to the surface. When these deep-seated tendencies combine with the emotional dependency in the marriage, the spouse-centered relationship shows up in all its vulnerability, and the partners have a seedbed for conflict and for communication breakdowns. This can easily become a vicious cycle that feeds upon itself because of the strong dependency each has on the other.

When you have a need dependency for the person you are in conflict with, both need and conflict are compounded. When a person's primary source of security, guidance, wisdom, and power is the relationship with his spouse, the circumstances we have indicated will produce distortions, overreactions, fighting-flighting tendencies, withdrawal, aggressiveness, the exercise of unrighteous dominion, impotency, frigidity, bitterness, resentment, hatred, clashing, warring, and cold competition. Each partner will then fall further back on background tendencies and habits (which may even be Church-centered or family-centered) in an effort to justify and defend himself and to attack the other in either active or passive ways.

Inevitably, anytime we are too vulnerable we feel the need to protect ourselves from further wounds. Often the best defense is a good offense, and sometimes this manifests itself in cynicism, the defense of the mind, for when we expect nothing we will never be disappointed. So the attack frequently manifests itself in sarcasm, in cutting humor, in sharpness of tongue, in criticalness, and in anything which will keep from exposing the soft, vulnerable, tenderness within. Each partner then will tend to wait upon the initiative of the other for love, only again to be disappointed but also to be confirmed as to the rightness of his or her own past accusations.

In a lovely beach setting I once took a walk with my wife when I was feeling angry with myself. Because of my lack of disciplined productivity in doing the writing I had scheduled for

The Lord is not only our advocate with the Father; he is our advocate with all of our Father's other children, unless we become our own advocate and defender.

myself, I was frustrated and annoyed, and I proceeded to "take it out" on my wife. Rather than deal with the major beam in my own eye, the two-by-four plank which was frustrating my whole soul, I focused upon the small mote which was making dust in my wife's eye, and in my clumsy effort to get it out, to correct her, I was overreactive, upset, and angry.

My wife said nothing in reply; she just listened and accepted me. When I couldn't engage her in coming back, in arguing or fighting or defending herself, another force came to bear upon me—the force of conscience. It takes two to fight, and if one partner does not fight back, soon the other's angry surliness spends itself. When my wife didn't punish me, the Lord did in his matchless way, and I ended up apologizing to my wife for acting out my frustrations on her. For the Lord is not only our advocate with the Father; he is our advocate with all of our Father's other children, unless we become our own advocate and defender. If we do that, when we are punished for our misbehavior as we really deserve we feel in a sense that we have really atoned for our own sins and we therefore tend to lose our sensitivity about the need to recognize the Savior's atonement and to turn back to him.

A LIGHT, NOT A JUDGE

I remember speaking at an Education Week in Phoenix when a lady came up to talk to me about the speech I had given the previous year at an Education Week in California on the subject of being a light and not a judge. She related to me her story of the intervening year.

She began by identifying how depressed she had been the year previous because of the lack of valiance in her husband's life-style. He had never caught fire in the gospel or the Church and was just barely getting along. She however had been illuminated with the gospel light and wanted the full blessings of the Lord on her entire family. She had tried every method she had heard of in an effort to influence her husband, all without success; and she had eventually succumbed to depression and cynicism.

Hearing my previous presentation, she was temporarily stimulated by the idea that her calling was to be a light, not a judge —in other words, a constant producer of good attitudes and behavior rather than a critic of her husband's poor attitudes and behavior. (After all, where in all the scriptures are we counseled to confess another's sins?) She decided to try it. She did so, and for several weeks she had a very difficult time in maintaining this new course.

As an example, she recounted that one time when she was preparing to go to church with the children, none of whom was very enthusiastic to go, she asked her husband in the middle of the TV program if he would join her in going to church and would help her with the children. He said he didn't want to go, that he wanted to finish watching his television program, and added, "You should let the kids stay and watch it and not force them to go to church." She swallowed hard and remembered she was striving to be a light, not a judge; a model, not a critic. Normally she would snip at him at the end of the encounter by saying something like, "Well, if these kids don't turn out right, you know whose fault it is"—then she would immediately leave, giving him no opportunity for a rejoinder. She always tried to get in the last word and couch it in the language of the scriptures. It was her way of getting some kind of justice.

This time, however, she said nothing as she left, but merely took the children along with her and drove to church. While driving, she condemned herself for not performing her traditional judgment act on her husband for his lack of valiance, and the withdrawal pains she experienced were severe. She was breaking a deeply impacted habit that was addicting to her—the habit of getting back, of justifying, of having the last word, of putting down. She persisted with this changed behavior, even though she experienced great internal emotional turmoil for several weeks. At one point she was about to abandon the entire project, but fortunately she counseled with her bishop. He encouraged her to keep it up, and she did.

At the Arizona Education Week she now pointed out her husband, who was across the hall, and said, "There's my husband. He is now a member of the bishopric." I asked her if she would mind if I talked with her husband regarding what had happened. She felt good about it and so did he, and he described the process.

He said he had felt completely justified in his relative lack of commitment to the gospel, because apparently there were no real, powerful fruits of it in her life. She wasn't really changed because of the gospel and the Church. Further, she would punish him from time to time in various ways, and that made him feel justified in his minor rebellions. She paid him off, and this gave him the "right" to do it some more. He even sensed her new method—be a light, not a judge—and her striving not to answer back or fight or yell or criticize. But he knew what she was really thinking and feeling inside, and to some degree he enjoyed her being punished, as she had been punishing him for such a long time.

At this point in his account he said something that struck me forcibly. "But she persisted until this new behavior became a habit to her, and I began to sense that she was changing inside also; she wasn't punishing or manipulating me any longer, and she derived no more satisfaction from the encounters." He added, "She became an angel, Brother Covey, and how do you live with an angel?"

Well, eventually you can't live with an angel unless you change to a like condition. You eventually shape up or ship out. Whatever good there is in one person is appealed to by the angelic nature of the other. Most people have a great deal of good within them, and if only others would perceive it and treat them accordingly, this would tend to bring it out. There is no guarantee of this, however, for it will take great time and patience, and oftentimes a person's life center is so strongly embedded in other things besides his spouse that the behavior of the spouse may be only a secondary-influence force.

WORK-CENTEREDNESS, MONEY-MAKING-CENTEREDNESS

Another logical and extremely common center to people's lives, particularly the breadwinners, is work, *gainful work*. It is the source of a person's livelihood and in a sense is so basic to life that one's opportunity to do much on any other dimension is powerfully influenced by it. In a hierarchy or continuum of needs, physical survival or security would come first. Other needs would not even be activated until that lower need was satisfied, at least to a minimum extent.

Most people face economic worries. There are many forces in the wider culture which can and do act upon a person's or a family's economic situation, causing or threatening such disruption to their life-style that they often experience an undercurrent of concern and worry even though this may not always rise to the conscious surface. Many people think and worry a great deal about the factors and forces which play upon their employment or income situation, and they become economically very defensive.

It seems to me there is a great encouragement in our culture to become work-centered or money-making-centered. Usually the excuse or reason given for it is the desire to take care of one's family better or, in the case of Latter-day Saints, to provide more opportunity for service in the Church. But as with other alternative centers or frames of reference identified in this chapter, this too will bring about its own undoing. Consider again the four life-support factors of security, guidance, wisdom, and power. Many people derive much of their security from their employment situation or from their income or net worth. And since many factors affect these economic foundations, people become anxious and uneasy, protective and defensive, about anything which may affect those foundations. When a person's sense of personal worth comes from his net worth, when it is the ground of his being, then he is totally vulnerable to anything that will affect that net worth. But work and money per se provide no wisdom, no guidance, and only a limited degree of power and security. All it takes to bring to the surface the limitations of a material world is a crisis in a person's life or in the life of a loved one. Man truly does not live by bread alone, unless perhaps that's all he has to live by, and that too will let him down in the last day.

We have all seen many people who have become work-centered or money-making-centered and how skewing and distorting such a map of life can be. When work demands come, they can easily put aside a family or Church commitment with the expression, "Well, I have to," which is based on the implicit assumption that everyone will understand that work expectations come first: he has to do what he has to do, and the practical world of work dictates this "have to."

On the other hand, one father promised to take his children to the circus, then an important call came from work for him to be there instead. He turned down the work call. His wife, who had listened to him on the phone, afterwards commented, "Maybe you'd better go to work." He responded, "The work will come again, but childhood won't." For the rest of their lives his children remembered this little act of priority setting, not only as an object lesson in their minds but as an expression of love in their hearts.

POSSESSION-CENTEREDNESS

Closely allied to the money center, and one of the most common worldly centers and driving forces of worldly people, is that of possessions. I speak particularly of material possessions, but the intangible possession of fame or glory or social prominence carries similar seeds of instability and disillusionment. Through experience most of us are aware how singularly flawed this center is, simply because it can vanish rapidly and it is influenced by a multitude of forces that can play upon it.

When a person's sense of security lies in his reputation or in having things, his or her life will be in a constant state of threat and jeopardy that these possessions may be lost or stolen or devalued. When his wealth is equated with his net worth, how does he feel in the presence of someone of greater wealth and net worth? Obviously, inferior. And in the presence of a person of lesser wealth or net worth? Obviously, superior. Thus his sense of self-worth fluctuates from superior one moment to inferior the next moment. Similarly with the intangibles of position, fame, status—the sense of self-worth depends on whom the person is with. This situation does not permit any feeling of constancy or anchorage or persistent selfhood. It becomes a life of constant threat and worry and of developing various ways of trying to protect and insure these assets, properties, or securities, this position or reputation.

We have all heard stories of people committing suicide after losing their fortunes in a significant stock decline or their fame in a political reversal. But perhaps the more subtle material vanities have to do with the fashionableness of our clothing, our good looks, the status symbols we surround ourselves with—elegant homes, cars, boats, jewelry, and so on. We simply cannot safely build our security upon such transitory things. "Vanity of vanities, saith the Preacher . . . all is vanity" (Ecclesiastes 1:2). The Savior's incomparable language summarizes it:

> Lay not up for yourselves treasures upon earth, where moth and rust doth corrupt, and where thieves break through and steal:
> But lay up for yourselves treasures in heaven, where neither moth nor rust doth corrupt, and where thieves do not break through nor steal.

For where your treasure is, there will your heart be also. (Matthew 6:19-21.)

And when the rich young ruler inquired what he needed to do to obtain eternal life, the Lord looked at him, discerned his spirit, and said, "Sell whatsoever thou hast, and give to the poor, and thou shalt have treasure in heaven: and come, take up the cross, and follow me." And the man went away sorrowing, because he was possessed by his possessions. (See Mark 10:17-22.)

One who is guided by a heavily developed material or social conscience loses the sense of who he really is and of what life is really about. For him, everything becomes unbalanced and distorted; even people become objects to be controlled, manipulated, and possessed. His is the "have" mentality; he wants to "have" things, "have" people as he wants them to be, "have" his own way — or else he becomes frustrated, angered, accusatory, and thoroughly spoiled.

From the poet Shelley comes a poem which epitomizes the ephemeral nature of possessions and position:

Ozymandias

I met a traveller from an antique land
Who said: Two vast and trunkless legs of stone
Stand in the desert. Near them, on the sand,
Half sunk, a shattered visage lies, whose frown,
And wrinkled lip, and sneer of cold command,
Tell that its sculptor well those passions read
Which yet survive (stamped on these lifeless things),
The hand that mocked them and the heart that fed;
And on the pedestal these words appear:
"My name is Ozymandias, king of kings;
Look on my works, ye Mighty, and despair!"
Nothing beside remains. Round the decay
Of that colossal wreck, boundless and bare,
The lone and level sands stretch far away.

PLEASURE-CENTEREDNESS

Another very common worldly center, closely allied with material possessions, is that of fun and pleasure. We live in a world where instant gratification is available. Some become impatient with the law of the harvest, the law of justice. They don't plan to wait for any harvest, or indeed to reap only what they sow. They want what they want, and they want it now. If they don't get it they scream and pout, or they intimidate and condemn and manipulate.

Television perhaps has been the major modern influence in increasing people's expectations for material things and for the pleasures of the world. Its vivid images are powerfully and dramatically drawn upon our minds. It portrays graphically what other people have and can do in living the life of ease and "fun." The very watching of television itself is a worldly pleasure which, if carried to an extreme, becomes highly addictive. Some people, if deprived of it for a period of time, literally experience withdrawal pangs. The "plug-in drug" is certainly an apt description for this pastime when it is carried to an extreme. When we consider the number of hours that even the average person in America is reckoned to spend in front of the TV every day, what a tremendous waste of time and energy and talent this represents! Over a lifetime it would amount to many years, probably more than most people spend in school, church, and significant family activities combined.

Innocent pleasures are proper in moderation for the relaxation of body and mind and the fostering of family and other relationships. But pleasure per se offers no deep-down, lasting satisfaction or sense of fulfillment. Consequently the pleasure-centered person, too soon bored with each succeeding level or kind of "fun," constantly cries for more and more. So the next new pleasure has to be bigger and better than the last, more exciting, with a bigger "high" in it. A person in this state becomes almost entirely narcissistic, interpreting all of life in terms of the pleasures it provides to self here and now — or at latest tomorrow. But he can't delay gratification too long, or he will become easily diverted into another pleasure sidepath. This surely is a poor altar to worship at.

Too many vacations, vacations lasting too long, too many movies, too much TV, too much video-game playing, too much undisciplined leisure time in which a person continually takes the course of least resistance—this kind of thing gradually wastes a life, wastes a family. It ensures that one's capacities stay dormant, God-given talents remain undeveloped, the mind and spirit become lethargic, and the heart is unfulfilled. Such a life gives no service, makes no contribution, enjoys no larger vision; and short of repentance and change, it slips down to spiritual decay and death. And the rejection of all the promise and potential of that soul will some day bring the recognition indicated by Whittier's verse:

> Of all sad words of tongue and pen,
> The saddest are these—"It might have been."

LEADER-CENTEREDNESS

Another possible center or frame of reference is *leaders* or *heroes*. Many people are very tender inside, very susceptible to the teachings and examples of people who embody the values they admire. They identify with these people. This is particularly the case in the Church. Because the Church is divine in origin and direction, many tend to assume that leaders within the Church, general as well as local, are a lot further along the path to perfection than in fact they are. They then build their security on such expectations and hopes and thereby become dependent and vulnerable. They can be terribly hurt and disillusioned when a particular leader, teacher, mentor, or hero of some kind "doesn't come through." They forget or do not understand that almost everyone has his Achilles' heel and therefore may not be able to measure up to the standard of perfection in every observed situation.

I recall the circumstances of a friend of mine, a colleague at Brigham Young University, who loved teaching at BYU but

> I am convinced that in the long run no one can hurt another without the other's consent; that is, hurt him in a deeply significant, personal, internal sense. This is because we always have the power to choose a response to what someone else does to us. This may be one reason why failure to forgive someone else is a greater sin than that which he has done to us.

became distraught because of the weaknesses of a particular administrator there. He allowed himself to think about it constantly until eventually it became an obsession with him. It so preoccupied him that it affected the quality of his relationships with his family and with the Church. He came to the conclusion that he had to leave BYU and accept a teaching opportunity at another university.

I asked him, "Wouldn't you really prefer to teach at the Y, if that administrator was not here?"

He answered, "Yes, but as long as he is here, then my staying is too disruptive to everything in life, and I must go."

I asked him why he worshipped this administrator. He was shocked by this question and denied any such worship. I pressed by suggesting that he was indeed worshipping him, for the administrator had become an object of mental and emotional focusing of a kind of negative devotion. I told my friend that he was allowing one individual and his weaknesses to distort his entire map of life, to undermine his faith in the Church and the quality of his relationship with his loved ones. He admitted that this individual had had such an impact on him, but he denied that he himself had made all these choices. He attributed the responsibility for these unhappy fruits to the administrator; therefore, he himself was not responsible.

As we talked, little by little he came to realize that he was indeed responsible, but that because he did not handle this responsibility correctly he was being irresponsible. He had centered his life on this leader. He had almost made him an enemy (another category or alternative center we'll explore later).

YOU CAN CHOOSE THE RESPONSE

I am convinced that in the long run no one can hurt another without the other's consent; that is, hurt him in a deeply significant, personal, internal sense. This is because we always have the power to choose a response to what someone else does to us. This may be one reason why failure to forgive someone else is a greater sin than that which he has done to us. That is, it causes more damage to the unforgiving one—a damage in the mind and heart—than that caused by what the other person may do to him externally. The latter damage doesn't necessarily have to affect the mind and the heart.

> My disciples, in days of old, sought occasion against one another and forgave not one another in their hearts; and for this evil they were afflicted and sorely chastened.
>
> Wherefore, I say unto you, that ye ought to forgive one another; for he that forgiveth not his brother his trespasses standeth condemned before the Lord; for there remaineth in him the greater sin.
>
> I, the Lord, will forgive whom I will forgive, but of you it is required to forgive all men. (D&C 64:8-10.)

VULNERABILITY TO DISILLUSIONMENT

New converts to the Church are particularly susceptible and vulnerable to disillusionment when they observe the imperfections of others. Frequently they have come into the Church with very unrealistic expectations, and when they experience what they interpret as hypocrisy, rejection, criticism, or judgment, they recoil. Often they "choose" an extreme reaction, either by complete withdrawal in a self-justifying way or by becoming extremely critical and joining with others who feel similarly. In the latter case they form with those others their own "we" group who can talk about the "theys" out there. They may get hung up on some particular Church doctrine or practice that they use to lever themselves over others. It is a kind of religious fanaticism. It seemingly has a vertical dimension to it—between man and God, that is—but no horizontal dimension.

I used to work with the devotional program at Brigham Young University and in that capacity was involved in inviting General Authorities to come and speak. I became well acquainted with their dislikes, their likes, and their idiosyncrasies. One time I was visiting with President Marion G. Romney about this, and he half jokingly said, "Stephen, don't get so close to the Brethren that you lose your testimony."

In that same mood of the half jest, I responded, "Well, they never gave me my testimony; they couldn't take it away."

He was fully serious in his comeback. "That's right, and don't you ever forget it."

I once knew a man who had taken his family out of the Church because of, as he expressed it, "the unscrupulous behavior of my bishop." He had always admired his bishop until they were involved in some kind of a business transaction, but he felt that in that transaction the bishop had taken advantage of him. "I just couldn't believe it, to think that my bishop would do such a thing as that. I couldn't get over it. I'm not over it yet. I can't get over it. It is so wrong." Then he would go on in some kind of circular reasoning process to explain that if the Church produces that kind of a person, what good is it all anyway?

FRIEND-CENTEREDNESS

Young people are particularly susceptible to becoming *friend-centered*. Acceptance and belonging to a peer group can become almost supremely important to a young person. Anything that would cause embarrassment to self or to the group becomes the supreme sin. In that situation the person's frame of reference becomes more like a straightjacket, through which he deals with life. Often this results, finally, in his losing the very thing desired, as he strives to become all things to all people. He ends up becoming nothing to everyone, including himself.

Focusing on one particular friend can be even worse, if that were possible. A young man who was very dear to me came to me one day distraught because of the possible loss of his girl friend. They had gone together for several years and had continually planned their futures together. But little by little her natural interest had somewhat declined. Even though they were still going steadily together, he could sense something was wrong.

This was tearing him apart emotionally. He lost interest in his school work and dropped out unofficially. He dropped out of church meetings, out of scripture study, out of prayer. He became a loner, withdrawn and isolated. The only outside interest was his girl friend. He was so girl-friend-centered that he wrested his own sense of personal identity and security out of that human relationship and would force the natural processes in it. This she resented. He would have visits he called "where we stand" visits. After expressing his feelings to her, he would press her to know where she stood regarding him. He would tell her, "Here I have expressed my feelings to you, and you haven't responded. It just isn't right or fair for me to continually be open and expressive and for you to say nothing in return." She would half-heartedly respond that nothing had happened, that she still felt the same way. But he could sense the lack of spontaneity, enthusiasm, and commitment in her expression, so he pressed her even more.

I pointed out to him that he had become girl-friend-centered and consequently had a completely inadequate source of security, guidance, wisdom, and power to build upon. He could see that this had happened, but his desire to change was so low that he simply lacked the power to do whatever was necessary to come back, or so it seemed to him. I had to take him through a teaching process as a missionary does a new contact who has low desires or power.

Eventually he agreed to read the scriptures out loud for a few minutes each day. He kept that commitment and then moved on to another one and then another one, until he returned to his priesthood meeting, his school, and finally to prayer. (He had been refusing to pray until he felt a higher level of worthiness.) Little by little, he came to realize that he was, indeed, losing his girl. He was forcing natural processes and violating her stewardship. He was even claiming answers to her prayers. He was becoming possessive and jealous, controlling and dominating to the point of being upset by her interest in others or in anything of which he was not the center.

ENEMY-CENTEREDNESS

How about putting an *enemy* at the center of one's life? Many would never think of this, and probably no one would do so consciously. Nevertheless, enemy-centering is a very common thing, particularly when there is frequent interaction between people who are in a real conflict with each other. When someone feels he has been unjustly dealt with by an emotionally or socially significant person, it is very easy for him to become preoccupied with the injustice and make the other person the center of his life.

SOME MODERN ENEMY CENTERS

In organization life, some become obsessed with the particular weaknesses of their bosses or their working associates — almost paranoid in some instances. They think and talk of almost nothing else, constantly looking for evidence, reading in motives, seeking validation and sympathy from others, planning defensive maneuvers, and so forth.

For instance, one man would phone me at 3:30 A.M. to report on "the latest" regarding his business partner. Without any explanation for such a late call, without even a greeting, he would start with, "Want to hear what he did today?" In other visits too his constant preoccupation (his frame of reference, his lens) was this business partner. In their early association as partners, when things in the business went fairly well, their relationship did also, but when either financial windfalls or reverses took place, gradually accusation replaced communication. This spawned suspicion, manipulation, cover-up, and self-justification.

When this man and I "stood apart" together and observed what was happening, he acknowledged that his partner had gradually become his enemy and the center of his life, significantly reducing his wisdom and power and negatively affecting his family relationships and business effectiveness. He took marriage counseling but found it to be working on leaves, not roots. And he felt, as he expressed it, "as if I'm operating on only two or three cylinders in business."

Many divorced people fall into a similar pattern. They are still consumed with anger and bitterness and self-justification regarding their ex-spouses. In a negative sense, psychologically they are still married — they each need the weaknesses of the former partner to justify their accusations.

Many "older" children go through life either secretly or openly hating their parents. They blame them for past abuses, neglect, favoritism, and so on, and they justify themselves accordingly. In a like way many parents become almost paranoid over a particularly testy child, reading all kinds of motives and bad seed into that "spoiled, selfish, ungrateful brat," using sophisticated adult language to explain and justify themselves to the child, and making sacrifices in condescending and manipulating ways to prove (protest) true parental love.

NEPHI PERHAPS TEMPORARILY ENEMY-CENTERED

From the record we have, even young Nephi might well have been a classic case of enemy-centered behavior. As I study his soliloquy in 2 Nephi 4, it looks to me as if, for a period of time, the faithful Nephi began to become centered on Laman and Lemuel, causing his strength to be slackened and his heart to be tinged with anger. In other words, Nephi was being engaged by Laman and Lemuel so much that it began to obsess him. He began to be more controlled by his enemies, it seems, than by the Lord. (See 2 Nephi 4:17-27.) He began to lose his power base. Laman and Lemuel were providing his direction and guidance, and he exhibited this in a defensive way. He began to lose his sense of security, and when he came to himself he acknowledged what had happened and resolved never to put his faith in the arm of flesh again, for it had decimated his strength and power and had darkened his mind. It had brought out all the weaknesses of the flesh. Listen to his determination and resolve to become God-centered again.

Awake, my soul! No longer droop in sin. Rejoice, O my heart, and give place no more for the enemy of my soul.

Do not anger again because of mine enemies. Do not slacken my strength because of mine afflictions.

Rejoice, O my heart, and cry unto the Lord, and say: O Lord, I will praise thee forever; yea, my soul will rejoice in thee, my God, and the rock of my salvation.

O Lord, wilt thou redeem my soul? Wilt thou deliver me out of the hands of mine enemies? Wilt thou make me that I may shake at the appearance of sin?

May the gates of hell be shut continually before me, because that my heart is broken and my spirit is contrite! O Lord, wilt thou not shut the gates of thy righteousness before me, that I may walk in the path of the low valley, that I may be strict in the plain road!

O Lord, wilt thou encircle me around in the robe of thy righteousness! O Lord, wilt thou make a way for mine escape before mine enemies! Wilt thou make my path straight before me! Wilt thou not place a stumbling block in my way—but that thou wouldst clear my way before me, and hedge not up my way, but the ways of mine enemy.

O Lord, I have trusted in thee, and I will trust in thee forever. I will not put my trust in the arm of flesh; for I know that cursed is he that putteth his trust in the arm of flesh. Yea, cursed is he that putteth his trust in man or maketh flesh his arm.

Yea, I know that God will give liberally to him that asketh. Yea, my God will give me, if I ask not amiss; therefore I will lift up my voice unto thee; yea, I will cry unto thee, my God, the rock of my righteousness. Behold, my voice shall forever ascend up unto thee, my rock and mine everlasting God. Amen. (2 Nephi 4:28-35.)

Immediately after this resolve was made, Laman and Lemuel increased their anger and their murderous ways. No longer would Nephi allow himself to move onto their territory and be afflicted by them. Consequently a permanent separation took place between the Nephites and the Lamanites.

DON'T FIGHT ON SATAN'S TERRITORY

The adversary would love to have us engaged with him, to fight him on his territory. He would rather have us be angry toward him than ignore him and be involved in our own work on the Lord's territory. If he can engage us, he can win. But if we have nothing to do with him, there is no way in which he can win. He is a parasite. Jesus said:

> When the unclean spirit is gone out of a man, he walketh through dry places, seeking rest; and finding none, he saith, I will return unto my house whence I came out.
> And when he cometh, he findeth it swept and garnished.
> Then goeth he and taketh to him seven other spirits more wicked than himself; and they enter in, and dwell there: and the last state of that man is worse than the first. (Luke 11:24-26.)

Evil survives by festering the good until it becomes evil. That is why it is critically important that whenever we overcome some bad tendency or habit, we immediately fill that void with good habits. The only way to overcome evil is with good. We must never resort to the adversary's tactics or methods in order to fight him, for then we will have joined him unwittingly and participated in an ugly and destructive union. We don't tell a lie in order to catch another's lie. We don't manipulate in order to expose the manipulations of others.

I remember several times in the mission field when missionaries and members became engrossed in discussing Satan and his ways. We had some experiences with evil spirits, but by the power of the priesthood we cast them out. In one instance we did this only to find that the spirit returned within a short period of time. Again we cast the spirit out and it left, only to come back later. I became acquainted with that spirit and became aware that it came back because of the desire and willingness of the victim to have it back. The victim was having some kind of twisted curiosity satisfied, even perhaps a masochistic enjoyment from it all, and was receiving a great deal of attention. Some people prefer attention, at any price, to being ignored.

We counseled our missionaries and the members to stop talking and thinking about the adversary and his ways, since one of his ways is to engage our minds in contemplating his own dark mysteries and preoccupy our spirits with his tactics. We needed to simply become occupied with our work and with doing good. Then the adversary could have no hold upon us.

THE LORD'S WAY

Doing good of course implies doing things the Lord's way, the way of honesty and integrity, with a total absence of manipulation and insincerity of any kind. An experience I was slightly involved in illustrates the positive results of such a course.

While serving as a mission representative of the First Council of the Seventy and the Quorum of the Twelve, at one point I was responsible for helping to introduce, emphasize, and teach a new set of missionary discussions to the four missions I was working with on the east coast. The following experience illustrates the power of complete integrity and openness in the mind and heart and the importance of our always dealing with people on the basis of such principles.

We were having a two-day conference with the missionaries in the Pennsylvania Mission. On the first day we handed out copies of the new discussions to all of the missionaries and discussed them conceptually, with particular emphasis on the teaching principles they embodied. The missionaries were to take this material, continue to study it that afternoon and evening if they had time, then bring it back the next day for the second day of our conference.

When the meeting began the next morning, a missionary raised his hand and asked if he might relate an experience he had had with the discussions since we had adjourned on the previous day. Here is my paraphrase of his story:

"My companion and I took the discussions with us on our teaching appointments last night, thinking we might have some time to study them or they might be of some other use to us. Accidentally we left the discussions in a home where we had taught several times before. We completely forgot about this until this morning, when we had to find the discussions to study them in preparation for today's meeting. When we couldn't find them, we remembered we had left them in the home of the investigating family the night before, and we were embarrassed and chagrined by this. We went this morning to pick them up.

"The man of the house met us at the door. He asked us to come in and said he wanted to discuss something with us. He told us that after we left the night before, he noticed we had left some materials. Being curious, he said, he picked them up and started to read them, only to find that they were the discussions we would be teaching his family, together with some counsel to the missionaries on how to teach the discussions, how to overcome objections, how to deal with problems, and so forth.

"At that point we became concerned, thinking that some of those instructions might be offensive to him. But he continued by saying he was greatly impressed with the discussions and was even more impressed by the counsel given to the missionaries on how to teach the discussions and how to deal with problems that might arise. In fact, he said, he was so impressed that he was convinced that we represented the true church, and he was seriously considering asking for baptism.

"We asked what it was in the materials that had had this kind of impact upon him. He responded that the interesting content of the discussions had kept him up reading it for much of the night, but that what impressed him most was the counsel that whenever the missionary had to deal with some serious obstacles or objections or problems, as the ultimate test, the court of last resort, the missionaries were to ask the investigator to go to his God and inquire in deep, sincere prayer and in the name of Jesus Christ. He said, 'I could hardly believe that you would have such confidence that God would confirm the truth of your teachings,

> **Ends and means are completely inseparable. In fact, ends preexist in the means. There is no way in which a person can truly accomplish a worthy end by using unworthy means.**

and you couldn't have that confidence unless your message was indeed absolutely true.' "

In other words, that man got hold of our best missionary instructional material, which was not intended for his eyes, and found in it no effort to manipulate, to pressure, to lie, to cover up, to conceal, or to distort in order to gain our own ends or add another member to the Church. He found instead that we were completely honest and caring and were absolutely reliant on the Spirit of God in guiding the investigator, in developing his understanding, and in confirming the truth of all that we were teaching him. He knew that our means and our ends were totally worthy and compatible.

Ends and means are completely inseparable. In fact, ends preexist in the means. There is no way in which a person can truly accomplish a worthy end by using unworthy means. When people are pure in their motives and intentions and they work within correct principles toward divine purposes they have the optimum teaching combination to draw down the powers of heaven in the teaching process. Then if the other person is likewise honest in his heart, is desirous and open-minded and sincere in his investigation, true divine communication will take place. Both will be edified. "Wherefore, he that preacheth and he that receiveth, understand one another, and both are edified and rejoice together" (D&C 50:22). And this principle works not only in missionary endeavor but in all situations in which we strive to help another improve his understanding and his life.

The Lord's way of resisting evil is not to oppose it with evil but to overcome it with good within the framework of correct principles. That constitutes "fighting" on the Lord's territory rather than the devil's. Said the Savior, "I say unto you, That ye resist not evil: but whosoever shall smite thee on thy right cheek, turn to him the other also." (Matthew 5:39.)

THE GREATER SIN

One time I talked on the idea that the forgiveness of others is the frail, thin pathway we ourselves must walk in order to receive our own forgiveness. I quoted Doctrine and Covenants 64:9, which indicates that the greater sin lies in the one who won't forgive. After my discourse, a sister came up and told me she was determined to go to a certain Church leader and seek forgiveness. She did this, and reported that through her actions she had gained an entirely new perspective of the problem. She had become almost paranoid in her feelings that she was being persecuted by this leader. And she had poisoned the hearts and minds of her children against him, his family, and his business. Though she herself had since repented, she was heartsick over the many seeds she had sown in the hearts of her children. She wondered what she could do to repent of the consequences of her attitude. It was a very good question, and I am not certain I gave her a very good answer to it. That contained in chapter 5 would be my answer to her today.

SELF-CENTEREDNESS

Another possible frame of reference, perhaps the most common one today, is *self-centeredness.* It lies at the foundation of most or all of the centers already described. We tend to equate self-centeredness with selfishness, which we think of as bad. Yet oddly enough, if we closely examine many of the popular approaches to growth, enlightenment, and self-fulfillment, we often find self-centering at their core. Nevertheless the approaches continue to find public acceptance. It is as if self-centeredness in the raw—as in a husband indulging his expensive tastes while denying his wife necessities—is clearly objectionable, while giving it another name and clothing it in clever articulation endows it with respectability. "How could it be wrong when it feels so good?" "You do your thing and I'll do mine."

Consider a continuum of self-centeredness. At the lower end is a kind of egocentrism wherein the person is concerned only with his own activities and wants. Near the lower end too would be a kind of philanthropic hedonism or pleasure seeking, an attempt to satisfy one's own wants in the guise of helping others.

HUMANISM

The higher forms of humanism would be at the upper end of the continuum. Even though the altruistic or humanistic approach appears to be other-centered, in that it focuses on doing good to others, its basic method is still self-centered. The dictionary defines *humanism* as "a philosophy that asserts the dignity and worth of man and his capacity for self realization through reason and that often rejects supernaturalism." Thus humanism is essentially a self-effort approach to improvement or self-actualization. It is based upon the assumption that through man's own efforts in schooling and education, as well as through social legislation, man can be saved; that he can make himself into another kind of person.

To a degree this is true, and that fact probably accounts for the nature of much of the terrestrial world, the world of honorable people who have not accepted the gospel (D&C 76:75). However, the terrestrial world itself is governed by the Spirit of Christ. Though the atheistic humanist does not recognize this, his real value system and power come initially from the Spirit. But the ultimate changing of one's nature and the partaking of a divine nature requires acquisition of divine powers, and this is possible only through obedience to the laws and ordinances of the gospel.

We all tend to reap where we have not sown. Frequently, the good aspects of humanism are reapings from the sowing of earlier religious training and values. The next generation reaps a harvest of self-centeredness and egocentrism at the low end of the continuum, as a result of humanistic values which, though sown nearer the high end, are not now rooted in God.

TREND IN SUCCESS LITERATURE

The findings of several reviews made of the success literature published over the last two hundred years underscore this point. They make plain that the secularization of culture accounts for, or at least has gone hand in hand with, the deterioration in religious values and beliefs which is evident almost everywhere in society today. For the first 150 of the years surveyed, the primary focus in the popular success literature was the *character ethic*, and this was seen largely through the lens of religious values and faith in God. The character ethic deals with the development of fundamental traits in the personality, traits such as service, honesty, industry, charity, chastity, patriotism, integrity, benevolence, thrift, self-discipline, self-sacrifice, and so on.

About thirty to fifty years ago, a highly significant new trend began to eclipse or subordinate this character ethic, and the trend has continued (though lip service was and occasionally is still given to the character ethic). The new trend might be called the *personality ethic*. It focuses primarily on human relations techniques, on influence strategies, on image building, on getting what you want, on self-actualization, on assertiveness skills, on PMA (Positive Mental Attitude), on success programming and people manipulation tactics. With this trend many self-centered cults and fads have moved into the literature and into life, promising their adherents self-realization, enlightenment, peace of mind, or vital health.

Each of these concepts and systems may have some genuine merit to commend it, but when they become ends in themselves —almost a definition of salvation—they create an absolute distortion of life, an aberrant behavior and addiction.

COMBINATION-CENTEREDNESS

I believe that combination-centeredness is the most common condition. Many people are so much a function of the influences that play upon their lives that their center often becomes a blending or mixing of many of the centers discussed above. Depending upon what condition (external and / or internal) the person may be in, different centers are activated until each is played out as the person's underlying needs are satisfied, then another center becomes the compelling force. Such fluctuations may take place even on the same day.

One of the main problems with an eclectic-approach or combination center is the continual shifting of the perspective of the map, resulting in relativism and a lack of consistency in basic values, standards and direction. It is like roller-coasting through life: high one moment, low the next, making efforts to compensate for one weakness by borrowing strength from another weakness. It offers no consistent sense of direction, no persistent wisdom, no steady power supply or sense of personal, intrinsic worth and identity. "For he that wavereth is like a wave of the sea driven with the wind and tossed" (James 1:6).

(See chapter 1 for the purpose of this picture.)

The Unreal Dilemma

Chapter 3

*He that loveth father or mother more than
me is not worthy of me: and he that loveth son
or daughter more than me is not worthy
of me. (Matthew 10:37.)*

In the previous chapter we discussed several possible maps or
frames of reference, any one or a combination of which we
might make the center of our lives. We saw that none of them is
adequate, that none give the security, guidance, wisdom, and
power we truly need. I have left to this point the discussion of
two other centers which rightly are dear to the Latter-day Saint's
heart and one or the other of which many Church members assert
as the proper center of our lives. I refer to the Church and the
family.

THE CHURCH-CENTERED LIFE

Suppose, then, that we consider putting the Church at the
center of our lives. This has the appearance of logic for
Church members, for certainly the Church is God's kingdom on
earth. It is the divine organization that has been established to
teach the gospel to people everywhere and to administer its
sacred ordinances to them. It has the loftiest and most progres-
sive ideas, being designed to give opportunities for infinite
development to all people, regardless of when they have lived or
will live upon the earth, by means of the opportunity to receive
and live the gospel of Jesus Christ. The purpose of the Church is
to help save all the living and all the dead. To do this it has three
essential missions: to preach the gospel to those who have not
received it; to perfect the Saints, or those who have received it;
and to redeem the dead.

A MEANS, NOT AN END

These surely are noble aims, and no other organization on earth comes close to the Church in its power to bless mankind. Nevertheless it is apparent that the Church is a means to an end, not an end in itself. The Church is the instrument. It is the vehicle, the conveyer, having the three-fold mission and role mentioned above. But by itself it cannot be a person's effective center, because it is itself dependent. As the vehicle for making the gospel available on earth, it reaches back to the central or fulcrum doctrine, the most significant event in the history of the world, the atonement of the Lord Jesus Christ. All of the Church's principles and ordinances derive their efficacy from the fact that Jesus Christ worked out the great, infinite atonement, the benefits of which we receive through faith in him and conformity with his gospel. These benefits include repentance, covenant making in the waters of baptism for the forgiveness of sins, and as renewed in partaking of the sacrament, and the gift of the Holy Ghost by the laying on of hands.

It is of critical importance that we see the Church as a means to an end and not as an end in itself. Most members of the Church know in their hearts that *there is a very clear and distinct difference between being active in the Church and being active in the gospel.* The latter embodies the former, but the converse is not necessarily true. It is my observation that generally speaking the more active a person is in the Church and the more substantial his responsibilities are in it, the more clearly he sees the difference between activity in the Church and activity in the gospel. The more active member grows increasingly sensitive to the Spirit and realizes that going through motions or perfunctorily fulfilling one's calling in order to meet minimum expectations is insufficient in doing the work of the Lord and blessing the lives of others.

In the narrow sense, activity in the Church is an occasional thing—basically meaning attending meetings and living certain well-defined and minimal laws such as tithing and the Word of Wisdom. Activity in the gospel, on the other hand, is a constant

> There is a very clear and distinct difference between being active in the Church and being active in the gospel. The latter embodies the former, but the converse is not necessarily true.

and a growing thing. It has to do with the heart and mind of man as well as the location of his body. It's fairly easy to attend Church meetings and yet be mentally and emotionally elsewhere. As they run from meeting to meeting or interview to interview, such Mormons are often characterized as poor Christians, bad neighbors, and insensitive to pressing human needs.

CHURCH-CENTERED SPOUSES

Many LDS marriages are in real jeopardy even though both parties are very active in the Church in the narrow sense described above. In these marriages husband and wife have even learned to use Church words and theological concepts to accuse and belittle and criticize and judge each other. They are constantly opening the door of justice for the Lord to come in and make right the wrongs others have committed against them, while all the time the Lord is knocking on the door of mercy which they have cemented up with pride, bitterness, resentment, and self-justification.

There are Church-centered people who escape from the more rigorous responsibilities in the marriage and the family by saying, "I'm going to do the work of the Church" (or "the work of the kingdom," or "the work of the Lord"). Attending meetings, interviewing others regarding their worthiness, or conducting worthwhile programs for others may be much easier than confronting and solving a difficult emotional situation at home with the spouse or the teenage son or daughter. Sometimes such a member, of whatever leadership position, will fully rationalize family neglect in the name of the Church. But such rationaliza-

It takes more nobility of character in the form of humility, patience, understanding, and courage to do whatever is necessary to build that one relationship—the family—than to labor diligently and faithfully for the many others outside of it.

tions are empty and hollow, and one day if and when the person reaches the top rung of whatever ladder he is climbing, he will look about him and see that it was leaning against the wrong wall.

In 1965, President David O. McKay made the following statement to a group of Church employees:

"Let me assure you, Brethren, that some day you will have a personal priesthood interview with the Savior himself. If you are interested, I will tell you the order in which he will ask you to account for your earthly responsibilities.

"First, he will request an accountability report about your relationship with your wife. Have you actively been engaged in making her happy and ensuring that her needs have been met as an individual?

"Second, he will want an accountability report about each of your children individually. He will not attempt to have this for simply a family stewardship but will request information about your relationship to each and every child.

"Third, he will want to know what you personally have done with the talents you were given in the preexistence.

"Fourth, he will want a summary of your activity in your Church assignments. He will not be necessarily interested in what assignments you have had, for in his eyes the home teacher and a mission president are probably equals, but he will request a summary of how you have been of service to your fellow man in your Church assignments.

"Fifth, he will have no interest in how you earned your living but if you were honest in all your dealings.

"Sixth, he will ask for an accountability on what you have done to contribute in a positive manner to your community, state, country, and the world." (Reported by Cloyd Hofheins in a talk to the seventies quorum of Provo Utah Oak Hills Stake, May 16, 1982.)

THE IMAGE OF ACTIVITY

In the Church-centered life it can happen also that portraying the active-Church-member image or appearance becomes the person's dominant consideration. In that situation hypocrisy is not far ahead. This undermines his personal security and intrinsic sense of worth. In spite of many divine sources of self-definition, his self-map now becomes socially defined. His guidance too comes from such a social conscience, and he tends to label everybody in terms of this Church-centeredness — active, inactive, liberal, orthodox, conservative, and so on.

There is now a danger that he will become an idealist or a perfectionist, unaware of or unwilling to deal with the practical, step-by-step processes of moving from real situations toward worthy ends. In that case he loses his sense of timing as to when to do what, talking in abstract principles and theological concepts in Church phrases. He develops a sense of powerlessness. He transfers responsibility from himself to his environment. He may also become increasingly aware of his hypocrisy and make occasional efforts to repent and to become more gospel-centered, but he is in the bondage of an incorrect map or pair of glasses, so that these sincere efforts are likely to fatigue him fast, and he sooner or later will fall back to going through the motions.

EFFECT ON FAMILY

All the while, he is repressing a great deal of feeling and sensing, and this eats into his personal security. These repressed feelings come forth in ugly ways later, perhaps in other contexts or merely in anger toward the family or withdrawal from it. Yet he still may fully rationalize the family neglect in the name of the Church.

Dag Hammarskjold, former secretary-general of the United

Nations, once said, "It is more noble to give oneself to one individual than to labor diligently for the salvation of the masses." A man could be very involved six or seven days a week, spending twelve to fourteen hours a day doing good things for other people, and yet not have a loving and meaningful relationship and communication with his wife or child or business partner; and it would take more nobility of character in the form of humility, patience, understanding, and courage to do whatever is necessary to rebuild that one relationship — to create a new and higher level of love and communication in the family — than to continue to labor diligently and faithfully for the many others outside of it. Ironically, bringing healing to this internal family or other vital relationship is often the most important key in being effective with the many. Going after the one is often the key to the ninety-nine. What a person *is* teaches far more eloquently than what a person *says* or even *does.* It communicates quietly, subtly; it is a constant radiation, and others, though unable to identify or articulate it, still understand it, sense it, absorb it, and respond to it.

EFFECT ON OCCUPATION

A Church-centered individual may also excuse mediocrity in work or professional endeavor, all in the name of the Church. He thinks he is giving his energies to the more important work, but he is unaware that his slipshod, mediocre performance is a powerful communicator of the true quality of his character. He may get by with it for a while, but eventually the disjointedness of his life will catch up with him and will produce a bitter harvest. As one put it, "It is the harvest and not the Master that will accuse the slothful servant." A lack of proper centering will cause inconsistent self-discipline, which will eventually be revealed as hypocrisy or inconsistency. Negligence in small things leads both to and from neglecting large things.

EFFECT ON CHURCH MEMBERSHIP

I remember speaking to a group of Protestant ministers at

their ministerial graduation exercises, and after the exercises were over I found one of the ministers to be a former Mormon. I asked him if he would tell me his story and explain why he did not find satisfaction in the Church and had therefore sought it elsewhere.

His response clearly indicated that he had been and still was a church-centered person. For many years he had been highly involved in the programs of the Church, rushing from meeting to meeting and never having any deep, rich, spiritual life. The Church had become an end in itself, and of course it had provided him with very little sense of satisfaction, security, peace, and power. He had confused means and ends. On the other hand, his present church provided a more peaceful life-style and an encouragement to seek the inner life. Though he and his wife had been married in the temple, and though they admired the Church for its aims and efforts, they claimed to experience more peace and satisfaction in their new church. They just felt that the Mormon church wasn't for them. During and after my visit with them I felt there were many other factors that had not been mentioned which would help to explain the situation; but also I was increasingly aware of the importance of not confusing means and ends.

As a mission president I once attempted tactfully to release a person from his Church position, but without success. The net effect was to release him from the Church. He had been Church-centered for too long, and most of his satisfactions had come from his Church position, to the point that he became emotionally dependent upon that position and highly vulnerable to any change in it. When a change was made and another assignment given him, his security base was disrupted. He had been thrown off the treadmill he was on, and he felt totally uncomfortable in his new situation. Gradually, little by little, he withdrew into himself and into inactivity. He justified his response intellectually by criticizing and finding fault, often using scriptural and religious words in the self-justifying effort. Actually, a good percentage of those who left the Church in this dispensation went out confessing the sins of others—and in the name of God, at that.

I remember once visiting a returned missionary in jail who had a most impressive track record of accomplishments in the Church. These included the Duty to God award, the Eagle Scout award, and so-called high positions in the mission field. But his Church-centeredness did not penetrate far enough to unravel a dishonest streak in his nature. He was always pushing things to the legal limits, passing over moral and ethical considerations, until one day he far surpassed the legal limits and the law caught up with him.

STRENGTH AND WEAKNESS

Why is Church-centering so weakening to the human character when obviously the Church is so strong a power for good? Consider the four factors—security, guidance, wisdom, and power—and you can come to understand why this is so. Remember that whatever is the center of a person's life becomes the source of his security, his guidance, his wisdom, and his power.

The Church is a formal organization made up of policies and programs and practices and people, and of itself therefore it cannot give a person any deep, permanent security, any sense of intrinsic worth. The gospel taught by the Church *can* do this, but the organization alone cannot. As indicated earlier, a Church security base would lead a person to identify himself with a label as being active or orthodox, and to label many others as inactive or unorthodox. Such artificial definitions obscure two realities: 1) in a sense virtually all Church members are inactive—it just depends on the context, on which commandment you are considering; and 2) activity lies on a continuum and embodies many dimensions, including activity in the Church. None of us is justified in throwing stones. As already mentioned, activity in the Church is necessary to activity in the gospel but is insufficient alone. As the above examples show, it cannot provide the type or degree of security we all need.

Nor can the Church give a person a constant sense of guidance. This is obtainable only through the gospel the Church teaches and through the Spirit. Consequently, a Church-centered person can easily live in compartments, acting and thinking and feeling in certain ways on the Sabbath and in totally different ways on weekdays and in non-Church environments. Such a lack of wholeness or unity or integrity is a further threat to the security dimension, thus creating the need for increased labeling and self-justifying.

This confusion of means and ends that we are calling Church-centeredness certainly undermines a person's wisdom or perspective and sense of balance. Though he might give lip service to the priority of people over programs, his actual behavior tends to invert this concept. He may draw an unusual sense of security from developing some expertise in the Church—say, a special knowledge of doctrine. In such a case it is common for great distortions to take place in the person's "doctrinal" knowledge, and this not only clouds his perspective and sense of balance but also weakens his knowledge and understanding of truth and thereby the foundations of wisdom. To use Elder Boyd K. Packer's excellent metaphor, if you were to continually pound one piano key, your very strength would become your weakness, your undoing. Most of us perhaps have attended a priesthood class or Sunday School class wherein we sensed that celestial principles were being discussed in a telestial spirit, a spirit in which abstract knowledge essentially eclipses love. Love is a higher and greater principle than knowledge, but it operates only under the influence of the Spirit, and that is not an attribute of the Church-centered life as we are defining it.

As regards the power factor or dimension, the Church teaches people about the real power source but does not claim to be that power source itself. It is a vessel or a vehicle through which the divine power can be channeled into man's nature. Speaking of gospel ordinances, which are available only through the Church, the Lord said: "Therefore, in the ordinances thereof, the power of godliness is manifest. And without the ordinances thereof, and the authority of the priesthood, the power of godliness is not manifest unto men in the flesh; for without this no man can see the face of God, even the Father, and live." (D&C 84:20-22.)

GOSPEL PRINCIPLES THE KEY

Power, then, in this narrow sense, does not come from the Church itself. The Church does not even have the power to help us overcome our faults and sins. Until a person taps the ultimate power source, he may experience some social sorrow for his sins because of the possibility of being found out or because of unhappy consequences, but he will find himself unable to stop the sinning. This is particularly true if the sinful habits, either of omission or commission, are deeply embedded in his character. The reason is that the Atonement and the forgiveness it offers to the repentant are *gospel* principles rather than Church principles, source-oriented rather than instrument-oriented.

At the April 2, 1982, Regional Representatives Seminar, Elder Bruce R. McConkie distinguished the separate roles of the Church and the gospel:

> Our tendency—it is an almost universal practice among most Church leaders—is to get so involved with the operation of the institutional Church that we never gain faith like the ancients, simply because we do not involve ourselves in the basic gospel matters that were the center of their lives.
>
> We are so wound up in programs and statistics and trends, in properties, lands, and mammon, and in achieving goals that will highlight the excellence of our work, that we "have omitted the weightier matters of the law." And as Jesus would have said: "These [weightier things] ought ye to have done, and not to leave the other undone." (Matthew 23:23.)
>
> Let us be reminded of the great basic verities upon which all Church programs and all Church organization rest.
>
> We are not saved by Church programs as such, by Church organizations alone, or even by the Church itself. It is the gospel that saves. The gospel is "the power of God unto salvation." (Romans 1:16.)
>
> Salvation comes because "Jesus Christ," as Paul said, "hath abolished death, and hath brought life and immortality to light

through the gospel." (2 Timothy 1:10.) It is the gospel that raises men "in immortality" and "unto eternal life." (D&C 29:43.) The gospel is the plan of salvation by which we can change the souls we possess into the kind of souls who can go where God and Christ are.

But the Church and the priesthood administer the gospel. There must be an institutional Church so there will be order and system in all things. There neither is nor can be salvation without the Church. The Church is the service agency, the organization, the earthly kingdom which makes salvation available to men.

Nothing that is said above is to be construed as minimizing or downgrading the value of the Church in our lives. The Church is indispensable to us as the divinely inspired organization that brings the gospel to all God's children—not merely to those seeking baptism and membership but also to members of all spiritual levels. It is the vehicle for growth in service as well as for a loving communion and worship as the body of believers. It is, however, still the vehicle, the instrument, and as such is insufficient as a life center.

THE FAMILY-CENTERED LIFE

If Church-centeredness is not right for us, how about family-centeredness? Surely that is a logical approach. After all, we are continually told by our Church leaders that the family is the most important organization both in time and in eternity. And we all can glibly quote two Church presidents on this theme: "No other success can compensate for failure in the home" (President David O. McKay), and "the most important of the Lord's work that you will ever do will be the work you do within the walls of your own home" (President Harold B. Lee).

WRONG CRITERIA SUBSTITUTED

These statements are true and proper, but they imply a center (the source of the teaching) other than the family. Ironically, the ultimate result of family-centeredness can be the loss of the family. As an example, a family-centered person may come to

Outside of the gospel there is no deep,
permanent power to keep families together,
particularly when the temptations of the
world thrust themselves on our young people
during the tempestuous teenage period.
Family life belongs, ultimately, to the celestial
kingdom and can be made secure for us only
by obedience to celestial laws.

resent Church demands and callings and may become almost a
law unto himself in judging and turning down properly inspired
calls. For him, gospel principles and standards may not be the
criteria for decision making; instead he may substitute his own
criteria in an effort to keep the family satisfied, together, and
harmonious.

I personally know of several individuals who each put his
family first, who made continuous efforts to keep the family
happy and together, but who in the process neglected Church
responsibilities, priesthood duties, Sabbath observance, home
night teaching, and the modeling of service and sacrifice outside
the family. These individuals do not have strong gospel-oriented
families any longer, because they were built too much on family
conveniences and pleasures instead of on gospel principles. "Me
and mine" can be as selfish as "me."

My wife and I had an experience one Sunday afternoon when
returning from sacrament meeting, where we had been figura-
tively (and to some degree literally) wrestling with our children.
It was late in the afternoon after I had attended several meetings
that day and had two more yet to come that evening. On our
way home we stopped to talk to a friend who was just pulling up
at his home, returning from a pleasure outing with his family,
and his children excitedly related to us what they had been
doing and how much fun they had been having. I remember
thinking about the contrast and momentarily wondering whether

it was all worth it, almost wishing we too had had a pleasant time in enjoyable recreation as a family that Sunday afternoon.

These contrasting experiences for the two families took place Sunday after Sunday until the other family's habit pattern, like ours, became addictive. The final chapter in either family has not been written, but I am personally persuaded that outside of the gospel there is no deep, permanent power to keep families together, particularly when the temptations of the world thrust themselves on our young people during the tempestuous teenage period. Family life belongs, ultimately, to the celestial kingdom and can be made secure for us only by obedience to celestial laws. And the Church, with its priesthood keys held by prophets, is the earthly repository of those laws.

DEPENDENCE AND COUNTERDEPENDENCE

Usually a family-centered person's sense of security or personal worth comes primarily from the family tradition and culture, and this makes him vulnerable to many changes in that tradition or culture. Being wrongly centered, as often as not he will love his children conditionally rather than unconditionally, in which case they will become emotionally dependent; or, in order to protect themselves from being wounded any further, they may become counterdependent and go opposite to the way they were reared. Both dependency and counterdependency are manifestations that the family is still controlling, one in the conforming way and the other in a negative conforming way.

As mission president, many times I welcomed to the mission field missionaries who had either been Church-centered or family-centered, and I sensed how lost they were in a totally new environment. They had been thrown out of their "comfort zone," and they now made every effort to try to regain that zone, even by living vicariously in the past or expectantly in the future. They had become dependent on certain practices which were totally inappropriate in the new situation. They had little orientation to principles or to the Spirit's whispering of new practices based on those principles.

One missionary had essentially been told how to do everything for almost his entire life to that point, and his own capacity to make independent decisions consequently remained dormant. His mother told him at the farewell airport scene that he was now on his own and would need to make his own decisions. Since he would probably feel somewhat lost, she handed him a long checklist of what to do in handling as many foreseeable situations as she could possibly identify. She sent his missionary funds to me so that I could manage them for him virtually on a weekly basis. He was sent out a cripple—overmothered, possessed, dominated, and smothered. It took many months before he was capable of making his own decisions based on correct principles, and the process of achieving that level of competency involved his changing to the correct life center.

INSECURITY A POOR TEACHING BASE

Family-centering can subtly destroy the eternal family in other ways as well. Without proper centering, security is lost. When insecure people begin to feel emotionally upset and threatened, they often become desperate and frantic and are guided by the emotions of the moment, spontaneously reacting to their immediate circumstances. Their lives are not usually disciplined, orderly, or regular. They often yell and scream at their children. They overreact and punish out of a bad temper, despite the fact that teaching is never powerful, in the ultimate sense, when accompanied by a spirit of anger.

People simply do not and will not learn when they are defensive. In fact, the best way at that point for them to maintain their sense of personal worth, however shaky that may be, their sense of integrity and identity, is to identify with the opposite of the teaching. This is because when people teach at a time when they are angry with someone being taught, they are essentially overreactive, and then the main message is rejection of the one taught. The teaching is the secondary message. So to handle the main message, the person often turns against the secondary message, because this gives him a feeling of asserting himself—

"I matter, I count, I'm important, separate and apart from my behavior." Such a reaction, of course, which is the second over-reaction, only feeds more fuel into the fire of negative collusion between teacher and taught, and the vicious cycle begins again at a deeper and more congealed level.

Such teaching comes from a position of weak, poorly founded wisdom. A parent who tries to teach celestial doctrine with a telestial spirit in his home simply will not succeed. Most of us have had the experience of coming to family home evening prepared to teach a lesson on love, patience, or some similar kindly theme, only to have some negative element intervene. Perhaps as the family assembles, a teenage daughter receives a lengthy phone call from a boy she "just can't cut off short"; or the family dog surges in at a crucial point of focus, and four children must each take personal responsibility for subduing and removing him; or a child returns from the bathroom with news that the water has been left running and is overflowing from the washbasin (into the basement, as it turns out). At such a moment it requires a strong self-control plus considerable help from the Spirit to control anger or frustration, settle down our feelings, and give an effective lesson on a celestial principle.

But at least a reasonable, striving parent can generally make the conditions right once a week. On the other hand, the parent who habitually teaches on a day-to-day basis from the weak position of angry reaction (or overreaction) to circumstances, as indicated above, will find again and again that one of the best ways in which others, particularly young people, defend their own sense of security, identity, and integrity is to resist the very teachings given to them. Until people see and feel, they will not hear. If they see a model contrary to what they hear—if they feel anger or rejection breathing behind words of love—they will be confused. Their confusion will create insecurity in them, and the whole process may be carried over to the next generation. Yet all the while their parents may be active in the Church and concerned for their families.

This situation is sad but true. We *all* know it.

Teaching is 90 percent modeling and relating and 10 percent telling. It is as with the iceberg—the tip of the iceberg, the seen part, is very small compared to the unseen part. The great unseen mass under the water represents what our children, our students, our followers, our investigators see and feel about us. The visible tip represents what they hear. If what they see and feel is in harmony with what they hear, it will take; they will indeed hear. If it is out of harmony, it will not take. If they hear at all, they will be confused. As Emerson put it, "What you are shouts so loudly in my ears, I cannot hear what you say." One other cliché applies here: "I don't care how much you know until I know how much you care."

What is the solution? The answer of course is the correct map or life center. While love and concern for family, like allegiance to the Church, are proper and necessary for the happy life, neither provides the requisite security, guidance, wisdom, or power *in and of itself.* For this, we must look beyond these two organizations to the only satisfactory life center for the Latter-day Saint.

That center is the focus of the discussion for the remainder of this book.

The Divine Center

Chapter 4

*And now, my sons, remember, remember
that it is upon the rock of our Redeemer,
who is Christ, the son of God, that ye
must build your foundation; that when the
devil shall send forth his mighty winds, yea,
his shafts in the whirlwind, yea, when all
his hail and his mighty storm shall beat
upon you, it shall have no power over you
to drag you down to the gulf of misery and
endless wo, because of the rock upon which
ye are built, which is a sure foundation,
a foundation whereon if men build they
cannot fall. (Helaman 5:12.)*

In the two previous chapters we considered several life centers
or maps, frames of reference from which to view one's world.
These we measured somewhat against our need for security,
guidance, wisdom, and power. I hope the discussion convinced
you that every one of those centers is inadequate.

Two of them — Church and family — seemed initially to have
a higher level of credibility than the others (and of course they
have!), since they are revered and honored by every convinced
Latter-day Saint. If those two are found wanting, what is there
left to grasp as our center?

My answer to this is: God and Jesus Christ. I will try to
explain why and in what sense I say this.

Let me first make clear the sense or senses in which I am *not*
suggesting the Savior in this connection. I am not indicating any
kind of "special" relationship with him or any other approach

that scriptures and modern prophets would not clearly sanction. My approach to this entire topic, as anyone's should be, is one of worshipful reverence with no idea of familiarity or intimacy such as between human friends. In several places in the Doctrine and Covenants, it is true, the Savior calls his faithful servants of that day his friends. I interpret that, however, as a gracious expression of approval and acceptance which, though sincere, is not to be construed as bringing him down to our level but perhaps rather as hinting at the possibility of our one day rising closer to his. Even those who achieve the highest reward hereafter, that of co-inheritor with Jesus Christ, will doubtless eternally hold him, along with his Father, in a special reverence.

THE CENTRALITY OF JESUS CHRIST

For all that, he is indeed our greatest friend. No mortal being has done or could have done for us anything for our benefit which is remotely comparable to the Atonement, to mention only the Savior's greatest act of love and sacrifice on our behalf. By any reasonable interpretation, along with the Father who gave us the plan of salvation, he is our loving friend.

I sometimes think that in our efforts to avoid "sectarianism" we Latter-day Saints get nervous and defensive on this matter of our expressions about Jesus Christ. We overreact, as it were. Conscious of the Savior's words to Joseph Smith condemning the various creeds, we subconsciously tend to negate also the emphasis which much of sectarian Christianity places on Christ-centeredness. Rather naturally we associate that emphasis with such false concepts as easy salvation by grace alone. But we ought not to "throw the baby out with the bath water." We should not allow apostate doctrines and interpretations to preempt in any degree the unquestioned centrality of the Savior to the true gospel we enjoy and to our individual lives. We should not be self-conscious or defensive about this concept merely because it has been misused by others who are not blessed with our knowledge or our gospel ordinances and covenants.

For truly, Jesus Christ is at the center of our hopes and aspirations, eternally speaking. The Father's gospel is called by the name of Jesus Christ. The first principle of that gospel is faith in him. Because he atoned for our sins he is our Redeemer and Savior and our Mediator with the Father. Hence, as Peter said under inspiration, "there is none other name under heaven given among men, whereby we must be saved" (Acts 4:12).

Those who properly receive the gospel ordinances of baptism and the laying on of hands for the gift of the Holy Ghost and are born of the Spirit to a newness of life become the sons and daughters of Jesus Christ. This is the sense in which he is our father. (See Moses 6:66, 68; Mosiah 5:7.) They take upon them his name (Mosiah 5:8; D&C 20:77), "for by this name shall ye be called at the last day" (3 Nephi 27:5). In renewing their baptismal covenants at the sacrament table, they recommit to take upon themselves the name of Jesus Christ. He is, as he said, "the way, the truth, and the life" (John 14:6). Our ultimate hope is to dwell with him and the Father; but, as he told us, "no man cometh unto the Father, but by me" (John 14:6).

THE TERM "CENTER"

The scriptures use different physical or space words to communicate the supremely important, the preeminent, the highest priority, the organizing or integrating principle, the governing source. Without exception these expressions all refer to God and Christ. Helaman used *foundation* (Helaman 5:15). Paul used *head* and *chief cornerstone* (Ephesians 2:20; 4:15). Old Testament prophets and Christ himself used *water, bread,* and so forth (Psalm 105:40; Isaiah 55:1; John 4:10-11; 6:58).

As a young man I was greatly impressed and inspired in hearing President David O. McKay counsel us to center our lives around God. It seemed to give me a handle on everything, a focus around which to organize all else. President Spencer W. Kimball stressed the centrality of Christ in our lives at a special student fireside, as reported in the April 1980 *New Era* article titled "The Savior: Center of Our Lives."

For many years the word *center* has seemed to communicate powerfully to me and to others. I like it because of its double role. As both a noun and an action verb, it implies a governing state of mind (the mind of Christ) and also an activity (getting centered) to achieve it.

THE SUPERLATIVE HERO-MODEL

I might have suggested the gospel as the true center of our lives. In theory this would be acceptable. But this is a behavior book, intended to be practical. In the minds of many (too many) the term *gospel* is too abstract for our purpose. It is also impersonal. The abstract and impersonal has less power to move us than the concrete and personal. What moves people is the gospel *in action*, the gospel exemplified rather than the gospel in theory. And which life moves and motivates us as much as that of Jesus Christ? As the single perfect example for all time, he is the model, as represented by the scriptural record of his life on earth. We all need a hero-model, and no record exists for us of any perfect hero-model except Jesus Christ. As he is the central fact and figure of the gospel, to center our lives on the gospel in our present context is to fail to sharpen the focus. As the point of focus, Jesus Christ is a "natural."

THE GODHEAD

When I speak of the Savior as the center of our lives, I mean this center to include also our Heavenly Father and the Holy Ghost. In the full sense, I mean the entire Godhead. This is the divine center. "We believe in God, the Eternal Father, and in His Son, Jesus Christ, and in the Holy Ghost" (first article of faith). In purpose these three members of the Godhead are one, yet they perform different functions or roles in accomplishing that singular purpose—that of bringing "to pass the immortality and eternal life of man" (Moses 1:39). The Savior said: "I and the Father are one" (John 10:30). "He that hath seen me hath seen the Father" (John 14:9). "I am in the Father and the Father in me"

(John 14:10). Certainly the center of the Savior's life was the Father: he was continually led by the Father in everything he said and did. Gradually, line upon line and precept upon precept, the Father's mind became his mind. He probably acquired a testimony of his own divine Sonship as he moved from grace to grace (see and study D&C 93). The Holy Ghost is the member of the Godhead who testifies of the Father and the Son to our souls, who continues to reveal their mind and will to us, who quickens our understandings and enlightens our minds, who teaches us and comforts us and confirms the Father's promises to us, who helps in purifying and sanctifying our souls. Our calling is to worship the Father in the name of the Son through the Holy Ghost, to pray to the Father in the name of the Son through the Holy Ghost, to serve in the name of the Son by the power of the Holy Ghost.

OUR RELATIONSHIP WITH THE GODHEAD

Elder Bruce R. McConkie, speaking at a BYU devotional on March 2, 1982, asked and answered the question, What is and should be our relationship to the members of the Godhead? Here is his answer:

> First, be it remembered, that most scriptures that speak of God or of the Lord do not even bother to distinguish the Father from the Son, simply because it doesn't make any difference which God is involved. They are one. The words or deeds of either of them would be the words and deeds of the other in the same circumstance.
>
> Further, if a revelation comes from, or by the power of the Holy Ghost, ordinarily the words will be those of the Son, though what the Son says will be what the Father would say, and the words may thus be considered as the Father's.
>
> And thus any feelings of love, praise, awe, or worship that may fill our hearts when we receive the divine word will be the same no matter who is thought or known to be the author of them.
>
> And yet we do have a proper relationship to each member of the Godhead, in part at least because there are separate and severable functions which each performs, and also because of what they as one Godhead have done for us.

Our relationship with the Father is supreme, paramount, and pre-eminent over all others. He is the God we worship. It is his gospel that saves and exalts. He ordained and established the plan of salvation. He is the one who was once as we are now. The life he lives is eternal life, and if we are to gain this greatest of all the gifts of God, it will be because we become like him.

Our relationship with the Father is one of parent and child. He is the one who gave us our agency. It was his plan that provided for a fall and an atonement. And it is to him that we must be reconciled if we are to gain salvation. He is the one to whom we have direct access by prayer, and if there were some need — which there is not! — to single out one member of the Godhead for a special relationship, the Father, not the Son, would be the one to choose.

Our relationship with the Son is one of brother or sister in the pre-mortal life and one of being led to the Father by him while in this mortal sphere. He is the Lord Jehovah who championed our cause before the foundations of the earth were laid. He is the God of Israel, the Promised Messiah, and the Redeemer of the world.

By faith we are adopted into his family and become his children. We take upon ourselves his name, keep his commandments, and rejoice in the cleansing power of his blood. Salvation comes by him. From Creation's dawn, as long as eternity endures, there neither has been nor will be any act of such transcendent power and import as his atoning sacrifice.

We do not have a fraction of the power we need to properly praise his holy name and ascribe unto him the honor and power and might and glory and dominion that is his. He is our Lord, our God, and our King.

Our relationship with the Holy Spirit is quite another thing. This holy personage is a revelator and a sanctifier. He bears record of the Father and the Son. He dispenses spiritual gifts to the faithful. Those of us who have received the gift of the Holy Ghost have the right to his constant companionship.

TERMINOLOGY FOR CENTER

How to express in a brief but effective term the highest center for our lives, at which we should be constantly aiming, is a question I have struggled with in writing this book. As we have seen, the term must be concrete and personal to be appropriately

What does it mean to put God and Christ at the center of one's life? The sense of this is seeing our world through the eyes of Christ, with the same kind of perception or map or frame of reference that he has. It is informed admiration and emulation of Jesus Christ, with the intent of reaching for his map, his frame of reference (which of course is identical with that of the other two members of the Godhead).

motivational, yet it must not convey or suggest incorrect impressions as to focus or as to a proper relationship with Deity. In keeping with these needs and in light of what is said above about the oneness of Godhead members and their complete identity of action in any given circumstances, I have decided to use the term *God/Christ-centered.*

This term may at first seem a little awkward to some, largely perhaps because it is "different." I used it hesitantly myself at first. But on balance I believe it is the appropriate and accurate expression for the meaning and purpose intended, and that as you read on you will quickly come to accept it. You will see too that throughout the subsequent chapters I vary the expression with such terms as *God-centered, Christ-centered,* and *divinely centered,* all with the same meaning and intent.

MEANING OF CENTERING

What do I have in mind when speaking of putting God and Christ at the center of one's life? The sense of this is seeing our world through the eyes of Christ, with the same kind of perception or map or frame of reference that he has. This sense is akin to Paul's expression made in speaking to the former-day Saints. Contrasting the spiritual discernment of the spiritually oriented with its lack in the natural man, he said, "We have the mind of Christ" (1 Corinthians 2:16). To have that mind is to be in harmony in all respects with the mind of the Father, as is clear from the Savior's own words: "I do nothing of myself; but as my Father hath taught me, I speak these things" (John 8:28). And again, "The Son can do nothing of himself, but what he seeth the Father do" (John 5:19).

As you will have gathered from our previous chapters, we see the world not as *it* is, but as *we* are. To change our perception, to improve our discernment, if you will, we need to change our spectacles, our frame of reference. The old one is the result of our environment, our previous conditioning and the attitudes we have developed or allowed to develop as a result.

When King Benjamin's people received the spiritual rebirth during his great sermon, their map was changed immediately and dramatically. The record does not show that change in all its detail, but one recorded result summarizes it in the participants' own words: "The Spirit . . . has wrought a mighty change in us . . . that we have no more disposition to do evil, but to do good continually" (Mosiah 5:2). We may fairly say, it seems to me, that as a result of this spiritual transformation they now had or were much nearer having the ability to see the world as if with the Savior's eyes. They had cast off their previous map or frame of reference in favor of the correct one.

Theirs was a sudden change, like Paul's or the Younger Alma's. More often, perhaps, it comes gradually as a person puts forth continual spiritual effort over the years. The ingredients of this effort are well known: prayer, scripture study, Church activity, service to others, and keeping the Lord's commandments — doing all such in meekness and love, in a spirit of dedication, and earnestly seeking the companionship of the Spirit. But something else is needed, I feel, and that is a strong model; one whose life and teachings match and are clearly visible; a totally reliable model who will never let you down. As I have suggested above, only one can fill that bill.

This informed admiration and emulation of Jesus Christ, with the intent of reaching for *his* map, *his* frame of reference (which of course is identical with that of the other two members of the Godhead), is what I mean by putting God and Christ at the center of your life.

THE COMPUTER METAPHOR

From the point of view of personal growth, it is extremely important that we have a proper relationship with the Father, the Son, and the Holy Ghost and a clear understanding of their different roles in accomplishing the same purpose—"to bring to pass the immortality and eternal life of man" (Moses 1:39).

I will suggest another physical analogy or metaphor to help communicate the nature of our relationship with the Father and the Son and in what sense we become spiritually begotten children, sons and daughters, of Jesus Christ. May I ask those of you who are not familiar with computer language to concentrate to understand this metaphor, for once it is understood you will find it extremely helpful in clarifying what this book is attempting to communicate (just as the metaphors of the map and glasses were, I hope, helpful to you).

I acknowledge the limitations of physical analogies or metaphors, of course. If they are pushed too far they will break down. So I am only using them for the purposes of facilitating communication between us in developing a "shorthand" vocabulary that will express considerable meaning in just a few words. The Savior's parables served a similar purpose; they drew a picture in people's minds which listeners could easily relate to, each of the listeners perceiving at the level of his own experience and understanding the essential truth of the principle being taught. A good metaphor will do the same thing.

HARDWARE AND SOFTWARE

As we move from the industrial age into the informational age, the primary tool is the computer. Many are mystified, even intimidated, by the computer, but the broad theory as to its essential parts and functions is simple to understand. The computer is made up basically of two parts: the machine itself, which is referred to as the hardware, and the programming fed into the machine, which is known as the software. Software means the directions or set of instructions given to the machine in processing information, and such programs or instructions can be added to, replaced, changed, or modified by the programmer without changing the hardware or machine.

For instance, when I work with a business organization in my capacity as a professional trainer and consultant, I frequently use a computer in combination with special data-gathering instruments such as questionnaires. Individuals each complete the questionnaire, then their answers are typed onto small cards the computer can "read," and in this way the information is fed into the computer. The software inside the computer processes this information, organizes it, and categorizes it according to the set of instructions the software has previously been given, and then it gives a "printout"—a typed document that is organized into a usable format for evaluation and study with organizational improvement in mind. Actually I am ignorant technically about how a computer works, how it is programmed, and really what hardware and software consists of. But I am aware of the invaluable power and usefulness of this amazing and continually developing tool, which is undoubtedly changing both the content and the quality of all of our lives in many ways.

THE HARDWARE

Let's now lead into a computer metaphor we can relate to our own lives. We know that God the Eternal Father is the father of each person's spirit body and that that person's earthly parents are the parents of his physical body. We know that the soul consists of the combined physical and spiritual bodies. In mortality these are separable by death. Eventually one will die and the other will go on to the spirit world, but at the resurrection they will reunite and become inseparable, eternally fused together to comprise the eternal soul. With Heavenly Father as the father of our spiritual body, and our earthly parents as the parents of our physical body, we have what we will call (for the purposes of our metaphor) the hardware, the basic spiritual-physical machine. In this combination we each inherit the potentialities and capacities of both God the Eternal Father and our earthly parents. This means that if we obey spiritual laws, we eventually can become literally like Heavenly Father; we can become perfect, just as he and our elder brother, Jesus Christ, are perfect. It also means that we are mortal; we are subject to the mortal processes of the decay and eventual death of the physical body. In addition, some may have certain genetic imperfections or weaknesses that limit the full release of their divine potentialities as long as they have a mortal body.

RESULTS GOVERNED BY SOFTWARE—THE PROGRAM

It will be evident now that, however complicated or sophisticated a computer itself is—the hardware—it is no better than its software—its programming. It simply cannot operate outside its software, for it is the software put into any particular computer that imposes the limitation on that computer. Even though the computer may have enormous potential—the capacity to handle many, many more software programs—in its functions and results it is completely limited to the set or sets of instructions given it. The rest of its capacity lies dormant, unawakened until more programs or sets of instructions are fed into it.

OTHER PROGRAMS FLAWED

A little reflection will show the vividness of this metaphor. We have seen some of the weaknesses and deficiencies inherent in all the other life centers except the divine one. If we identify with the human hero, for example, his weaknesses will constitute a flaw in the software of our mind and will preclude all except a small release of the potential capacity of our spirit, a basic hardware element. Similarly, if we identify with an institution, its weaknesses will tend to be transferred to us.

The software of the other centers too is defective in both quality and quantity. The spouse center may program in marital love, for instance, but not charity, the pure love of Christ. The hero center may model strength and courage while lacking compassion. Faith may be programmed without its essential partner, hope. Such software quality defects, inevitable in human institutions and relationships, are compounded by the quantity factor. A computer may have a capacity for, say, 1,000 software programs while it is programmed with only 20, in which case 980 are unused, are merely latent. For the superb computer of the human soul, this is a tragic waste. Yet no other center but the divine one can program the myriad qualities and characteristics, all to perfection, that the soul cries out for in its finest moments.

DIVINE PROGRAM ELIMINATES LIMITATIONS

Following our metaphor, then, I suggest that Jesus Christ is the equivalent of the software. He is the model, the embodied set of divine principles, obedience to which will release the full potential contained within the hardware of our spirits. (We recognize again certain inherited physical limitations — the Church does not even baptize severely mentally deficient people, since they are not self-aware, therefore not accountable.)

As we work to program our computer with the software represented by Jesus Christ, then, we are removing all imposed limitations of former programs. *This program contains the fulness or perfection,* because Christ obtained that fulness (D&C 93:16). Those who receive Christ and obey the gospel shall receive "all that my Father hath" (D&C 84:36-39). They become joint heirs with Christ himself (Romans 8:17).

The world generally regards this as impossible, but the world is wrong. As one who, like us, comes from the family of God the Eternal Father, Jesus Christ was the first begotten in the spirit and the Only Begotten in the flesh. He shows each of us that we can do it because he did it. He was born to this earth of a mortal mother, as we were. He probably had infancy and childhood experiences similar to ours. He did not receive of the fulness at first, but he received line upon line, precept upon precept, here a little, there a little — just as we do. He received grace for grace and grew from grace to grace until eventually he received of the fulness. (See D&C 93:12-13.) He is the path; he is the way. "What manner of men ought ye to be?" he asked his Nephite disciples. And he answered that question, "Verily I say unto you, even as I am." (3 Nephi 27:27.)

In effect, he says to us: "You can do it. I will help you. I will live a perfect life and work out the great and infinite atoning sacrifice to pay for your sins and enable you, if you obey the laws and ordinances of the gospel, to become like me and our Father. I will be both your advocate and mediator with the Father. Just as I did it, you can do it too. Don't be dismayed or discouraged—you are not another species, you are not like animals who are completely programmed by instinct and/or training; you are literally the children of God the Eternal Father; he is my God and Father too. I am your elder brother. Watch with me, that ye enter not into temptation. Follow me. No man cometh unto the Father, but by me. You cannot release the fulness of the divine potential built into your spirit body except by me, by following my example, by entering into a covenant relationship with me, by being directed throughout your life by the Holy Spirit in all that you do, say, and think, by becoming a co-worker with me in helping other of our Heavenly Father's children to understand these divine purposes and principles, to understand who they truly are, to have a correct, divine map of themselves, and to see me as the means, the way, the method, the life, the light, and the power."

To program our computer we must try to empathize with the frame of mind and heart of the Savior as he might thus speak to us. Elder Neal A. Maxwell wrote: "Since Jesus is at the very center of it all, we must make Him and His ways the light by which we steer and the light that we hold up to others." (*Wherefore, Ye Must Press Forward,* Deseret Book Co., 1977, page 28.)

THE SAVIOR'S TRANSCENDENT QUALIFICATIONS

The Savior's "hardware" was different from that of everyone else's. Our totally mortal parentage, physically speaking, implants in us the seeds of death. From his mortal mother Jesus inherited the *capacity* for death, but being physically begotten of our Eternal Father, who is an immortal being, he was not a *subject* of death, not under its bondage, as we are. For the same reason, after death he could go on to be resurrected. Without his divine parentage he could not have become "the resurrection and the life" (John 11:25) and our Redeemer.

But his different hardware did not smooth his earthly path in any way. His mortal heritage made him subject to all of the other earthly, physical, temporal processes of life. Thus he "[suffered] pains and afflictions and temptations of every kind" (Alma 7:11), being "in all points tempted like as we are" (Hebrews 4:15). But by obeying the software of his mind, that is, every instruction and directive that the Father gave him, he went beneath and then rose above every temptation. In this way he earned the right to work out the great atoning sacrifice—that is, to suffer and die for the sins of all mankind. In the process he perfected his soul and his character, leaving the adversary with no claim on him. He had overcome the world. At the end of his life he could say, "The prince of this world cometh, and hath nothing in me" (John 14:30).

The Savior's perfect life also gave him the right to become our perfect model, for while he confronted temptations, obstacles, and problems that were far greater than any of us have ever dealt with, he was superior to them all and his life from start to finish was totally sinless. This gives power and efficacy to his statement, "I would that ye should be perfect even as I, or your Father who is in heaven is perfect" (3 Nephi 12:48). These are no abstract, idle words. The goal, though not easy, is realistic, attainable. And the process of accomplishment is clearly given: by following in his footsteps, using him as our software, the father of our mind, of our steering system, our interpretation system, our governing system, our control system; as the map of our mind, our frame of reference, our pair of glasses.

Carefully consider each phrase in this testimony of Paul's:

> And he is the head of the body, the church: who is the beginning, the firstborn from the dead; that in all things he might have the preeminence.

For it pleased the Father that in him should all fulness dwell. (Colossians 1:18-19.)

It is through Christ that we can receive the fulness of the Father. He shows us the way to come to that fulness, which really means the fulness of that which is within us, since we are literally the Father's children. With God and Christ at the center there are no limitations; every one of the thousand software programs can be activated. By this means, we too can attain a fulness. We too can literally become perfect even as he is perfect.

APOSTATE MAP OF GODHEAD

Because of the incorrect map inherited through centuries of apostasy, the sectarian world does not understand the above concepts. The map so distorts the knowledge of who we really are, who our Father in Heaven really is, who Jesus Christ really is, and who the Holy Ghost really is, that it imposes enormous limitations on the software program of those who "buy into it." It also impels their minds to great accusation and criticism of those who are correctly programmed in these matters. They call the Latter-day Saint concept of an anthropomorphic God arrogant, presumptuous, and narcissistic. Their concepts drastically reduce man's ultimate potential. To them, that potential is not to become like God, not to have eternal life —that is, to have the kind of life and character that God has, to become perfected as he is—but instead to become his eternal robots, worshipping him in a saved condition throughout all eternity. This rules out the celestial family stewardship, the opportunity to become eternal co-inheritors of all that the Father has, and the eventual opportunity to become like the Father, a god, capable of eternal increase, of spiritual procreation.

The true map, on the other hand, tells us what Elder Lorenzo Snow summarized in his couplet:

As man now is, God once was;
As God now is, man may become.

Through the divine-center approach we
recognize the literal relationship we have with
our Eternal Father and with our elder brother,
Jesus Christ. Christ is the one who created the
world under the Father's direction and who
made redemption and salvation available to
mankind by living a perfect, sinless life and
by working out the infinite atoning sacrifice.
The Holy Ghost is given to us to guide us,
testify to us, sanctify us, and reveal to us the
mind and will of the Father and the Son.

LITERAL-CHILDREN CONCEPT LOST

One of the great behavioral consequences of the apostate
doctrine of the Trinity, in which the one God manifests himself
in different ways, is to lead people to believe that we are a
creation of God rather than his *literal offspring*. Even though
some holding that concept may speak of being made in the image
of God and being the children of God, they mean this in a symbolic or figurative or spiritual sense; they do not deeply believe
they are *literally the spiritually begotten sons and daughters of
God.* They do not believe in a premortal existence; that there an
eternal intelligence was clothed in each case with a newly begotten spirit body; and that we agreed to the eternal plan of our
coming to mortality to receive a physical body and to see if we
would obey God's commandments and thus keep this second
estate, this probationary estate, so that we could go on to a
fulness of joy, a fulness of growth and potential, and a fulness of
the opportunity to contribute eternally within the great plan.

THE TERRESTRIAL LEVEL

The sectarian doctrine on this would limit us to at best the
terrestrial level; that is, we might live good and noble lives and
become worshippers of Jesus Christ our Savior, who reconciles

us to God the Father, but really not become like him in the full sense. This is one of the major flaws in the sectarian Christ-centered doctrine. They do not see that we are the children of Elohim, capable of becoming like him by following our elder brother, our model, Jesus Christ. Instead they see us as grasped from death and hell by Jesus Christ, as we accept him as our Savior and Redeemer. The terrestrial world, which the millennial state will be, will be a Christ-centered world. Christ will be here personally upon the earth during the entire millennium. But the terrestrial world, or the millennial world, is not the celestial world, where both the Father and the Son are present, where the fulness of our potential can be realized, where we and our sealed posterity will be members of God's eternal family and go on to perfection, to become like him in all respects.

DIVINE CENTER THE PROPER APPROACH

Now we can see why the Christ-only approach is inappropriate for Latter-day Saints and for this book. One reason is that that approach can too easily give such emphasis to one member of the Godhead as to distort the essential balance among the three members and their respective roles. Another reason is that the Christ-only approach can come to verge on the sectarian one, wherein limiting terrestrial concepts are highlighted at the expense of the great truth that we are begotten children of our Eternal Father *and therefore capable of becoming like him.* The divine-center approach, though, recognizes that literal relationship, along with that which we have with our elder brother, Jesus Christ; that he is the one who created the world under the Father's direction and who made redemption and salvation available to mankind by living a perfect, sinless life and by working out the infinite atoning sacrifice; and that the Holy Ghost is given to us to guide us, testify to us, sanctify us, and reveal to us the mind and will of the Father and the Son.

There is, however, the "on the other hand," briefly mentioned earlier in this chapter. In our desire to avoid "sectarianism," we must not overreact. Let us never stray from forcefully, clearly, explicitly declaring our faith in Jesus Christ as the first principle of the gospel, as the foundation principle, as the principle from which all other gospel principles derive their power and efficacy, as the integrating, organizing, unifying, harmonizing principle. Let us not be fearful of being "guilty by association" in talking about Jesus Christ. He is the head of our church. It bears his name. We belong to his kingdom. He is the Truth (correct map), the Way (model), the Life (power), the Light (guidance). He is our advocate and mediator, our Savior and Redeemer (security). We have taken upon ourselves his name. Through the gospel and the spiritual rebirth we become his children, his sons and daughters. He is the driving force of our lives. Let us be sure we do not allow the fear of guilt by association with counterfeit doctrines to separate us from the vital, central reality that Jesus Christ constitutes in the totality of our lives, both in time and in eternity.

In the God/Christ-centered life, then, our Heavenly Father is the father of the spiritual hardware and our earthly parents are the parents of our physical hardware. Jesus Christ is the father of our software, the father of our mind. He is our frame of reference, our pair of glasses, the source of the correct map. And the Holy Ghost testifies of the Father and the Son and reveals to us their mind and powers.

(See chapter 1 for the purpose of this picture.)

The Intrinsic Solutions *Chapter 5*

*I am the light of the world: he that
followeth me shall not walk in darkness, but
shall have the light of life. (John 8:12.)
I am come that they might have life, and
that they might have it more abundantly.
(John 10:10.)*

In chapters 2 and 3 we considered several possible centers or
frames of reference and suggested reasons why they do not
satisfy a person's needs for security, guidance, wisdom, and
power. That is not to say they are without value, albeit for some
of them the value is only temporary. But ironically *their true
value and importance can be realized only when viewed through
the God/Christ-centered lens.* To take a most significant
example of this, consider what happens to your relationship to
the Church when you take a divine-centered approach. Notice
how your feelings change as the map comes more clearly into
focus—how you perceive the Church and its members, for
example.

When you put God at the center you become more diligent
and far more effective in the Church, not less. You appreciate
and love the Church more, not less. You cease overreacting to
the weaknesses of leaders or members or to changes in programs
or procedures, and you develop a flexible stance and carry your
comfort zone with you. You are always able to accommodate
new changes, new people, new environments, because you
understand and appreciate the over-arching divine purposes and
principles which the Church teaches and which never change.
The Spirit is the lubricant.

"I am come that they might have life," said the Savior, "and that they might have it more abundantly." Let's now look at each of the centers previously discussed and briefly indicate by comparison the advantages of the God / Christ-centered approach. The bottom line is that through this approach we will have each good part of life more abundantly.

SPOUSE-CENTEREDNESS

First, the *spouse-centered* life. We mentioned a major problem of emotional dependence and how devastating it can be when the two partners are in a falling-out pattern and harsh words are exchanged — as can happen in any marriage when the conditions are "right" for it. In their hurt condition perhaps each licks his wounds and resolves to stay quiet as a protective measure and also as a mutely hurtful one — the silent treatment. At this point they each need the healing power of each other's love, but each waits upon the initiative of the other. And since the life center is that other partner, who now is equally insecure and powerless, each may wait a long time.

UNCONDITIONAL LOVE NECESSARY

The reason is that now they each need a love that doesn't await the "right" conditions — an unconditional love. But to show love initially and unconditionally one must have a love supply source which is independent of the human object of that love, one which itself came freely — without request or demand — and unconditionally. For us, Christ alone is that power source. ("We love him, because he *first* loved us" [1 John 4:19].) His love and that of our Father in Heaven comes freely, without request, and unconditionally to all mortal beings; and even though most of them never receive that which is given, it is nevertheless given ceaselessly and in a thousand different ways. No mortal being, regardless of how wonderful and consistent and solid he or she may seem, can even approach the degree of firm security and faithfulness and unconditional love and greatness of the Father and the Son. The implications for a person's security, guidance, wisdom, and power are obvious.

THREE-WAY PARTNERSHIP

A woman once confronted me with the statement, "Well, I am told to put my husband first, to put him at the center of my life, and that he is to put the Lord at the center of his life." I asked her, "Who is the ultimate source of that teaching and counsel to you as a wife?" She answered, "The Lord."

Her own answer was sufficient to show that ultimately it is only a God / Christ-centered life that can establish and maintain a celestial relationship with a husband. It is a three-way partnership. God is the center and the core of that partnership for either party; otherwise, where would a wife get the power to love an unrighteous husband? Her own security must come from not the human relationship but the divine. Then she will have the guidance through the still, small voice and the wisdom or perspective to see the larger picture in facing the nitty-gritty difficulties of each day. And she will also have the power source with which courageously to carry through in acting upon that wisdom.

The difficulty of one spouse's making significant changes in a marriage relationship while the other partner carries on the old hostilities is only too obvious. Other people remember and keep labels on us even though we may be repentant. It is their way of defending themselves against being vulnerable and hurt again, for it is easy to deal with a label; but it is difficult to deal with a changing, growing person.

LABELS

I have seen partners in marriage relationships begin to behave according to the spouses' nagging labels. The labeling became so deeply set that any effort toward change was met with remarks like, "Oh, come on, I know what you're really like—stop trying to put on; stop trying to fake. I know you." Unless the labeled person became God / Christ-centered, he often gave in to this kind of verbal punishment and returned to his old way of

> **When we love God and Christ first, we will love our spouse more, not less—with more true love, more wisdom, and more charity. Divine-centeredness is literally the key to a celestial relationship. If we are true and faithful to the covenants we make with the Lord, we will have the security, guidance, wisdom, and power to deal with problems in the marriage.**

behaving, which only supplied the awaited evidence to the labeler and gave him reason to jab again with, "I knew it all the time."

Some of the serious obstacles we all face in attempting to change our behavior are the labels other people put on us. Others may not want to change these labels, their safe categorization around which they have already developed their defenses. Unless they change and put God at the center themselves, they will derive a modicum of security from these labels and stereotypes. It is important to lubricate the change processes in ourselves by telling others authentically what we are trying to do, why, and how difficult it may be, so that they can see us grow before their eyes, as it were. If we persist, and if they test our sincerity and find that the change is real and the growth solid, they may well come to change their labels of us and still feel safe, even though they may not yet be oriented to the divine center.

When we love God and Christ first, we will love our spouse more, not less—with more true love, more wisdom, and more charity. Charity, the pure love of Christ—that is the key. Consider Mormon's beautiful expression:

> Wherefore, my beloved brethren, pray unto the Father with all the energy of heart, that ye may be filled with this love, which he hath bestowed upon all who are true followers of his Son, Jesus Christ; that ye may become the sons of God; that when he shall

appear we shall be like him, for we shall see him as he is; that we may have this hope; that we may be purified even as he is pure. Amen. (Moroni 7:48.)

Divine-centeredness is literally the key to a celestial marriage. Just as in the temple we receive the endowment by covenants we make with the Lord before we enter into the new and everlasting covenant of marriage, so, if we are true and faithful to the covenants we make with the Lord, we will have the security, guidance, wisdom, and power to deal with problems in the marriage. Ideally, of course, it would be best if both husband and wife were God/Christ-centered and were living true to the covenants of the endowment, so that the spirit of the gospel lubricated the problem-solving processes in the marriage. But this is generally not the case. Usually, it is one of the parties who is more faithful to the covenants than the other. In other words, they are unequally yoked together.

"TAKE MY YOKE. . . ."

Unequally yoked to whom? To Christ. And that is the very point. If the marriage partners see themselves as primarily yoked to each other rather than to Christ, they will feel straightjacketed, controlled, governed, dominated, possessed, intimidated, nagged, held down, by the other. Then they will fall into a pattern of collusion with each other wherein weaknesses of each confirm the other's perceptions. This vicious cycle feeds upon itself and grows into deeper bitterness, stronger self-justification, more anxious validation from the outside, and more confirmed accusation of the other. Rather than sidestepping negative energy, the partners engage it and collude with it and magnify it.

But there is a better way—the yoke of Christ. The Savior said: "Come unto me, all ye that labor and are heavy laden, and I will give you rest. Take my yoke upon you, and learn of me; for I am meek and lowly of heart: and ye shall find rest unto your souls. For my yoke is easy, and my burden is light." (Matthew 11:28-30.)

In a class of six-year-olds where the above scripture was read, one of them asked, "What is a yoke?" The teacher immediately began composing in her mind an answer about animals being yoked together to pull a wagon, and about a frame for the shoulders that would help a person carry milk cans or some other burden. But before she could respond to the question, a little girl spoke up in a soft voice.

"Jesus' yoke is when he puts his arms around your neck," she said.

And so it is, for his yoke truly brings "rest unto your souls." If even one of the partners in an unequally yoked marriage is truly centered on Christ and yoked up to him primarily, then that person's entire perception of the situation will change. He or she will have the security, guidance, wisdom, and power to do whatever is necessary in the Lord's way and in the Lord's time for as long as necessary in an effort to bless the other and help and inspire him to become equally yoked to Christ.

In the process, the person yoked to Christ will perceive the other's weaknesses with compassion rather than with accusation. He will give grace in the form of kindness, patience, understanding, and unconditional love. Such attitudes and behavior will not guarantee that the other will ultimately respond in kind, but they will maximize that likelihood. There may be a few exceptional situations in which the other person simply will not respond, evil having completely congealed the wrong map. In these circumstances the righteous party can receive divine guidance and wisdom to justifiably explore other alternatives. The point is that when God and Christ are truly preeminent in our marriage, we will see the entire problem situation differently from before. When they are not, we will fall to the same level we accuse the other partner of being on.

TREAT HIM LIKE AN INVESTIGATOR

An older woman, a friend, phoned me once about her deep unhappiness in not being able to go on a couple mission with her husband, as many of her friends had been doing as couples. This was because of her husband's lack of activity and belief in the Church. As we talked, she gradually came to understand that she was already on a full-time mission and had been for almost her entire married life, and that her husband was her investigator. For the first time she saw the entire situation differently. This new perspective affected her in two ways: it somewhat depressed her, because she now recognized the years of waste in which she had acted on the old accusatory, self-justification perception; and it thrilled and excited her with a new energy and sense of hope. She came to understand the miracle of forgiveness through the power of repentance and the Atonement. The second attitude essentially eclipsed the first, and she enthusiastically went to work on the problem.

This suggestion to her was of a part with a comment I once heard President N. Eldon Tanner make. He said that the key to raising faithful children is to treat them always as investigators. Anyone who has ever done missionary work will know what you do to reach an investigator. You do literally anything necessary, consistent with correct principles. You fast and pray, you sidestep negative energy and answer it with positive energy; you show love in as many ways as possible; you show almost endless patience; and so on. All this you need to do with your child too, perceiving him to be at least as important as an investigator would be. But watch how your behavior and attitude changes when you perceive your child as being disobedient, rebellious, or indifferent!

How you see things is transcendently important. Becoming divinely centered is the key to seeing them as the Lord does.

WORK-CENTEREDNESS

Another common life-center we discussed is *work*, an important part of character but dangerous as a frame of reference. While financial strivings are a normal and proper part of life, enough was said earlier to indicate the frailty even of "economic security," whether of net worth or solid gainful employment or any other economically oriented factor. Certainly they ought not to govern one's life.

The man who took his family to the circus as planned rather than respond to an unscheduled work call was sure he had his priorities right. There may be other situations in which the person should do the opposite—respond to the work demand and put off a family or Church demand. To make such a decision correctly, however, requires a God-centeredness, making one sensitive to the still, small voice in determining such a priority.

The question, therefore, is never one of choosing between Church and family, or family and work. It is not a matter of asking which comes first. The Lord should always come first, and if we truly put him in that position he will tell us which comes "second." Sometimes it will be the Church, sometimes family, sometimes work. This situation may not seem as cut and dried as some of us would like it, but the great advantage is the constant source of guidance on the matter and the peace and security and wisdom which come from following that guidance.

LEADER-CENTEREDNESS

Why is it that missionaries and teachers continually teach Christ-centeredness? It is so that investigators and converts don't become too emotionally founded and dependent on the human teachers. They are to develop their direct power source rather than rely upon the other human one, as may be appropriate for a short period of time. People are often first converted to the missionaries and the quality of their hearts and lives. This is all right and natural, for they are responding to the fruits of the gospel. But eventually they need to develop their own personal testimony from the divine source, so that no matter what happens in the lives of their teachers, they will be anchored within themselves.

The respect and admiration for leaders or missionaries, as we have seen, can be carried to extremes in the form of centering one's life-support system upon them. Too often then, a real or imagined flaw discovered in the behavior of such a center brings a shattering disillusionment which may even carry the former admirer into an embittered inactivity. A good barometer of a person's center or source of security, then, is a close examination as to what causes him to feel offended or deeply disappointed or

> **The question is never one of choosing between Church and family, or family and work. It is not a matter of asking which comes first. The Lord should always come first, and if we truly put him in that position he will tell us what comes "second."**

controlled or manipulated. Any center outside of God can lead a person into suffering innumerable offenses and disappointments and thereby cause his attitude to crystalize into cynicism and skepticism. Jesus said, "Blessed is he, whosoever shall not be offended in me" (Matthew 11:6). The divinely centered person will seek not to take offense but rather to forgive if an offense is offered.

THE POWER OF TRUST
Sometimes the hero-leader has indeed fallen, if only temporarily, but by still imposing trust in him, or reminding him of his trust, the admirer may assist him to rise again.

A close missionary friend of mine was a powerful teacher and was the primary human instrument in bringing an outstanding man into the Church. This man went through several stages of conversion, until finally he was deeply converted to the Lord Jesus Christ and his holy gospel. Having received such a conversion, he was "free" not to be offended or overreactive at the weaknesses of others in the Church. Little by little he received increasingly responsible assignments until he became a Church leader in his area. This took several years.

Meanwhile the teaching missionary fell into inactivity and intellectual apostasy or pride. He pursued a different life-style. As a Church leader, his convert was invited to general conference, so he made arrangements to visit the former missionary on his way home after conference. They scheduled themselves so that they could be together for two to three hours, but because of changed plane schedules it transpired that they literally had only five minutes in which to see each other.

95

The leader knew about the former missionary's inactivity and was very unhappy about it. He wanted to tactfully and appropriately broach the subject. He had planned to socialize politely for a while and then, later in the conversation, to inquire about what had happened to the missionary's faith. But with only five minutes available he was perplexed as to what he should do.

He sought the Lord's guidance and received it. When the two met, after they had shaken hands and exchanged a cordial greeting, this leader said, "Elder, I have given my entire life now to the Church and the gospel you brought me into. Tell me, Elder, have I made a mistake?"

The elder stared at him momentarily and then broke right down, "No, you haven't, but I have," he said. He then reaffirmed his testimony and the necessity for personal repentance.

The two men embraced and parted, but the impact had been profound and unmistakable upon both when the leader placed his trust momentarily again with the missionary. The missionary, driven by a deep but buried divine conscience, responded faithfully in acknowledging the truth about the Church, the gospel, and himself.

Trust is a powerful tool for lifting and building. The more a person is God/Christ-centered, the more he can give trust clearly and even one-sidedly. He can then do so conditionally, as it is sometimes necessary to do. This is possible because he is anchored to the unconditional source of love and security.

FRIEND-CENTEREDNESS

Another center we mentioned in chapter 2 is that of *friends.* True friendship is a noble and uplifting quality, fully justifying the verse attributed to Samuel Johnson:

> Friendship, peculiar boon of heaven,
> The noble mind's delight and pride;
> To men and angels only given,
> To all the lower world denied.

True love is found in the affirmation of another person's identity and stewardship, in seeking his or her growth and good, not in interpreting all the other person's responses in terms of one's own needs, hungers, or desires.

Nevertheless, even the best of human friendships are limited in their contribution to one's needs for security, guidance, wisdom, and power. And lower down the scale, where the friends are less mature or less committed, the contribution may not only be merely temporary but may in fact range from minor to insignificant — or even go into the negative side.

We referred to the friend-centeredness of young people and the tight restrictions of conformity to peer customs that their urge to be liked and accepted frequently imposes. Questionable or wrong behavior is a common result. On the other hand, the young person whose center is the Father and the Son will take a more courageous path. He will value the trust and respect of others more than their mere liking him. This course generally ends up in increased liking as well as respect.

A person who becomes friend-centered will find that his social conscience will gradually subordinate his divine conscience. He will find it almost impossible to forgive himself of some wrongdoing, even though he is doing it no more. Social conscience remembers the wrong, the punishment being getting caught instead of or more than the intrinsic repulsion of the act itself.

The young man in chapter 2 who was girl-friend-centered was in a bad case. His was a kind of sick, twisted love wherein he needed the girl so much that he loved her, rather than vice versa. On the other hand, true love is found in the affirmation of another person's identity and stewardship, in seeking his or her growth and good, not in interpreting all the other person's responses in terms of one's own needs, hungers, or desires. True

| The key is to see others, particularly so-called enemies, as they truly are—children of our Heavenly Father, for whose sins the Savior also atoned as he did for ours.

love is not possessive or manipulative or conspiratorial or forced in any way. *But it requires an unconditional love supply source.*

The young man was vulnerable at all depths. Interestingly, a person can allow himself to be vulnerable on the surface of his life if he still retains a deep God/Christ-centered invulnerability. Then he can afford to be gentle and soft, to give and take, to give love without demanding anything in return—and that of course leaves him open to rebuffs and disappointments on occasion. But when a person is deeply vulnerable, centered on something other than God and therefore not securely rooted, he can't afford to be vulnerable on the surface, or he risks being simply wiped out.

People develop various defenses in controlling and manipulating strategies to get what they want, and in his insecure position, with the moorings shifting all the time, this is what my young friend did. Notice his strategy of trying to plumb the girl's feelings—baring his own soul and then insisting that she bare hers. Whenever a person loses a sense of his own identity, and consequently the power to choose his response to his associates' feelings, moods, or thoughts, he tends to lose an awareness of their stewardships. He begins to force natural processes. Eventually he loses the thing he most desires. It is only in orienting his life to the divine center that a person can secure anything else he desires and yet not be based upon it. Only then will he have the internal security, guidance, wisdom, and power to cultivate and enhance true friendships.

In the example I have given, my friend did what was necessary to become divinely anchored and centered, and this gave him the security and guidance to deal wisely with the fracturing human relationship. He affirmed the girl unconditionally, and little by little all that had originally attracted her to him did so again. Their relationship blossomed and flowered. Later he told me, "I hope the relationship works out. I love her so much. But if it doesn't it won't wipe me out as it did before—as long as I stay with the Lord."

ENEMY-CENTEREDNESS

As to *enemy-centering* (being possessed by hatred and vindictiveness, or at least being obsessed with the other person's weaknesses), I referred to this possibility even in such an exemplary character as Nephi, who certainly had immense provocation. I told too of my experience with the woman who had repented of her persecution mania and wanted desperately to remove the seeds of criticism and bitterness she had sown in her children's hearts against the leader concerned, and to remove the consequences of her former attitude.

I noted that I might not have helped her much with my answer. But if I were asked the question now I would counsel her to describe the entire process to her children and to listen fully to their feelings, then to take time to teach them to forgive those who trespass against them, first by her modeling and second by precept. In order to do this, it would be necessary to turn to the Lord with all her heart, might, mind, and strength. In other words, it would be necessary to become God/Christ-centered.

Christ himself gave the ultimate prescription for avoiding enemy-centering. In fact, this prescription was an important part of the teachings which produced a beautiful Zion society on the American continent, a society in which perfect love and peace reigned for over two hundred years.

> Therefore, if ye shall come unto me, or shall desire to come unto me, and rememberest that thy brother hath aught against thee—
> Go thy way unto thy brother, and first be reconciled unto thy brother, and then come unto me with full purpose of heart, and I will receive you. (3 Nephi 12:23-24.)

The key is to see others, particularly so-called enemies, as they truly are—children of our Heavenly Father, for whose sins the Savior also atoned, as he did for ours. They are literally our brothers and sisters. Again the answer lies in the perception.

POSSESSION-CENTEREDNESS AND FUN / PLEASURE-CENTEREDNESS

Both possession-centeredness and fun / pleasure-centeredness are obviously weak centers from the very outset and require little further analysis to emphasize this point. Nevertheless, perhaps these two centers combined categorize the life-style of the great majority of the people in the relatively affluent part of the world (survival being the dominant mode in the other part).

How does God / Christ-centeredness deal with these two popular centers? As with the other centers, it puts them in their proper perspective (and they definitely have an important role in life to play). It first consecrates them to the Lord and then receives them back as a stewardship to serve divine purposes— fundamental to which is supplying basic needs and justified wants of one's family and then using these possessions in the service of our Heavenly Father's other children.

When controlled from the divine center, pleasure and fun become a phase of life that serves the purposes of recreation, renewal, relaxation, and enjoyment. They play a legitimate role in a balanced, integrated life, but they do not dominate that life; they are not carried to excess. Proper use of them is analogous to what is called Preparation Day in the mission field, in which the missionaries take a break from the proselyting routine to do other needed things, to recoup energy, to relax and engage in wholesome fun, as well as to make plans and preparations for the work ahead.

God / Christ-centeredness gives a proper perspective on fun and pleasure. William Moore Allred told the following story about the Prophet Joseph Smith's response to some who felt he should not indulge in sports.

I have played ball with him many times. But it was quite a stumbling block to some. After some had found fault about it, he was preaching one day and told a story about a certain prophet who was sitting under the shade of a tree amusing himself in some way. A hunter came along and reproved him. The prophet asked the hunter if he always kept his bow strung up. "Oh, no," said he.

"Why not?"

"Because it would lose its elasticity."

Said the prophet: "It is just so with my mind. I do not want it strung up all the time." (Hyrum L. and Helen Mae Andrus, compilers, *They Knew the Prophet*, Bookcraft, 1974, page 140.)

CHURCH-CENTEREDNESS, FAMILY-CENTEREDNESS

For our purposes the most significant of the non-God-centered maps or frames of reference are the *Church* and the *family*. First, we are on hallowed ground, so to speak, when we discuss them, because of their divine origin. Second, it is frequently supposed that one of these two must have top priority (must be our life center, that is) and all else must be subordinate to it. Third, it is the demands of these two that seem most often to require resolution in the lives of actively involved Church members.

Most of us will readily admit that we are occasionally, if not frequently, torn between meeting the demands and expectations of the Church and responding to the needs and demands of the family. On the surface it becomes a practical matter of time allocation, but more often, down deep, it becomes a matter of loyalty or priority. Many feel guilty in one direction or another, and often in both directions simultaneously. That is, if they do a really good job in their Church work at the expense of family time and relationships, they may feel reinforced by Church leaders and members; but inwardly a gnawing guilt eats at them about their not spending quality time, or perhaps enough of any time, with the family. On the other hand, many will go in the other direction and give that quantity and quality of time to the family and do a mediocre job in Church responsibilities and feel guilty in the other direction. Many, in trying to do both jobs well, end up doing neither to the level of expectations of Church leaders or family members or self.

The Savior himself used one of these primary loyalties—the family—to illustrate the ultimate cost of discipleship to him. In working miracle after miracle, teaching marvelous insights, blessing many lives, he became extremely popular during parts of his ministry. Multitudes would follow after him. Once he turned and said to them: "He that loveth father or mother more than me is not worthy of me: and he that loveth son or daughter more than me is not worthy of me" (Matthew 10:37). In another similar quotation (Luke 14:26) he includes wife also.

In these two statements the Savior apparently was speaking of the highest priority of centralness, of the most basic loyalty, of the driving force and frame of reference of a person's life. In essence, he was saying, "Unless my Father and I come first, unless you view life in this particular way, you cannot be my disciple." And he drew the most forceful and telling analogy he could with people who cared greatly about their families by telling them that unless they put him first, they could not be his disciples.

He clearly spelled out the cost:

> And whosoever doth not bear his cross, and come after me, cannot be my disciple.
>
> For which of you, intending to build a tower, sitteth not down first, and counteth the cost, whether he have sufficient to finish it?
>
> Lest haply, after he hath laid the foundation, and is not able to finish it, all that behold it begin to mock him.
>
> Saying, This man began to build, and was not able to finish. (Luke 14:27-30.)

"Come after me." "Be my disciple." Does this throw us back to the Church-centered position? Decidedly not. We have already seen what that will do for us and to us, and that the Church, important as it is, is the Lord's instrument, the means to help bring us to Christ and the Father, and not the end in itself. Surely the Savior was speaking of a deeper discipleship than that.

NO SEPARATION OF CHURCH AND FAMILY

The family vs. Church issue is an excellent case in point of how *hewing to the divine center gives us an entirely new perspective and understanding of the issue.* That centering essentially transcends this false dichotomy, this either-or situation, and dissolves the artificial compartmentalization which heavy cultural conditioning (or software, to use computer language) has programmed into Church members.

Simply put, the more God/Christ-centered a person becomes, the more he recognizes that family vs. Church is not an issue at all. The reason is that, properly considered, *there is absolutely no separation of the Church and the family.* Other than the individual soul, the family is the basic organizational unit in the Church. The ward and stake organization represents the "scaffolding," to use President Harold B. Lee's metaphor.

> Again and again has been repeated the statement that the home is the basis of a righteous life. With new and badly needed emphasis on the "how," we must not lose sight of the "why" we are so engaged. The priesthood programs operate in support of the home, the auxiliary programs render valuable assistance. Wise regional leadership can help us do our share in attaining God's overarching purpose "to bring to pass the immortality and eternal life of man." (Moses 1:39.) Both the revelations of God and the learning of men tell us how crucial the home is in shaping the individual's total life experience. You must have been impressed that running through all that has been said in this conference has been the urgency of impressing the importance of better teaching and greater parental responsibility in the home. Much of what we do organizationally, then, is scaffolding, as we seek to build the individual, and we must not mistake the scaffolding for the soul. (*Conference Report,* October 1967, page 107.)

The purpose of the "scaffolding" is to assist the family to live a life founded upon the gospel and the rock of revelation; also, to contribute through the priesthood correlation which takes place on the scaffolding—at the ward, the stake, the region, the area, and the general level—to bring the gospel to our Heavenly Father's other children, both living and dead, so that they too can have the blessings of family exaltation. The Church and the family are so interrelated that a person cannot be an effective worker and a leader on the scaffolding unless he has first dedicated himself to the family role—husband and father, wife and mother, son and brother, or daughter and sister.

Most of us are culturally programmed to think of the Church as being either (1) the ward or branch building where local meetings and programs take place or (2) the various levels of organization within The Church of Jesus Christ of Latter-day Saints *other than* the fundamental unit of the family. Our very semantics or word definitions contribute to that same connotation, and as we constantly use this language through daily and weekly repetition, Church members come to think in terms of two institutions: the Church and the family. They compartmentalize; they dichotomize; and the center of their life becomes essentially a composite of Church and family. The result of all this is that many times we give lip service to statements like President McKay's "No other success can compensate for failure in the home" or President Lee's "The most important of the Lord's work that you will ever do will be the work you do within the walls of your own home." We even preach these ideas over the pulpit, but when it comes down to day-to-day thinking, decision making, and acting, many people unwittingly fall right into the thinking of that false dichotomy or conflicting value system.

But as a person becomes God/Christ-centered, that is, has "the mind of Christ" (1 Corinthians 2:16), the issue takes on a totally different appearance. As he looks at it, it literally dissolves. It never becomes a matter of which to put first, the family or the Church. *The answer is always to put God first and to let him reveal what, at that particular moment, is to come second or next.*

"GETTING TO CHURCH ON TIME"

I have almost become convinced that the only way to effectively show what a false dichotomy this cultural programming has created in most of our minds is to use negative or contrasting examples which clearly show that the family, if based upon the gospel, is the fundamental unit of the Church.

Several times in my family life I have had the experience of trying to get my family gathered together so that we could get to church on time. (Reread the language of the previous sentence and you will perceive the semantics problem I have already mentioned: get the family together in order to get to church on time.) Sometimes I have become unpleasant and have raised my voice. "Come on, kids, let's go! We're going to be late!" or "You're making the entire family late! Let's go! Come on! Come on!" or "What's wrong with you? You knew earlier that you had to do that! Why didn't you get your clothes ready! Hurry and eat your breakfast! Stop spending so much time on your hair!" or other words to that effect. As a timesaver to speed our departure we have sometimes offered rather "hurry-up," routine prayers.

Since I have become aware of what a false dichotomy Church vs. family is, whenever I have found myself falling into those patterns I have tried to stand aside and see what was happening. It is then I have realized that I was yelling at my children to get them to go to church on time when, in fact, I was standing in church yelling at them to get to the "scaffolding" so that we could better learn, among other things, how to talk to each other with kindness, respect, and soft voices. Whenever I have really taken the time to gain this perspective, I have also tried to realize that it's better to be late for church than to lose the Spirit; and that human parenthood is an apprenticeship for godhood; and that a home is a place where love is taught to children; and that the most powerful form of example from which children learn takes place in watching parents under conditions of stress and pressure; and that perhaps I can teach more gospel by resolving the practical problems in quiet, kind, loving, and firm ways than by getting into an accusing mode and judging everybody. If I don't resolve the problems in gentle, loving ways, I teach the children two standards: one for the privacy of our own home, where we can talk in any way we wish, and the other for the public eye, where we try to maintain an image. Thus the conditioning—the programming, as the computer language has it—moves to the next generation and the whole foundation becomes hypocritical.

All the above realizations come to me clearer, and practicing them comes better, when I am earnestly striving for the God/Christ-centered approach. I love my wife more when I love the Lord first. Put another way, I love my wife more when I view her through the lens of the gospel with a correct map or pair of glasses. Our love then is more mature than conditional, because of the security base and power source provided. I find that I discipline my children with more effectiveness and consistency and love when I have on the right pair of glasses than when I do not, because then I am not underreactive or overreactive, depending largely on my fatigue level or my mood. I become more unconditional in my love and more consistent in my discipline (following through on earlier agreed-upon consequences).

Let me just add here that none of my above remarks relative to getting a family off to the meetinghouse should be taken as an excuse to be late for Church meetings. Normally, by planning and organizing properly it is possible to get there on time. And since in effect we have an appointment there with the Lord, we should by all means make the necessary effort to meet it promptly.

CHURCH WORK AT HOME

The concept of main base and scaffolding has some interesting implications. On one occasion a ward auxiliary leader approached me about whether I thought my wife was too busy to give some help on a forthcoming special ward program. I said, "Perhaps she can, but I know she's very busy."

His response was, "Well, we know she's very busy too, and we didn't want to overburden her. How many Church jobs does she have?"

"Twelve," I answered.

"Twelve? I've never heard of anyone having that many

Church jobs. What are they?"

"Well, there's Cynthia, Maria, Stephen, Sean, David—"

He interrupted, "Oh, I mean *Church* jobs."

"Well, consider little Colleen," I said. "Would you consider her a Church job? The time you would spend preparing for a Sunday School lesson—do you think this child would deserve this amount of private time, or perhaps more?"

"Oh, I know how important the family is," he responded, "but I was asking about *Church* jobs."

"Oh," I said, "you mean jobs on the scaffolding. Yes, she has one at the ward level of the scaffolding, teaching the Spiritual Living course in the Relief Society. She has one at the stake level of the scaffolding, in the presidency of the Mutual. With nine children and a husband, that equals twelve Church jobs. Each one is separate and different and requires individual attention and has needs that must be met. Each one takes time, effort, energy, and loyalty."

Once while I was serving as a member of the Church Missionary Committee I was assigned to a stake conference in the Sacramento area where the stake presidency was to be reorganized. When Elder Harold B. Lee, then a member of the Quorum of the Twelve, set apart the new stake president, he asked me to assist him. Both in the setting apart blessing and after, Elder Lee emphasized to this new stake president that the most important Church work he would do would take place with the person at his side, his wife.

The new president responded, "Oh, I know how important my wife is. She's such a wonderful support to me. I appreciate her so much."

Elder Lee looked him in the eye and said, "You didn't quite get my message. The most important *Church* work you will do in this stake will be done with the person standing next to you" —and he placed emphasis on the word *church.*

When Elder A. Theodore Tuttle of the First Quorum of the Seventy was supervising the Regional Representatives and mission presidents in Utah, in a meeting of all the Regional Representatives he counseled us to make certain that our meetings began and ended on time and that we encouraged stake and ward leaders to do similarly, so that the leaders concerned did not make excessive demands on people's time and budgets. At one point he said, in essence: "If a high council meeting was supposed to end at nine o'clock, make certain that it does end at nine o'clock, because it could well be that a high councilor has a date at nine-fifteen to take his wife out to get some ice cream, and that date is as important as anything which took place in the meeting." As he said this his voice broke and he momentarily struggled to control his emotions, as if the principle underlying this remark had been building up in him for some time. And everyone there was stunned into silence with the realization of what he was really saying.

Elder Tuttle also counseled us to work with the inactive fathers through home teaching by clearly communicating to them that our goal was to help them become the spiritual leaders of their homes. At the time I wondered if that was totally honest, but I was viewing his comment from the "software" of a heavy cultural tradition, in which I saw the purpose of home teaching the inactive members as getting them to come back to Church meetings so that they would be active in the Church again. But since the family *is* the Church, or at least the foundational unit of the Church, if it is based upon the gospel, then Elder Tuttle's comment was thoroughly honest.

We really are there to help the fathers become the spiritual leaders of the homes, and if we can encourage them to lead the family in family prayer and conduct family home evenings and so on, they will inevitably feel their incapacity and their need for assistance from the priesthood quorum and the Church auxiliaries. After all, the Lord places the full responsibility of teaching the gospel to children upon the parents, not upon the auxiliary organizations. Nor do the home teachers have this responsibility. President Marion G. Romney said: "Home teaching should not be confused with the Lord's program for teaching the gospel in the home by parents. It is not intended, nor would it be proper, for home teachers to take the place of the family head in teaching the gospel in the home." (Priesthood Home Teaching Committee Meeting, General Conference, April 8, 1966.)

Over the past several years the Church has given increasing emphasis to the importance of the gospel-centered family life as the central purpose of all other Church programs and activities and the criterion by which decisions about them are to be made. This does not mean by any stretch of the imagination that the scaffolding work is not important. I believe that a very large percentage of our lives should be spent on the scaffolding and that *LDS parents need to model to their children the importance of sacrificing for the sake of bringing gospel-centered family life to other people* in the Church through home teaching, to those outside the Church through missionary work, and to those in the spirit world through genealogical research and temple work. The scaffolding is the extension of home life, so we should always be recommitting ourselves to the principles of gospel-centered living as well as to the outreach effort to take the scaffolding to all of our Heavenly Father's children so that they too can have the same blessings.

Consider the following prophetic counsel from President Joseph F. Smith and Elder Harold B. Lee:

Government in the home and in the Church constitutes an important part in the lives of the people, and the government in the home is the basis of all successful government in church or state. (Joseph F. Smith, *Gospel Doctrine*, page 290.)

The home is the basis of a righteous life, and no other instrumentality can take its place nor fulfill its essential functions. (Harold B. Lee, *Conference Report*, October 6, 1962, page 72.)

It seems clear to me that the Church has no choice — and never has had — but to do more to assist the family in carrying out its divine mission . . . to help improve the quality of life in the Latter-day Saint homes. As important as our many programs and organizational efforts are, these should not supplant the home; they should support the home. (Harold B. Lee, *Ensign*, March 1971, page 3.)

EFFECTS & IMPLICATIONS OF ALTERNATIVE CENTERS

Alternative Centers	Dimensions of Personality	
	SECURITY	GUIDANCE
GOD / CHRIST	"Being" mentality Built on rock Divine definition Internally rooted Person valued intrinsically Unconditionally loved	The Light Spirit-directed Divine purpose Principles, promptings and practices
SPOUSE	Based on treatment by spouse Possible goal / role expectation conflicts Dependency-vulnerability-defensiveness cycle	My needs and expectations: the other's needs and wants
FAMILY	Founded on family acceptance and fulfilling family expectations As volatile as the family Family-reputation based	"What's good for my family?" is criterion May exclude sacrifice and service Practices, coming from upbringing family, extremely limited as to guidance. Inflexible in own family
CHURCH	Dependent on ward / branch acceptance and leader treatment May lead to Pharisaism "Belonging" mentality	Judges, labels, categorizes others as active or inactive, orthodox or liberal, using "in" wor Practices come from Church models
WORK	Defines self by occupational role Economically defensive Obsolescence mentality	Work needs and expectations Material, economic, secular criteria Work role models guidelines
LEADERS / HEROES	Dependent on leader meeting expectations Achilles' heel mentality	From imperfect leaders' vision, methods, reactions

WISDOM	POWER
Service orientation Eternal perspective Eternal values Idealistic and realistic The Way (correct map)	The Life / Abundant Life The driving force Taps sources of infinite power to achieve and to help others achieve eternal life
Extremely limited — our marriage, my mate	Finally limited by weakness in spouse or self
"Me and mine," almost as selfish as "me" The nuclear family	Limited by family models and personal comfort zone
Confuses means and ends As limited as Church experience Inflexibility, rigidity	If active in the Church and inactive in the gospel, good Mormon, bad Christian Mechanical, hypocritical Short-lived willpower change efforts bring discouragement, cynicism
Myopic (work alone) vision Lives by "bread alone"	Limited by work role models, occupational opportunities, organizational constraints, the boss's weaknesses, willpower
Interprets life through a social lens	Only reflected light, like the moon Limited by human role models

EFFECTS & IMPLICATIONS OF ALTERNATIVE CENTERS

Dimensions of Personality

Alternative Centers	SECURITY	GUIDANCE
FRIENDS	Socially defined Fickle, changing Straightjacketed by human weaknesses High dependency on others' opinions	"What will they think?" Embarrassment mentality
ENEMIES	Volatile — function of enemies' movements Fear / self-justification mentality	Self-justification and accusation — seeks validation from likeminded "What are they doing? Planning?"
POSSESSIONS	Net worth = personal worth "Having" mentality	Protect, enlarge, increase, display, pose, hide behind
FUN / PLEASURE	Short-lived, anesthetizing Fun mentality Dependent on environment	"More, more!"
SELF	Constantly changing, shifting Arm of flesh	"If it feels good. . . ." "What I want" "What I need" "What's in it for me?"
COMBINATION	Externally anchored "Tossed to and fro . . . with every wind of doctrine" Arm of flesh Built on sand	Vacillating guidelines

WISDOM	POWER
Everything seen through a social lens	Limited by social comfort zone As fickle as opinion
Narrow — defensive, overreactive Distorted judgment Paranoia	Anger, envy, resentment, vengeance wither human potentialities and conceal bad habits Negative energy shrivels and destroys
"Mammon" view of life	Limited by extent of but only one dimension of life
"What's in it for me?" "What have you done for me lately?"	Almost negligible — momentary, fickle
Shortsighted, narcissistic mentality "How will it affect me?"	As far as willpower, talent, and education can carry (humanism)
Changing, shifting — long view, short view	Like electricity intermittently plugged in and out

INACTIVE OR ACTIVE?

I was once home teaching a family whose son had strayed from "the Church," and the parents were beside themselves with grief over what to do. At one point I said, "I notice that your son frequently visits with you, and this shows a lot of love and loyalty to the family." The parents responded, "Yes, he's a very good person in that way. We only wish he would be more active in the Church."

I then taught the concept discussed above and explained that their son was active in certain aspects of the fundamental unit of the Church but was not at this point engaged in the scaffolding work. I told them that they should not condemn or label their son, because these labels tend to become self-fulfilling and they frequently are inaccurate anyway. By loving the son unconditionally and setting a good example themselves and trying to be understanding, I suggested, they would be modeling gospel values; then, little by little, with patience and prayer, they would probably see the son become increasingly active in the gospel and on the scaffolding. And this did come to pass.

RECONCILING CHURCH AND FAMILY STEWARDSHIPS

Once I was explaining these ideas in a priesthood meeting, and one good brother spoke up and said, "Well, this sounds good and idealistic, but it just isn't realistic."

I asked him to explain what he meant by that.

He began, "When I was called to be a bishop, I told the Lord I would completely devote myself to his work if he would take care of my family."

"What happened?" I asked.

"I did devote myself to his work," he replied.

"And then what happened?"

"I lost my two sons."

"In your heart," I said, "you really feel that the Lord has let you down, don't you, that he didn't take care of your family?"

"Well, in a sense, perhaps, but I would hesitate to say that openly. Frankly, I'm disappointed and I don't know what to do about these two sons."

He went on to describe how during his bishopric years he would always sacrifice doing anything with his sons because of the many demands placed upon him in his bishop's role. Then he threw me right into the fire of his very experience when he said, "Okay, what do you do? Your son needs to visit with you but you've got a bishopric meeting you need to go to."

This gave me an opportunity to explain what God / Christ-centeredness means. It means basically that we get our guidance from the Spirit. It could well be that in the situation posed the son is very tender and open for the first time in many months, and the Spirit says to you, "Counsel with your son." So you walk over to the phone, pick it up, call your first counselor, and essentially say, "Please carry on the bishopric work on the scaffolding. I've got some special Church work I need to do." Then you give yourself to your son as the Spirit directs.

This does not mean you shouldn't try to organize yourself to do both jobs exceptionally well. I believe that the Lord will make us equal to the burden that will be placed upon our shoulders, that he will enlarge our capacities if we will enlarge our dedication, but I also believe that it is partially a matter of our self-discipline and time management. We need to learn to properly establish and honor the stewardships of other people. In fact, I am convinced that *if people are consistently overburdened* in their so-called "Church work" or their family activities or their professional and business activities, it is because *they are not properly establishing or honoring stewardships.* I have no question that the Lord can enlarge our capacities so we can achieve excellence in all of our activities, but I admit it is very difficult for people with the cultural programming of today to accept this concept.

PARENT-CENTERED OR CHILD-CENTERED FAMILY LIFE?

One of the pendulums many parents swing on is whether the family should be parent-centered or child-centered. If we survey the popular literature of the past forty years it becomes very clear that the emphasis has shifted back and forth on this

> **In a God/Christ-centered home, correct principles will first govern the parents and they will teach them to their children, primarily by example and secondarily by precept, so that their children are also governed by them. The parents will perceive their children as their most sacred stewardship in time and in eternity. They will not perceive them as their possessions, for their children are really the spiritually begotten children of God the Eternal Father and are thus the brothers and sisters of their own mortal parents.**

pendulum. We are often told that the rebellion of the 'sixties was essentially a fruit of the permissiveness of the 'forties and the 'fifties. Many educators and parents are being influenced by the approaches of modern humanists. Much of the literature in the 'seventies and 'eighties attempts to address this problem by encouraging families to be more parent-centered and less indulging of their children's wants, whims, and desires — to dare to discipline, to teach values, to counsel, to direct, to set limits, to follow through, and so forth. However, much of this literature focuses on teaching values that are different from the basic values taught in the parent-centered literature of the first century and a half of United States history, which focused on hard work, honesty, thrift, responsibility, integrity, fidelity, humility, sincerity, and related qualities.

The parent-centered or child-centered question is simply another false dichotomy, a false way of viewing the problem. The key is to cultivate not a parent-centered home or a child-centered home but a divinely centered home, one in which the Lord guides in all aspects of home life.

Admittedly, when the children are young it might seem that the centering in what the parents call a God/Christ-centered home comes initially from the parents themselves, thus making it a parent-centered home. But this is an altogether different kind of parent-centered home from one in which the Father and the Son are not the center of their lives. In a God/Christ-centered home, correct principles will first govern the parents and they will teach them to their children, primarily by example and secondarily by precept, so that their children are also governed by them. The parents will perceive their children as their most sacred steward-ship in time and in eternity. They will not perceive them as their possessions, for their children are really the spiritually begotten children of God the Eternal Father and are thus the brothers and sisters of their own mortal parents. Their parents have given to them their physical bodies and have covenanted with the father of their spirit bodies to raise them in the nurture of the Lord.

What a 180-degree perception difference this is as compared with talking, thinking, and acting in terms of "my children," "my ways," "my will," "my wants," "my possessions," "my time"!

SACRIFICE OF FAMILY ACTIVITIES

When our parental role is directed from the divine center, the Spirit may sometimes guide us to sacrifice family pleasures and activities, even family companionship for a time, so that we may build the kingdom of God or for that matter engage in other worthy projects. *By up-front and continuous communication and by involving family members,* even little ones, in decision making and problem solving, we can help them sense the larger purpose and come to understand and accept separations and inconveniences and also to feel to share in the sacrifice. Such family involvement and sacrifice will literally help save (strengthen, unify, sanctify) the family. As so many missionaries discover, they had never really found their families until they left them!

I believe that the Savior's incomparable statement—"He that findeth his life shall lose it: and he that loseth his life for my sake shall find it" (Matthew 10:39) — pertains to family as well as to individuals.

Sacrifice truly "brings forth the blessings of heaven," and succeeding generations will probably continue the pattern and modeling of selfless service and sacrifice. Children learn these things primarily from their main models, their parents.

TOUGH LOVE

Clearly, in the God/Christ-centered home the atmosphere is one of love. Love is kindness, patience, affirmation of the other person's worth. In saying this, however, we are not saying that love is permissiveness, softness, "nice-guyness." True love, divine love — charity, or the love of Christ — is "tough." It involves standards, expectations, requirements, and disciplines. The criterion or essence of divine love is the growth and development of the person loved, not his temporary pleasure or one's own popularity. Sometimes the kindest thing we can do is to hold another to the responsible course while he is condemning us for doing so, or to allow natural and logical consequences to teach him accountability and responsibility. This "tough love," as some call it, communicates that we care more for and believe more in that person than he does in himself. We are saying we know he can do it, and that we will neither *give up on him* nor *give in to him.*

I have a friend who at one time felt he was losing his oldest son and who set about to rebuild the relationship. He later told me he felt he had achieved that rebuilding essentially by doing two things: 1) by increasing his demonstration of love for the son through more listening, kindness, patience, understanding, and shared activities; and 2) by simultaneously increasing the discipline on the son through clear teaching of correct principles, withholding permission to do certain things and associate with certain people, and holding the son responsible to meet family expectations and standards. He knew his son was old enough to go against his advice and teachings if he decided to, but instead the young man obeyed, though somewhat grudgingly. I believe his obedience came because of the father's increase in love. The limits helped the son to define who he was and was not, something that youthful peer acceptance cannot do.

The power to combine love and discipline or consideration and courage is, I suggest, rare. It is divinely rooted (whether this is acknowledged or not). It is fairly easy to be considerate without courage or to be courageous without consideration, but to be both simultaneously is the essence, and a good working definition, of maturity. Similarly, to love without discipline is fairly easy, also to discipline without love, but to combine them — that takes character and fortitude. That is tough love.

SACRIFICIAL LOVE

I draw attention here to another kind or facet of love, one that is perhaps on the highest plane of love. It involves walking with the other, sacrificing for the other, going the second mile with the other, simply doing more than the other would expect. This kind of love is not given with the intent of getting a particular response. It is unconditional in character and is a sacrificial kind of love. It partakes of the spirit of Jesus Christ, who laid down his life for others. It may take many creative and unique patterns, but it is always a kind of love that the Spirit can direct and inspire.

Family situations offer much opportunity for this divinely centered love. I came to know of one such experience. A friend of mine was serving as a stake president. His son didn't want to go on a mission, and this terribly concerned his father, who wanted his son to be a model to the stake as well as to have and give the blessings of missionary work. The father pleaded and urged and talked. He also tried to listen to the boy to understand him, all the while in the hope that the son would turn about and agree to go on a mission.

The subtle message he was communicating, I felt, was one of conditional love. The son felt that the father's desire for him to go on a mission in a sense outweighed the value he placed on him as a person and a son, and this, perhaps subconsciously, was terribly threatening. It stirred up a fight for the son's own identity and integrity, and he increased in his resolve not to go on a mission and to rationalize it away.

One day when the father was talking to me about this, I suggested that within himself he make a sacrifice of conditional love; that he come to terms and make peace with the idea that his son might choose not to go on a mission; and that the father should love the son unconditionally regardless of his choice. Also, that his wife should do the same, and that they should both do what was necessary within their hearts and minds to make such a sacrifice. It was an extremely difficult thing I was asking this couple to do, because for years they had planned on this mission. They had talked constantly about it. The boy had planned on it. He had even saved money for it in earlier years, but his interest had waned.

Now the father and mother went through a very difficult process of fasting and prayer and scripture study and, above all, the struggle to understand the nature of the unconditional love manifested in the atonement of Jesus Christ. Their own sacrificial offering was to be that of a broken heart and a contrite spirit (D&C 59:8). Little by little they received more and more of the spirit of unconditional love, until they were deeply confirmed within themselves that they had not loved their son unconditionally but were beginning to feel that love and wanted to express it. Then they communicated to the boy what they were doing and why, and told him they had come to the point at which they could say to him in honesty that whether he chose to go on a mission or not, it would not affect their complete feeling of unconditional love toward him. They didn't do this to manipulate the son, to try to get him to "shape up." They did it as the logical extension of their spiritual growth and character.

The son didn't give much of a response at the time, but the parents were in such a frame of mind now that it would have made no difference to their feelings for him. About a week later the son told his parents that he had prayerfully considered the matter and had decided not to go on a mission. While they would have been very happy if he had said instead that he would go, the parents were perfectly prepared for this response and they continued to show unconditional love for him. Now everything was settled and life went along normally.

One day the son was sitting in a large assembly room listening to one of the General Authorities give a devotional speech at Brigham Young University, when he felt the Spirit come upon him. It flooded his mind with the desire to serve a mission. The next thing his stake president father knew was the son coming in for an interview to go off on a mission, following his interview with his bishop. Again the father showed by his unconditional love that he fully accepted the son's decision. The son said that he realized that, and that that very realization had freed him from the unconscious or conscious fear of being pressured to serve a mission. Now that he had felt the Spirit inspire him to go on a mission, he really wanted to go with all his heart. His father was thrilled and happy, but he wasn't excessively elated, because he had truly sacrificed and had gone the second mile in a unique and creative way of showing love. And this had given him a deep sense of peace.

There are many other ways of going the second mile. Every situation is different. And while I suspect that not all relationship problems will respond to this principle, the unconditional love manifested cannot fail to have an effect on the receiver and will inevitably move the giver further along the divine-centered road.

ALL THINGS ARE SPIRITUAL

A marvelous thing about Mormonism is that it makes all good things sacred and spiritual. The Lord has said, "All things unto me are spiritual" (D&C 29:34). There are no secular activities. There are only secular minds and hearts. In the Church, there are essentially four points of emphasis: spiritual welfare, temporal welfare, genealogical work, and missionary work. The Church therefore has designated three essential missions: to preach the gospel, to perfect the Saints, and to redeem the dead. The perfecting of the Saints involves both the temporal and the spiritual welfare of the Saints, so the so-called temporal or physical or secular is really spiritual. It's a part of the Lord's work and kingdom.

STUDENT STEWARDSHIP

I try to teach this to my students at Brigham Young University — that their work as a student is a sacred stewardship. They have been given a great trust in that they are being largely supported and financed by the tithing funds of the Church, and that they should look on their student work in the same way that they look upon their so-called "Church work"; that excellence in their Church assignments is no excuse for mediocrity in their school assignments; and that any kind of a false compartmentalization or dichotomy needs to be transcended by increased centering on the Father and the Son.

FAMILY WELFARE FARM

If all things are spiritual to the Lord, certainly that is true of legitimate efforts to serve one's family. Once when I was serving as a Regional Representative, I was counseling with stake presidents regarding the choice of a regional welfare advisor. We came across a good man, and I asked his stake president about this man's track record on welfare. The president said that it was excellent; that the man understood the program and was very committed to it. But for some reason, he said, the man wouldn't come out on the stake welfare farm on Saturday afternoon with the rest of the brethren. I asked him what the man was doing at that time, and he said sarcastically, "Selling real estate," as if the man was going after filthy lucre and neglecting the work of the kingdom.

I looked the stake president in the eye and said, "President, you mean he's on the family welfare farm. Is that what you mean?"

The president asked, "What are you saying?"

I asked the stake president which would be the more serious

kind of apostasy—to neglect the family welfare farm or the stake welfare farm? He thought for a long time and said, "Well, I guess, the family welfare farm."

I said, "Yes, that's correct. 'He that will not provide . . . for his own . . . is worse than an infidel,' as the scripture teaches" (1 Timothy 5:8).

Now, I admit that normally a person can and should do both if he properly organizes and disciplines himself, but we need to be very careful about concluding that stake welfare farm work is work of the kingdom and a person properly taking care of his occupation is secular and self-serving.

The point is that we will never be released from our most important Church job, that of husband and father or wife and mother. It will be with us eternally. We will, however, be released from all of our work on the scaffolding from time to time. Eventually perhaps the scaffolding will be withdrawn and the eternal organization will be the patriarchal family.

I have mentioned the renewed and increased emphasis upon the family as the fundamental unit of the Church. Joseph Smith's leadership philosophy, "I teach them correct principles and they govern themselves," has also been emphasized in recent years. Thus more and more capacity is developed within the parents to carry on the program of the Church right within the home setting. Perhaps it will take another generation before this new software program fully takes, but all of us can see it happening. I believe that the closer we come to the Millennium, the more we will pick up momentum on focusing on fundamental principles such as the gospel and priesthood and the family and ordinances and quorums and scriptures and revelation and God-centered living.

FAMILY PATRIARCH'S STEWARDSHIP

Once the high priests group in a ward I was in invited a member of the elders presidency to make a presentation on welfare work. In making it, at one point the brother got sidetracked and said in essence that the high priests group was made up of high-powered, highly experienced individuals, but that we were essentially "on the shelf" and doing very little outside of home teaching, some temple work, and a little missionary work, while he and some of his elders were doing much, much more.

I asked him how many children he had. He said he had one and a half. I turned to two of the older high priests on the front row and asked them how many children they had. Five and eight were the answers. I asked them about their grandchildren and great-grandchildren. One had a posterity of over seventy, and the other's was in the thirties. Missionaries from both families were presently in the field. I turned back to the elder and said, "Are these men really on the shelf? They are natural family patriarchs, and that is the highest Church calling they will ever have, one that they will never be released from and one that consumes most of their energies in the evenings and on weekends. Should they feel guilty because they are not doing a lot of things that you're able to do with your evenings and weekends?"

I am citing all of these experiences and concepts to try to create a better perspective, a better balance. These improved perceptions come to us only as we make efforts to orient our lives to the divine center, however weak and faltering those efforts may be. Such perceptions cannot come from any other frame of reference. We have seen the total inadequacy of some of the common life centers. Even the seemingly most promising ones—Church and family—will not do, for either of these will at some time have us trying to walk eastward and westward at the same time.

I hope by now the prefacing scripture at the beginning of this chapter has taken on a great deal more meaning. "I am come that they might have life, and that they might have it more abundantly." Divine-centeredness is the key to properly preserving and enhancing every other center except the enemy one, and that one will essentially be diminished or eliminated by perceiving the "enemy" with compassion, forgiveness, and understanding, as one would look on a troubled investigator of the gospel.

It is not that Christ is just another center or object of worship. Rather it is that we view each life activity or space through the lens of this divine center and release the fulness of God's powers and gifts into every one of these compartments of life in such a way that they are integrated, harmonized, and balanced. Then, literally, all things work together for our good. A synergy takes place — the whole becomes more than the sum of its parts. It is the relationship between the parts that becomes more significant than the parts themselves. Everything becomes magnified, enlarged, increased, lifted up, and eventually exalted. The Lord wants his children to have a fulness, a richness of all that the earth's experience can provide in every direction. Only the divine center makes this possible.

ALTERNATIVE CENTERS & AREAS OF LIFE CHART

The purpose of the following chart (pages 128 through 143) is to graphically summarize possible reactions that would result from perceptions conditioned by different centers of life. Each *Alternative Center of Life* represents a different frame of reference or way in which we see the world. Remember that our reactions are a product of our perceptions, and our perceptions are a result of what is at the center of our life.

To understand the mechanics of this somewhat complex chart some explanation is required, and this is given below. If you will carefully study the chart and the explanation, I think you will be well rewarded for your efforts.

■ The twelve-matrix grid on the facing page represents the chart in total. The shaded and the open areas on the small matrix correspond to the material that appears on each double spread from pages 128 through 143. For example: the material on pages 128 and 129 corresponds to the upper left-hand shaded area of the small matrix. The small matrix is provided so that you can relate each double spread to the total configuration.

■ Each heading—God/Christ, Spouse, Family, etc.—appears as both an *Alternative Center of Life* and an *Area of Life.* They function both as a frame of reference or center to our life and as a field of thought, activity, or concern in life.

■ As you read horizontally across each *Alternative Center of Life* you will note that the regular type under each *Area of Life* heading represents one or more ways in which a person so centered might perceive that *Area of Life.* The italic type below that represents how that person might view that area or what his reactions might be if his expectations of that area (as defined by his center) are not met.

■ To use the chart, then, find the page containing the *Alternative
Center of Life* and the *Area of Life* you are interested in and read
from the appropriate square. Be creative and think up other
possible scenarios in addition to those on the chart.

Understanding the mechanics of the chart is one thing. The real
meaning will only become clear to you as you put your mind in a
frame that will allow you to empathize with a person who is
centered on whatever center you have chosen. The key is your
imagination. You must imagine how a person sees the world, and
then you will begin to understand how he thinks or feels. For we
see not so much with our eyes as with our minds and souls.

Alternative Centers \ Areas of Life	GOD/CHRIST	SPOUSE	FAMILY	CHURCH	WORK	LEADERS/HEROES	FRIENDS	ENEMIES	POSSESSIONS	FUN/PLEASURE	SELF	COMBINATION
GOD/CHRIST												
SPOUSE			128-129							130-131		
FAMILY												
CHURCH												
WORK			132-133							134-135		
LEADERS/HEROES												
FRIENDS												
ENEMIES			136-137							138-139		
POSSESSIONS												
FUN/PLEASURE												
SELF			140-141							142-143		
COMBINATION												

127

Alternative Centers		Areas of Life GOD / CHRIST	SPOUSE	FAMILY
GOD / CHRIST	*PERCEPTIONS*	Eternal Father Elder Brother Model, Savior Center, source	Eternal companion Potential king, queen in heaven	Eternal basic unit of the Church Building block of society
	REACTIONS	*Educate and obey conscience* *Exercise patience, diligence*	*Love unconditionally* *Become a light, not a judge* *Optimize each situation*	*Balance love with discipline* *Treat as if investigators*
SPOUSE	*PERCEPTIONS*	Source of marriage Unimportant or irrelevant	Main source of need satisfaction Highly vulnerable	Good in its place Children less important Common exciting project
	REACTIONS	*Upsetting but basically irrelevant* *Faith weakened*	*Confused, disillusioned, frustrated, upset, angry* *Accusation, manipulation*	*Frustrated* *Belittling* *"Children get in our way"*
FAMILY	*PERCEPTIONS*	Source of family Protectors, source of blessings Justifiers Unimportant	Part of the family	The highest priority "We and ours" Possessive
	REACTIONS	*"Why us?"* *Confused, faith weakened* *Assert self-sufficiency*	*Judge / accuse* *Reject* *Family may compensate*	*Alternate between judgment and guilt, authoritarianism and permissiveness*

CHURCH	WORK	LEADERS / HEROES	
The kingdom of God on earth	Family welfare farm	Servants	*Please turn the page for the continuation of Chart 1*
Family life highest Church activity	Means of service, contribution, modeling, talent development, attaining excellence	Human models Growing children of God	
Make personal sacrifices to build kingdom *Be active in the gospel as key to building*	*Be honest in all dealings* *Balance courage with consideration*	*Show respect for authority* *Build on strengths, make weaknesses irrelevant*	
Source of marriage Strengthening or weakening to marriage	Necessary to properly take care of spouse (necessary evil) Spouse co-worker	Relatively unimportant Admires some people	
Upsetting *Interfering* *Faith-weakening*	*Disruptive, upsetting to economic base*	*Interfering*	
A second priority Family supporter and unifier	Family economic support Temporal, secular Means to family ends	Family-oriented type models Source of family-life education	
Inconveniencing *Interrupting* *Confining*	*Disruptive, even destructive, of family plans*	*Disillusioned* *Upset*	

	Areas of Life		
Alternative Centers	FRIENDS	ENEMIES	POSSESSIONS
GOD / CHRIST — PERCEPTIONS	Dear confidants Service opportunity Social-emotional support	Children of God Personal growth test	Stewardship for service and sharing Blessings
REACTIONS	*Be understanding, accepting* *Believe in their potential* *Affirm their worth*	*Love, pray for them* *Don't give in, don't give up*	*Be grateful* *Consecrate*
PERCEPTIONS	Spouse best friend or only friend Enjoys some friends Not needed	Spouse worst enemy Source of marriage definition (common enemy)	Gifts are means to bless, impress, manipulate
REACTIONS	*New common enemies gained*	*Confused, terribly disturbed and threatened*	*Upset to degree spouse is possession-centered*
FAMILY — PERCEPTIONS	Friends of family Family oriented Supportive Competition, threat to strong family life	Defined by family Source of family strength and unity Possible threat to family strength	Family comforts and opportunities Relatively unimportant
REACTIONS	*Shaken, disturbed* *Strengthened, unified*	*Unimportant or confusing*	*Distressing if matter family-related, otherwise unimportant*

130

FUN / PLEASURE	SELF	COMBINATION
Renewing, refreshing	God's own child	All things are spiritual
Diversion	"Bought with a price"	All good things have a place
Relating with others		Everything in its place
"No big thing"	*Exercise humility, faith, obedience, sacrifice, consecration*	*Seek the Spirit*
Be adaptable		*See life as mission, not as career*
Mutual activity	Self-worth defined by spouse	Alternative common interests
Common unifying activity	Highly vulnerable	
Unimportant		
Frustrated, depending on importance to relationship	*Confused, shattered*	*Upset if combination important to relationship*
		Search for alternative pattern
Family activities	Vital part of but subordinate to family	Each serves to preserve and enhance family
Relatively unimportant		
Moderately upsetting when matter family-related — other areas compensate	*Disturbing — expect family to somehow compensate*	*Moderately upsetting*
		Search for family-support options

Alternative Centers		*Areas of Life* GOD / CHRIST	SPOUSE	FAMILY
CHURCH	PERCEPTIONS	Head and foundation of the Church Speak to our prophets	Vital part of the Church plan Secondary to Church callings	Needful for exaltation Secondary to Church callings
	REACTIONS	*Confused — "Why?"* *Mechanical prayers* *Hypocrisy — lip service*	*Judge, accuse, using Church words* *Manipulative* *Act as "martyr"* *Eventual rejection* *"I'll obey if he's righteous"*	*Judge, accuse* *Moralizing, preaching* *"Elder brother" syndrome* *Justify in Church terms*
WORK	PERCEPTIONS	Unnecessary, irrelevant Guilt producers or work justifiers	Helper or interferer in work	Help or interruption to work People to instruct on work ethic
	REACTIONS	*Upsetting, interfering* *"Unfair"* *Faith weakened*	*Hindrance* *Judge, accuse*	*Upset, angry, frustrated* *Judge, accuse* *Punish, ridicule*
LEADERS / HEROES	PERCEPTIONS	OK but unnecessary or irrelevant Compartmentalized	Of lesser value — worth attached to hero identification	A poor second Means of making impression or source of embarrassment
	REACTIONS	*Confused* *Disbelieving* *Rejecting*	*Upset, angry* *Judge, accuse* *Reject*	*Undermine explicit foundation (center), creating frustration and accusation*

CHURCH	WORK	LEADERS / HEROES	
God's kingdom First priority (family second) Primary source of security, guidance	Necessary secular activity to provide material needs Relatively unimportant	Idealized if in top Church positions, otherwise, "not much"	*Please turn the* *page for the* *continuation of* *Chart 2*
Pharisaism *Confusion* *Frustration* *Depression*	*Justify mediocrity* *Use double standard* *for work quality* *Judge / condemn unrighteous* *Take advantage, manipulate*	*Judge, reject* *Confused, shattered if* *Church leaders*	
Possible source of interruption to work, imposition Secondary loyalty	Source of satisfaction and fulfillment Highest ethic	Idolized if work oriented, otherwise ignored	
Very upsetting *Interfering* *Angry, rejecting*	*Devastating,* *emotional overreaction*	*"Feet of clay"* *Livelihood threatened* *Economically defensive*	
Idealized if heroes are Church leaders	Necessary evil Useful in impressing leaders / heroes	Heroes / ideals Worthy of adulation, almost worship	
Judge, compare *Offended — inactive*	*Upsetting, embarrassing*	*Shattered, confused* *Disappointed, angry* *Pities and condemns* *self, feels guilty*	

Alternative Centers		Areas of Life		
		FRIENDS	ENEMIES	POSSESSIONS
CHURCH	PERCEPTIONS	Good if Church members Co-Church workers and socializers	Enemies of God Deserving of judgment, rejection	Worldly Minimum necessary is evidence of righteousness
	REACTIONS	*Judge, reject as unfaithful*	*Confused* *Seek evidence to relabel* *Justify persecution*	*Upset, angry* *Judge, using Church language*
WORK	PERCEPTIONS	Developed from work setting Basically unnecessary	Obstacles	Tools to increase work effectiveness Fruits, badge of work
	REACTIONS	*Interrupting* *May threaten ricebowl*	*Relieved* *Confused*	*Upsetting loss to work effectiveness*
LEADERS / HEROES	PERCEPTIONS	Selected by leaders / heroes criterion	Help in defining leaders' strength	Means of making impression or source of embarrassment Opportunity factor
	REACTIONS	*Leaders / heroes the criterion for judging / rejecting friends*	*Confusion*	*Embarrassed* *Upset and angry* *Opportunity loss*

FUN / PLEASURE	SELF	COMBINATION
Essentially worthless Church socials, outings acceptable	Important in Church Means to greater Church end	Too complicated Confusing, worldly Duplicitous
Judge *Justify in Church terms*	*Judge self* *Condemn self* *Justify Church* *Be a "martyr"*	*See Church as justifying judgment*
Waste of time Interfere with work	Defined by job role	Unnecessary complication, interference
Interfering waste for "lazy"	*Devastating*	*Judge, accuse*
Worth defined by leaders / heroes tastes Unimportant Compartmentalized Day dreaming	Worth determined by leader acceptance	Usefulness defined by leaders / heroes style
Unimportant, thus of little effect	*Embarrassment* *Self-disgust, self-rejection*	*Judge, reject*

Alternative Centers		Areas of Life		
		GOD / CHRIST	SPOUSE	FAMILY
FRIENDS	PERCEPTIONS	Best friends or worst enemies Viewed with indifference	Possible friend or possible competitor Social status symbol	Source of need satisfaction or dissatisfaction
	REACTIONS	Loss of faith Generalized cynicism Increased dependency on friends	Embarrassed Angry Reject, isolate spouse	Anger, resentment, accusation toward interfering family member or activity
ENEMIES	PERCEPTIONS	Allies or deserters Viewed with indifference	Sympathizer One to blame (scapegoat)	Refuge or annoyance Emotional support Those to blame (scapegoat)
	REACTIONS	Unjust Faith weakened Depressions, paranoia	Angry release of pent-up hostility and guilt Another enemy	Judge, accuse, overreact Family a scapegoat
POSSESSIONS	PERCEPTIONS	Justifiers of "me" Source of unimportant or irrelevant	Main possession Assistant in acquiring	Possession to use, exploit, dominate, smother, control Showcase
	REACTIONS	Shattered, broken, insecure Lose faith or repent out of fear	Too self-willed Judge, accuse	Contention Belittle, berate, manipulate with things

CHURCH	WORK	LEADERS / HEROES	
Social gathering Social barrier	Source of economic and social good	Possible competition Viewed with jealousy mixed with admiration	*Please turn the page for the continuation of Chart 3*
Interference *Waste of time* *Of no importance*	*Interference* *Waste of time*	*Frustration* *Venting anger* *With common enemy, friendship now strengthened*	
Source of self-justification Emotional refuge or guilt trip	Interference or escape Means to fight with Support	Source of vindication or guilt Irrelevant Blameworthy (scapegoat)	
Fails to understand *Confusion, anger* *Church a scapegoat*	*Paranoia* *Self-pity or anger at self*	*Leaders have joined enemy ranks* *Cynicism*	
Institutional possession — "my church" "My people"	Another possession to control Key to increasing possessions Outlet for carrot-and-stick motivation	"Belong to me, I to them" Models Name-drop security	
Confused *Judge as unreliable* *Inactive*	*Shattered — leverage lost*	*"My" loss*	

Alternative Centers		*Areas of Life* FRIENDS	ENEMIES	POSSESSIONS
FRIENDS	PERCEPTIONS	Highest aspiration Crucial to be "in" (belong, be accepted, popular)	They're "out" Competitors Source of unity or self-definition	Social pleasures Means of buying friendship Means of entertaining
	REACTIONS	*Wiped out* *Depressed, confused, disoriented*	*Confusing* *Disunifying*	*Frustration* *Social fears*
ENEMIES	PERCEPTIONS	Emotional supporters and sympathizers	Objects of hate Stimuli to self-protection, self-justification	Fighting tools Means to secure allies An escape, refuge
	REACTIONS	*Devastated — Job-like* *New enemies* *Paranoia*	*Disoriented, suspicious, defensive, confused* *Feels manipulated*	*Evidence of conspiracy* *Depression*
POSSESSIONS	PERCEPTIONS	Personal objects Usable "Elite"	Takers, thieves Definers of "me" and "mine" "Trying to use me"	Status symbols "My things"
	REACTIONS	*Hurts "me"* *"How could they?"* *Vindictive*	*Confused* *"New way to control / possess me"*	*Identity, whole security base threatened*

FUN / PLEASURE	SELF	COMBINATION
Primary social events	Socially defined	Is it socially useful?
Enjoyed always with friends	Afraid of embarrassment / rejection	Is it manipulatable?
Frustration	*Depression*	*Disappointed*
	Confusion	*Shifting and searching*
	Insecurity	
R and R before next battle	Seeks justification, protection	Allies, supporters
Strategizing	Get even — revenge	
No pleasure in anything	*Self-condemnation*	*Loneliness*
Self-justification	*Self-flagellation*	*Cynicism, paranoia*
	Confused, wiped out	
Buying-shopping, club-joining, are form of possession, "my thing"	Closest possession is "me"	"Have" mentality in all circumstances
	"Needs" must be satisfied	
	Taking care of self	
Upsetting, frustrating	*"Couldn't control myself"*	*Threatened*
Retreat to things		*Shaken*

Alternative Centers		*Areas of Life* GOD / CHRIST	SPOUSE	FAMILY
FUN / PLEASURE	*PERCEPTIONS*	In the way or irrelevant	Companion in fun and pleasure or obstacle to it	Vehicle or interference
	REACTIONS	*Ignore / reject* *Repent from force of circumstances*	*Accuse-judge* *Escape*	*Responsibility too great* *Withdraw, neglect* *Escape* *Rationalize*
SELF	*PERCEPTIONS*	Irrelevant or justify "me" I more special to them than others	Possession Satisfier and pleaser	Possession Need satisfier
	REACTIONS	*Narcissistic* *"Why me?"* *Disbelief, cynicism*	*Extreme anger* *Accusation, self-justification* *Frustration valve*	*"Ungrateful, selfish brats"* *Scapegoat for any frustration*
COMBINATION	*PERCEPTIONS*	Depending on the nature of the combination, the applicable descriptions given above would combine in unique ways		
	REACTIONS	*Depending on the nature of the combination, the applicable descriptions given above would combine in unique ways*		

Chart 4

CHURCH	WORK	LEADERS / HEROES	
Vehicle or obstacle	Means to an end	Fun oriented — sports, party, celebrity types	*Please turn the page for the continuation of Chart 4*
Too "heavy"	"Fun" work OK		
"Fun" Church activities OK			
Frustration	*Disturbing main means to fun*	*Shift to other leaders / heroes*	
Escape or leave			
Rationalize inactivity			
Servant, comforter, protector, enhancer	Servant, protector	Justifier, helper, strengthener	
Possession — "my church, my people"	Need satisfier		
"Let me down, deserted me"	"How could they?"	*Confusion, dismay*	
"Unfair — poor me!"	"The whole world's turning against me"	*Total narcissism*	
Anger, self-justification			

Depending on the nature of the combination, the applicable descriptions given above would combine in unique ways

Depending on the nature of the combination, the applicable descriptions given above would combine in unique ways

Alternative Centers		Areas of Life FRIENDS	ENEMIES	POSSESSIONS
FUN / PLEASURE	PERCEPTIONS	Companions in fun "Fun" guys Fellow partners People to always be around	Take life too seriously Guilt trippers Destroyers	Objects of fun Means to more fun
	REACTIONS	Judgment — cutting humor, sarcasm	"What's going on?" Cynicism	"What can I do now?"
SELF	PERCEPTIONS	Supporter, provider "for me"	Source of self-definition, self-justification	Source of self-definition, protection, enhancement
	REACTIONS	Self-pity "You too?" "Why me?"	Confusion, cynicism Increased insecurity	Anger, accusation "Everything's happening to me! Take care of me!"
COMBINATION	PERCEPTIONS	Depending on the nature of the combination, the applicable descriptions given above would combine in unique ways		
	REACTIONS	Depending on the nature of the combination, the applicable descriptions given above would combine in unique ways		

FUN / PLEASURE	SELF	COMBINATION (two or more)
The supreme activity (end in life)	Main instrument for pleasure	Product of "It's fun" mentality Many different funs
Depression *Restlessness* *Search for bigger "highs"*	*Depression* *Restlessness*	*Upsetting* *Search for alternative pattern*
Deserved sensate satisfactions "My rights" "My needs"	More special "Me, myself and I" "My wants, my way, my time, etc."	For self needs and wants
Unhappiness *Selfishness*	*Self-hatred or self-justification*	*Anger, accusation* *Pouting, "martyrdom"*
Depending on the nature of the combination, the applicable descriptions given above would combine in unique ways		
Depending on the nature of the combination, the applicable descriptions given above would combine in unique ways		

The Centered Life

Chapter 6

> *But we all, with open face beholding as in a*
> *glass the glory of the Lord, are changed into*
> *the same image from glory to glory, even*
> *as by the Spirit of the Lord. (2 Corinthians 3:18.)*

All things unto me are spiritual" (D&C 29:34). This statement by the Savior is enormously significant. Ponder on it for a moment.

If to Christ all things are spiritual, one who has "the mind of Christ" (1 Corinthians 2:16) will see all things through spiritual eyes or spiritual understanding. To him there will be no compartments, no artificial separations that would equate with the different centers we have already explored and others we could explore. To the spiritual mind, the mind that emulates the perception of Christ, there is no separation between the sacred and the secular. "Unto the pure all things are pure" (Titus 1:15).

When a person has this map or frame of reference, the Lord and his work becomes the driving force of that person's life. It becomes the unifying and organizing principle, the center around which everything revolves. It is the anchor and root, the foundation and cornerstone of all his activities, relationships, and decisions. Such a person, having consecrated himself to the Lord, will have a divine sense of stewardship about everything in his life, including time, talents, money, possessions, relationships, his family, his body, and so forth. Even though some of these things are often thought of as "temporal," he knows they are spiritual, and he recognizes the need to use them for righteous purposes and, as a steward, to be accountable for their use.

DIVINE CENTER MAKES ALL THINGS SPIRITUAL

With such a perception, we bring spiritual values and applications to any honorable occupation or situation. It is not difficult, of course, to see how all things in a missionary's life are spiritual, including Preparation Day, recreation activity, eating, and sleeping, because it is all geared toward one end, that of building the kingdom. It is more difficult, although the principle still holds, to see how all things are spiritual to a businessman, a student, a housewife, an artist, an athlete.

Brigham Young once said: "We can serve God as much in one place as in another, whether we are working in a mercantile institution, or on our crops in the field, or preaching the gospel. We serve God as much in one place as in the other." Consider how this is so. This world is temporal; it is physical. To survive, we must make a living in it. The temporal welfare of the Saints is a very important part of the work of the kingdom. There are perhaps as many teachings and parables surrounding money and the making of a living as any other single subject. Often the greatest of the spiritual tests take place in this area of life, simply because it is so real, so practical, so immediate. How we conduct ourselves in this challenging area clearly shows what is truly preeminent in our lives.

In that sense, missionary work offers far less of a test, a temptation, than making a living does. To be honest in all our dealings and to maintain a spiritual perspective while making a living requires loyalty to a true, divine center; a true discipleship, a firm internal discipline. There are nowhere near as many external supports and disciplines on the one making a living as there are on the missionary in the mission field. The missionary is surrounded by a very powerful, cultural "law of Moses," as it were; that is, an external set of expectations, rules, and disciplines. These serve as the ancient law of Moses did—as a schoolmaster to bring the missionaries to Christ or to a higher law, so that they transcend the law of Moses and move into the law of Christ, where they are motivated by love, guided by correct principles, directed by the Spirit.

The student is in a similar case. He needs to be self-disciplined in managing his time and his life so as to meet the academic requirements of his classes in the development of his talents, both intellectual and emotional. His is a sacred stewardship; learning is sacred; it is divine; it enables us to be better prepared for the mission to which the Lord has called us. The Lord's words to earlier Saints apply likewise to us today:

> Teach ye diligently and my grace shall attend you, that you may be instructed more perfectly in theory, in principle, in doctrine, in the law of the gospel, in all things that pertain unto the kingdom of God, that are expedient for you to understand;
> Of things both in heaven and in the earth, and under the earth; things which have been, things which are, things which must shortly come to pass; things which are at home, things which are abroad; the wars and the perplexities of the nations, and the judgments which are on the land; and a knowledge also of countries and of kingdoms—
> That ye may be prepared in all things when I shall send you again to magnify the calling whereunto I have called you, and the mission with which I have commissioned you. (D&C 88:78-80.)

The mission to which we are called is the mission of mortality—that of teaching the gospel, perfecting the Saints, and redeeming the dead. Our church perhaps more than any other one has placed enormous emphasis upon the importance and the power of education, of continually improving one's knowledge and understanding. Strictly it is a misnomer to call such learning profane or secular in contrast to the more spiritual and sacred. This does not mean, of course, that there is not a hierarchy or a set of priorities in the field of education, as in any other field, as to what knowledge is most important. But it does mean that everything has its proper place, and that, when viewed with a spiritual mind, knowledge of all kinds and the educational process itself is intended to be spiritual.

THE CHRISTLIKE APPROACH

Naturally, this perception, approach, and application all move one toward a Christlike approach to human relationships.

On the matter of seeking to be Christlike, President David O. McKay said:

> The highest of all ideals are the teachings and particularly the life of Jesus of Nazareth, and that man is most truly great who is most Christlike.
>
> What you sincerely in your heart think of Christ will determine what you are, will largely determine what your acts will be. No person can study this divine personality, can accept his teachings, without becoming conscious of an uplifting and refining influence within himself. . . .
>
> Members of the Church of Jesus Christ are under obligation to make the sinless Son of Man their ideal — the one perfect Being who ever walked the earth. (*Gospel Ideals*, Improvement Era, 1953, pages 34-35.)

The Christlike approach is especially important in the usually difficult situation of suffering injustice or affliction. In keeping with Christ's example, if the God/Christ-centered person is offended, he blesses in return. He returns kindness for unkindness, patience for impatience. If he is afflicted, he chooses a response which enables him to grow and learn from the affliction, to suffer with meaning and nobility, a response which will have a greater influence on others than perhaps any other value, experiential or creative. If the person is praised, he gives thanks. If he is blamed, he appraises the matter to see whether there may be some blameworthiness in him, and if there is he plans self-improvement. But he does not overreact and either accuse or blame in return, or condemn himself.

And all the time he seeks to identify with Christ. Christ is his model. For instance, he studies the scriptural accounts of the Savior's earthly life, and as he does so he visualizes each of the situations recorded. He empathizes with the people involved, sees himself as part of the action, feels himself in the more positive, disciple-type roles. He creates in his mind his response to present-day situations based on living by the principles represented by the scriptural accounts. In this way he brings home to his heart the reality of each situation and its principles, and as he feels this

In addition to Christ being our advocate with the Father, in some special ways he can be our advocate with our Father's other children.

deeply his understanding and his love increase for the perfect one, the Master, the Savior of the world, the one who is our advocate and mediator with the Father and who manifests the Father's will in every regard. Gradually, as he comes to see the Savior as the perfect model and mentor, he identifies with that mental image and vision. In this way he acquires "the mind of Christ" and thus gradually learns to respond to life situations as *He* would have responded (which is as His Father would have responded), or perhaps more realistically as He would have him respond based on his present level of faith and understanding.

CHRIST OUR ADVOCATE WITH OTHERS

This God-centered approach is a highly practical thing. It endows one's life with calm and peace and the certainty of a sure anchorage, plus the understanding and the ability to respond as Christ would have him do. In addition the benefits carry over by example into the lives of others. As mentioned previously, for instance, I am convinced that, in addition to Christ being our advocate with the Father, in some special ways he can be our advocate with our Father's other children.

Let's use as an illustration a common experience in missionary work. Two missionaries out tracting knock on a door and a woman responds. This person is basically good—honest, God-fearing, family-loving, and so forth. But she has an inaccurate map about Mormonism, a map which has come from tradition, rumors, false reports, and suchlike. So she acts in terms of her map and tells the missionaries she is not interested in their message. The missionaries continue to communicate with kindness, patience, and empathy, with a reasonableness and courtesy. But the woman persists in showing no interest, so the missionaries are turned away at the door. Nevertheless their spirit remains cheerful and buoyant, pleasant and courteous, and in their parting comments they express appreciation for the privilege of the short visit and wish the woman a good day.

What happens to the woman when they are gone? Well, her conscience has been stirred. None of the things she had heard about Mormons was indicated by her experience with two of their representatives. These young men are courteous, gentlemanly, kind, understanding. They are not extreme, not religious zealots, not brainwashed cultists, not anti-Christ, but simply very fine, decent, reasonable, Christian people. This bothers her. She can't easily "write them off." It bothers her because, being a fine person, she has the Spirit of Christ in her life. She is not by any means "past feeling" (see 1 Nephi 17:45). Her conscience, her own personal Liahona, is directing her and giving her a sense of right and wrong. And in essence the Spirit of Christ is the voice of Christ. He has become those missionaries' advocate to this woman.

It would have been so much simpler and easier if the missionaries had been curt and sharp to her, as initially she was to them. In that case she would now feel confirmed in her prior judgment of Mormons. If only they had been insincere and more manipulative, less respectful and more pushy, less empathetic and more judgmental, then she wouldn't have this gnawing feeling in her conscience and in her heart. But as it is, she goes to the window to see the two missionaries walking away up the street. She sees one of them put his arm on the shoulder of the other, the one who had initially made the door approach, as if to say, "That's okay, Elder, you did a fine job. We tried our best. Let's keep going." This bothers her even more, because again the Savior works upon her through his voice, her conscience. Perhaps she can faintly remember or "feel" the scripture wherein the Savior said, "By this shall all men know that ye are my disciples, if ye have love one to another" (John 13:35).

Now take another case. Someone has offended you. In fact, this person seems frequently to offend you and offend your children by his abrupt ways, the judgmental labels he places upon you and your children. Perhaps it is a neighbor or a fellow Church worker, or an auxiliary teacher, or a high councilor assigned to your ward, where you are serving as a counselor in the bishopric. It would really make no difference what the context was, because the same principle would operate. That principle is that *when you consistently return kindness for unkindness,* patience in the face of impatience, good for evil, *you release the still, small voice inside of the other person to advocate your case,* and it will appeal to whatever good there is in that person.

Of course, there is no guarantee that this will result in a change in the offending person's behavior. As happens with many people in all kinds of situations, he may completely ignore the still, small voice. The point is that one of the main factors, perhaps the major one, influencing whether he will listen to the voice or ignore it will be your own behavior and attitude. The person who is striving for Christ-centeredness will seek to bless when being cursed, to turn the other cheek, to go the second mile, to forgive and forget, to move on in life with helpfulness and cheerfulness, believing in the potential goodness of people and the eventual triumph of truth and righteousness. And such a divinely centered behavior pattern arouses enticings to righteousness in the consciences of all those around him, representing an "upward temptation." In effect, he then has the Savior as his advocate.

Interestingly enough, the moment a person attempts to become his own advocate, he loses in part the Savior's advocacy. If he seeks to defend and justify himself, or to return in kind the treatment he is receiving, thus being caught up and cooperating in the negative exchange of energy, then he has forfeited the higher advocacy. Both parties then are on the same territory, and either fight or flight will be the probable outcome, whether in the

There is nothing as baffling to one who is full of tricks and duplicity as straightforward, simple honesty in another. It sets him in a war with himself, with his conscience, with his Savior.

form of smooth manipulations, pressures, violence, withdrawal, indifference, cold wars, or heated-up legal battles.

GENUINENESS ESSENTIAL

The desire and effort for God/Christ-centeredness must of course be genuine. A person can't just pretend to be seeking that center and expect to have the Savior as his advocate, because as soon as difficult circumstances arise, he simply won't have the inward security base and the source of guidance, power, and wisdom. He will be like the five foolish virgins, who had not taken the Holy Spirit for their guide—in other words, had no oil for their lamps—who believed that there was some kind of a shortcut they could take to get this oil, this Holy Spirit. So they rushed to the five wise virgins—who had the necessary oil and whose lamps could be quickly made ready—as if they could obtain the oil merely by asking for it, or could buy it at the last moment instead of paying the price of obedience and righteousness in advance, meriting the influence of the Holy Spirit day by day. (See Matthew 25:1-13; D&C 45:56-57.)

THE KEY: THE WHOLE ARMOR OF GOD

Lacking the inner security base, when faced with difficulty the foolish-virgin type will experience instead an internal void and will feel the need for some kind of armor or defense to defend and protect himself. This will result in ego battles. While admittedly it is not easy, and Satan constantly seeks to frustrate our efforts in this, the key is to put on the whole armor of God so that no such need exists for psychological and social defenses.

Such armor guarantees goodness and simplicity and self-forgetfulness, plus freedom from ego assertion and the need to claim one's so-called rights, as we seek to do when we take offense. Quoting Paul again, "Charity . . . seeketh not her own" (1 Corinthians 13:4-5), to which we might add something I once heard President N. Eldon Tanner say — "Never allow yourself to be offended by someone who is learning his job." (Aren't we all learning a job, in some sense?) There is nothing as baffling to one who is full of tricks and duplicity as straightforward, simple honesty in another. It sets him in a war with himself, with his conscience, with his Savior.

Admittedly, the offended one can continue to use psychological defenses such as rationalization, denial, isolation, and intellectualization to handle these situations. Or he may use social defenses, such as keeping the offender at a social distance through status symbols or authority levels or social stereotypes. There may be extreme circumstances in which there is a need to defend and protect oneself, even in legal ways, but this represents the court of last resort and comes about primarily because the offending people's consciences have been stifled or subordinated and they are resolutely determined to pursue some unworthy action or goal. Even in those cases, should we feel compelled to take such action, it is important that we feel divine insights and direction so that we don't become embroiled in a bitter process and then rationalize it in divine terms. You can usually tell when a person has received such guidance, because he will be at peace with himself, free of rancor or bitterness, hatred, envy, jealousy, or vindictiveness. He really is seeking the good in others, even in the person or persons who have been hurting or abusing him. Compassion has replaced accusation.

EMPATHY — THE ESSENCE OF COMPASSION

Compassion, a vital part of true Christian love, consists of a depth of feeling for others who are in distress or difficulty. To express this loving feeling, I suggest we need to empathize with the other person, to truly listen with an open mind and heart to what is inside him. When the Lord communicates with his children, he always does so within the frame of reference, the language, of his children, so that they will understand his meaning. It is futile to communicate words only which have no meaning in the frame of reference of the other person.

By deep, genuine listening, you make several things happen. First, you come to understand how the other person sees the world; you begin to perceive what has become the center of that person's life. Second, inevitably you feel increased reverence, humility, and respect, because you have sensed the uniqueness of another soul, the person's intrinsic worth. Third, any earlier tendencies you may have had to label and to judge subside, if they don't vanish altogether, because true understanding precludes judgment. You have no mind to judge, simply because you understand. Fourth, it's a therapeutic experience, because the other person can express how he feels without fear of ridicule, embarrassment, or censure; as Joseph Smith wrote, if God "would give liberally, and not upbraid, I might venture" (Joseph Smith — History 1:13). The whole key to human influence is first to be influenced, to understand another as he wishes to be understood, and to reflect that understanding empathetically so that he is then open to your own influence. Fifth and finally, because of the understanding you receive, you can adapt your presentation or your message to the internal mental and emotional realities of the other person's life.

We had a missionary in Ireland who became a very powerful teaching missionary, Elder Elray Lloyd from Gilmore, Texas. After his mission he suffered a terrible and fatal accident. I was asked to speak at the funeral service, and there I read what he had prepared before he left his mission: "My Blueprint for Life and My Most Cherished Missionary Experience." His most cherished missionary experience came when he learned to empathize, to listen in depth to other people. It happened shortly after he began his mission. He was filled with excitement, enthusiastic in sharing all that was within him, but he had not yet learned to understand what was within another person and to enable the person to ventilate it and thereby become open to what the missionary wanted to share in return.

In his record he told of the experience he had with a widow he and his companion were teaching. They were now on the fifth or sixth discussion. She had several children and was very teachable and open, but she was not living the commitments she had made, and the missionaries were rather frustrated. It was about this time that we emphasized to the missionaries the importance of listening with empathy, not listening with the intent to reply but listening with the intent to understand.

Elder Lloyd took this counsel to heart, and the next time he went into the home he said to the woman, in effect, "We have talked to you almost continuously. We would now like to listen to what you would like to share with us." She didn't quite know how to handle this, and it was a little awkward for a while, but gradually she began to open up and relate her story and her feelings. When she was through, it was clear that she felt deeply understood, for she turned to Elder Lloyd and said, "Never before have I felt anyone has understood me as you do. I want you to know, elders, that I will do anything you teach me to do."

In his account, Elder Lloyd continued: "We were so overpowered and humbled by that learning, by that listening experience and by her expression of confidence and trust, that we didn't feel we could teach at that time. We returned to our digs and sanctified ourselves and prepared extensively our next lesson. We did it with all of the subsequent (retaught) lessons, each of which she received fully, in turn living all of the commitments, including baptism."

It is highly instructive that repentance precedes covenant making. In a sense, repentance is getting "old wine" out before you attempt to put in "new wine"—new commitments, new covenants. Empathy—deep, genuine listening—is risky business, and unless we are inwardly secure we will not feel that we can afford that risk, but it is certainly one of the most powerful expressions of love. Perhaps this is partly the meaning of the words, "pure knowledge, which shall greatly enlarge the soul without hypocrisy, and without guile" (D&C 121:42).

I have not been able to discover who wrote the following piece. I quote it here because it communicates the tender feelings and the self-protective mechanisms of many people who hide their true feelings and need our empathy to bring them out. The title itself is poignant.

Please . . . Hear What I'm Not Saying

Don't be fooled by me. Don't be fooled by the mask I wear. For I wear a mask, I wear a thousand masks, masks that I'm afraid to take off, and none of them is me. Pretending is an art that is second nature with me, but don't be fooled.

I give the impression that I'm secure, that all is sunny and unruffled with me, within as well as without; that confidence is my name and coolness is my game; that the waters are calm and that I'm in command and I need no one. But don't believe it; please don't.

My surface may seem smooth, but my surface is my mask, my ever-varying and ever-concealing mask. Beneath lies no smugness, no coolness, no complacence. Beneath dwells the real me, in confusion, in fear, in loneliness. But I hide this; I don't want anybody to know it. I panic at the thought of my weakness being exposed. That's why I frantically create a mask to hide behind, a nonchalant, sophisticated facade to help me pretend, to shield me from the glance that knows. But such a glance is precisely my salvation. My only salvation. And I know it. It's the only thing that can liberate me from myself, from my own self-built prison walls, from the barriers that I so painstakingly erect. But I don't tell you this. I don't dare. I'm afraid to.

I'm afraid your glance will not be followed by love and acceptance. I'm afraid that you will think less of me, that you'll laugh, and your laugh will kill me. I'm afraid that deep down inside I'm nothing, that I'm just no good, and that you'll see and reject me. So I play my games, my desperate, pretending games, with a facade of assurance on the outside and a trembling child within. And so begins the parade of masks, the glittering but empty parade of masks. And my life becomes a front.

I idly chatter with you in the suave tones of surface talk. I tell you everything that's really nothing, nothing of what's crying within me. So when I'm going through my routine, don't be fooled by what I'm saying. Please listen carefully and try to hear what I'm *not* saying; what I'd like to be able to say; what, for survival, I need to say but I can't say. I dislike the hiding. Honestly I do. I dislike the superficial phony games I'm playing.

I'd really like to be genuine, spontaneous, and me; but you have to help me. You have to help me by holding out your hand, even when that's the last thing I seem to want or need. Each time you are kind and gentle and encouraging, each time you try to understand because you really care, my heart begins to grow wings. Very small wings. Very feeble wings. But wings. With your sensitivity and sympathy and your power of understanding, I can make it. You can breathe life into me. It will not be easy for you. A long conviction of worthlessness builds strong walls. But love is stronger than strong walls, and therein lies my hope. Please try to beat down those walls with firm hands, but with gentle hands, for a child is very sensitive, and I *am* a child.

Who am I, you may wonder. For I am every man, every woman, every child . . . every human you meet.

GRACE TO GRACE, GRACE FOR GRACE

This compassionate, honest, simple, loving approach to people and circumstances calls to mind section 93 of the Doctrine and Covenants (verses 12, 13, 20) which teaches us that we grow from "grace *to* grace" and also that we will receive "grace *for* grace." "Grace," writes Elder Bruce R. McConkie, "is granted to men proportionately as they conform to the standards of personal righteousness that are part of the gospel plan." (*Mormon Doctrine*, second edition, Bookcraft, 1966, page 339.) I have often interpreted the expression "you shall receive grace for grace" to mean that as we give grace to others, we receive more grace ourselves. That is, as we treat them affirmatively, love them, display a fundamental belief in their capacity or potential for growth and change and improvement, as we bless them, even when they are cursing or condemning or judging or labeling or hurting us — as we do these things we are really exemplifying the attitude and character of the Master, who worked out the great atoning sacrifice for all mankind. He gave and is giving grace to all people, whether they receive it or not, through the fact that he atoned for their sins. He gave and gives grace even though it is not deserved.

Now, his grace will not be efficacious, and we are not capable of receiving it, except through our obedience to gospel standards of righteousness. Nevertheless, it is still given. Similarly, others may not receive the kindness, the patience, the understanding, the blessing, the grace that we give to them; to do so, they also must obey the laws on which such reception is predicated. But the point is that we must continue the giving, and it makes no difference what the response may be. We are not doing it for the purpose of manipulation or to secure other ends. We are doing it because it is right, because it is the proper extension of our own personality and character and, in a sense, a reflection of who we are — a child of God. And we are doing it because the source of our power to behave in this way comes from God himself, as expressed in the example of Jesus Christ, humanity's supreme exemplar and model of this essential characteristic.

I once read the expression, "It is in the nature of plucked flowers to wither." If we were to pull true principles or practices out of their source, it would be comparable to pulling petals or leaves or flowers away from the stem and root. They would die and wither. "Abide in me, and I in you," said the Savior. "As the branch cannot bear fruit of itself, except it abide in the vine; no more can ye, except ye abide in me." (John 15:4.)

As many committed parents have learned the hard way, it is not enough to teach correct principles. We need to emphasize also their living, integrating source. The real key in maintaining life in gospel principles and practices, then, is the perfect Source, as exemplified by the person who fully embodied such principles and who makes available the Spirit which enables us to properly organize and orchestrate and harmonize and give priorities to all the divine principles and practices we are asked to follow. Some of these may be applicable in one instance but entirely inapplicable in other instances — the unique realities of differing situations call for varied responses. Unless a person is in contact with the Spirit, which gives guidance as to what practices are appropriate, based on correct principles, a person will be left to himself to figure out what to do. And if he does not have the mind of Christ, whatever else is at the center, whatever is his frame of reference, will be the basis of his guidance, wisdom, and power.

Through the Prophet Joseph Smith, the Lord told David Whitmer about this lack of proper guidance. Read this counsel carefully.

> Behold, I say unto you, David, that you have feared man and have not relied on me for strength as you ought.
>
> But your mind has been on the things of the earth more than on the things of me, your Maker, and the ministry whereunto you have been called; and you have not given heed unto my Spirit, and to those who were set over you, but have been persuaded by those whom I have not commanded.
>
> Wherefore, you are left to inquire for yourself at my hand, and ponder upon the things which you have received. (D&C 30:1-3.)

TRIALS PART OF THE PLAN

The next time someone offends you, strive for God/Christ-centeredness and bless them in return. Pray for those who persecute you and speak evil against you. Realize that this is one of the missions to which you have been called, and don't ask to be saved from it. When the Lord's disciple cut off the ear of the high priest's accusing, arresting servant, the Savior replaced it miraculously and rebuked his disciple with a question which implied, "Are you trying to save me from my hour?" (John 18:10-11.)

We exhibit the highest form of divine influence when we exemplify divine attitudes and attributes in the worst kind of situations and predicaments. Consider how often you have heard or read the statement of the Savior on the cross, "Forgive them, for they know not what they do." Consider the enormous impression those make who are in extremely difficult circumstances —say, suffering a terminal illness, or receiving obviously unjust treatment—yet do not respond in kind but instead bear it with dignity and grace and seek to bless rather than to curse. Elder Thomas S. Monson of the Council of the Twelve wrote:

> To live greatly, we must develop the capacity to face trouble with courage, disappointment with cheerfulness, and triumph with humility. You ask, "How might we achieve these goals?" I answer, "By getting a true perspective of who we really are!" We are sons and daughters of a living God in whose image we have been created. Think of that truth: "Created in the image of God." We cannot sincerely hold this conviction without experiencing a profound new sense of strength and power, even the strength to live the commandments of God, the power to resist the temptations of Satan. (*Pathways to Perfection*, Deseret Book Co., 1973, page 81.)

Peter wrote: "Beloved, think it not strange concerning the fiery trial which is to try you, as though some strange thing happened unto you; but rejoice, inasmuch as ye are partakers of Christ's sufferings; that, when his glory shall be revealed, ye may be glad also with exceeding joy" (1 Peter 4:12-13). A little before this he had written:

> For this is thankworthy, if a man for conscience toward God endure grief, suffering wrongfully.
>
> For what glory is it, if, when ye be buffeted for your faults, ye shall take it patiently? but if, when ye do well, and suffer for it, ye take it patiently, this is acceptable with God.
>
> For even hereunto were ye called: because Christ also suffered for us, leaving us an example, that ye should follow his steps:
>
> Who did no sin, neither was guile found in his mouth:
>
> Who, when he was reviled, reviled not again; when he suffered, he threatened not; but committed himself to him that judgeth righteously:
>
> Who his own self bare our sins in his own body on the tree, that we, being dead to sins, should live unto righteousness: by whose stripes ye were healed.
>
> For ye were as sheep going astray; but are now returned unto the Shepherd and Bishop of your souls. (1 Peter 2:19-25.)

PROPHETIC COUNSEL ON FAMILY VIRTUES

Peter emphasized that for wives who have the word and are dealing with husbands who don't have the word, the best way to win them to the word is without the use of the word. They are not to nag them, to accuse and verbally assault them, but instead to affirm their worth and bless them through the ornament of a meek and quiet spirit.

> Likewise, ye wives, be in subjection to your own husbands; that, if any obey not the word, they also may without the word be won by the conversation of the wives;
> While they behold your chaste conversation coupled with fear.
> Whose adorning let it not be that outward adorning of plaiting the hair, and of wearing of gold, or of putting on of apparel;
> But let it be the hidden man of the heart, in that which is not corruptible, even the ornament of a meek and quiet spirit, which is in the sight of God of great price.
> For after this manner in the old time the holy women also, who trusted in God, adorned themselves, being in subjection unto their own husbands. (1 Peter 3:1-5.)

Peter then went on to counsel husbands similarly, recognizing that the man and wife are heirs together of eternal life, that the husband should give honor to the wife, and that the efficacy of their prayers is dependent upon this kind of unity and mutual respect.

> Likewise, ye husbands, dwell with them according to knowledge, giving honour unto the wife, as unto the weaker vessel, and as being heirs together of the grace of life; that your prayers be not hindered. (1 Peter 3:7.)

Then to both husband and wife and to everyone he in effect reemphasized the importance of choosing to make righteous responses to unrighteous treatment and environments.

> Finally, be ye all of one mind, having compassion one of another, love as brethren, be pitiful, be courteous:
> Not rendering evil for evil, or railing for railing: but contrariwise blessing; knowing that ye are thereunto called, that ye should inherit a blessing.
> For he that will love life, and see good days, let him refrain his tongue from evil, and his lips that they speak no guile:
> Let him eschew evil, and do good; let him seek peace, and ensue it.
> For the eyes of the Lord are over the righteous, and his ears are

open unto their prayers: but the face of the Lord is against them that do evil.

And who is he that will harm you, if ye be followers of that which is good?

But and if ye suffer for righteousness' sake, happy are ye: and be not afraid of their terror, neither be troubled;

But sanctify the Lord God in your hearts: and be ready always to give an answer to every man that asketh you a reason of the hope that is in you with meekness and fear:

Having a good conscience; that, whereas they speak evil of you, as of evildoers, they may be ashamed that falsely accuse your good conversation in Christ.

For it is better, if the will of God be so, that ye suffer for well doing, than for evil doing.

For Christ also hath once suffered for sins, the just for the unjust, that he might bring us to God, being put to death in the flesh, but quickened by the Spirit. (1 Peter 3:8-18.)

The same modern prophet we quoted earlier on being Christ-like, President David O. McKay, had this to say about sacrificing self to assure harmony in the home.

[We have today] greater responsibility than ever before, as men of the priesthood, as women of the Church, to make our homes such as will radiate to our neighbors harmony, love, community duties, loyalty. Let our neighbors see it and hear it. Never must there be expressed in a Latter-day Saint home an oath, a condemnatory term, an expression of anger or jealousy or hatred. Control it! Do not express it! You do what you can to produce peace and harmony, no matter what you suffer. (*Improvement Era,* June 1963, page 535.)

SELF-MAP, SOCIAL MIRROR, DIVINE MIRROR

So far in this chapter we have discussed some of the positive effects of making God our center or frame of reference. Let us now consider the most significant negative effect any other center has on security, guidance, wisdom, and power. The effect I refer to is that of being anchored to and governed by the social mirror, that is, the reflection of the surrounding culture.

Most of us have visited the crazy mirror room at circuses or carnivals. There we stand in front of mirrors which reflect bizarre caricatures of our bodies. We laugh and are amused by the reflection simply because we know it is not a true one. It is an inaccurate map of the territory. We know this because each of us has a referent we can look at, a criterion to judge by: his body.

Now, consider what happens when the basic source of a person's definition of himself is the social mirror—that is, the reflection of how other people perceive him. He has no true referent point to compare with this social mirror. He isn't even aware it is a map. He thinks that the social reflection is the real self. He internalizes this self-view into a self-description or self-image or self-concept. It becomes his label. He believes it and accepts it. And even though he may be exposed to other views or maps of himself, including the divine one, he rejects them because they do not show the distortions he has come to accept as true. He feels more comfortable with a picture or label of himself with which he is familiar.

Stan Herman recasts this problem in poetic form:

> Ed said
> When men found the mirror
> They began to lose their souls
> The point, of course, is that
> They began to concern themselves
> With their images rather than
> Their selves
>
> Other men's eyes are mirrors
> But the most distorting kind
> For if you look to them you
>   can only see
> Reflections of your reflections
> Your warpings of their warpings

THE REAL POTENTIAL

From time to time I conduct a little experiment with my students. I ask them to take a blank piece of paper and divide it into two columns by drawing a line down the center. They head the left column "Social Mirror." In that column I have them list others' perceptions of them, according to their understanding, beginning with their parents, moving to their brothers and sisters, to other relatives who have been very important to them, and finally to friends and peers. This list may also include their understanding of the perceptions of various teachers and leaders in the school and in their local wards and branches.

The right column they title "Divine Mirror." There they write their understanding of the Lord's view of them: his opinion, his definition. They consider such sources as their patriarchal blessings (those who have received them); the Lord's description of them through prophets, ancient and modern; the supreme price the Lord paid for them in his atoning sacrifice; and the implicit assumptions built into the ordinances of the gospel concerning the person's true eternal nature and possibilities.

The next stage involves some deep introspection and self-analysis, wherein they each attempt to describe their own self-concept or map. They do this by describing their behavioral, attitudinal, and thinking habits. After studying both lists already written, the social and the divine, and comparing them with their self-map, each one is able to deduce from which source his self-map has primarily come. A good percentage of the students, over 50 percent, are quite shocked when they realize how much of their self-view has come from the social mirror. It has come slowly, gradually, imperceptibly, day by day, week by week, year by year, and now the self-concepts are deeply embedded, crystalized in their minds and hearts. These society-derived self-maps and labels distort a person's true nature, his true origin and destiny, as much as the crazy mirrors in the carnival distort his true appearance.

Yet these social perspectives have become a kind of comfort zone which a person may find difficult to leave. "Comfort zone" is a popular term which has been coined to describe the environment or behavior which has become so self-contenting that various kinds of tensions are triggered if a person finds himself removed from the setting or the familiar habits. The comfort zone serves like the thermostat on the wall, which regulates the temperature inside a room. When the room temperature reaches that at which the thermostat is set, perhaps seventy degrees for comfort, the heat or the air conditioning automatically turns off. Unless your self-map includes a knowledge of your true nature, it will serve as a comfort zone and will limit the achieving of your potential.

AFFIRMING ANOTHER'S WORTH

For most of us, one of the great needs in life is to be brought to visualize our potential and be motivated to reach for it.

The movie and play *The Man of La Mancha*, written by Dale Wasserman, portrays such an occurrence when a romantic, medieval knight comes into contact with a woman of the street, a prostitute. In spite of her degrading behavior, he perceives the beauty, the loveliness, and the virtue that is in her. His love is unconditional, and his faith and persistence eventually penetrate the mortal overlay, the "software" of her mind, the inaccurate map of herself, and she comes to feel her true identity and potential. As with the self-fulfilling prophecy, she starts to live in that way. The knight even gives her a new name, Dulcinea, so that she will constantly be reminded of her true identity and potential. When nearing his death, he looks her in the eye and says, "Never forget you're Dulcinea." And after he passes away, she sings a beautiful ballad about her new name.

To affirm a person's worth or potential in this way, you have to look at him with the eye of faith, the mind's eye, the soul's eye, so that your verbal expression is congruent and honest. Otherwise, the act would be hypocritical and manipulative. I am convinced that when we truly believe in Jesus Christ, we also believe in the unseen identity and potential of our Heavenly Father's other children; that faith in Christ, or God/Christ-centeredness, actually cultivates and nourishes such a perception of others. Then we don't have to treat them in terms of their behavior, but rather in terms of their potential, of what they can become. Goethe put it in this way, "Treat a man as he is and he will remain as he is; treat a man as he can and should be and he will become as he can and should be." None of this necessarily means that we trust the person unconditionally, but it does mean that at least we begin a process of trusting him conditionally. We start where he is now and attempt to lead him to the next step, then to the next, and thus gradually motivate him to the higher way.

USE GOD'S DEFINITION

Both academic psychology and popular psychology, in the latter case as reflected particularly in positive mental attitude books and other "success" literature, teach this same concept: to reach for your potential you must first understand your true nature. But these psychologies are essentially secular, and in themselves they do not teach man's true nature. What God has revealed about man is light years ahead of what man has discovered. The obvious course, then, is first to study what God says about man and then use his definition as a basis for evaluating what man says about himself.

The Prophet Joseph Smith taught, "If men do not comprehend the character of God, they do not comprehend themselves." (*Teachings of the Prophet Joseph Smith* [hereafter referred to as *TPJS*], Joseph Fielding Smith, compiler, Deseret Book Co., 1976, page 343.) Since we truly are sons and daughters of God the Eternal Father, we possess in embryo his nature and potential. When we study missionary activity, we see that the Lord, through his Church, is attempting to communicate to all peoples of the world who they truly are. Cultural traditions are set deeply in people's minds and hearts, and it takes a deeply sincere and sustained effort in prayerfully pondering the words of the Lord for this divine knowledge to seep in. Perhaps "to seep out" is a more accurate description—to seep out of the mortal overlay, out from deep, inner, spiritual, premortal awareness.

Our missionary work among the Lamanites is illustrative of this divine process of hearing and doing. As the prophets have indicated would happen, the Lamanites are gradually dropping

If we study and live to understand the character of the Lord, we will gradually and naturally be changed into a like character, the Spirit being the catalyst for change.

their disguise, changing their comfort zone, and coming to understand that they are Israelites, promised and blessed children of God. This new, divinely mirrored self-view is enabling them to take the higher path in life that will eventually lead them to the fulness of the Lord's blessings.

In general conference, Elder Spencer W. Kimball spoke of this day of the Lamanite:

> The day of the Lamanite brings opportunity. Millions farm the steep hillsides of the Andean ranges and market their produce with llamas and horses and burros. They must have the emancipating gospel. Millions serve in menial labor, eke out bare subsistence from soil and toil. They must hear the compelling truths of the gospel. Millions are tied to reservations, deprived, untrained, and less than they could be. They must have the enlightening gospel. It will break their fetters, stir their ambition, increase their vision, and open new worlds of opportunity to them. Their captivity will be at an end—captivity from misconceptions, illiteracy, superstition, fear. (*Improvement Era*, December 1965, page 1133.)

The Apostle Paul spoke of the solution with authority backed by authentic personal experience. He wrote: "But we all, with open face beholding as in a glass the glory of the Lord, are changed into the same image from glory to glory, even as by the Spirit of the Lord." (2 Corinthians 3:18.) In other words, if we study and live to understand the character of the Lord, we will gradually and naturally be changed into a like character, the Spirit being the change catalyst.

James used the divine-mirror type of metaphor, stressing constancy in doing as well as hearing:

> But be ye doers of the word, and not hearers only, deceiving your own selves.
> For if any be a hearer of the word, and not a doer, he is like

unto a man beholding his natural face in a glass:

For he beholdeth himself, and goeth his way, and straightway forgetteth what manner of man he was.

But whoso looketh into the perfect law of liberty, and continueth therein, he being not a forgetful hearer, but a doer of the work, this man shall be blessed in his deed. (James 1:22-25.)

TRANSITION PERSONS

A friend of mine invented a term I like: *transition figure.* It denotes someone who is a change catalyst, someone who sparks in his family or a larger group the change which brings the perception of man's divine identity and thereby opens the way to true self-realization.

We have mentioned previously the satanic taking away of "light and truth, through disobedience, from the children of men, and because of the tradition of their fathers" (D&C 93:39). The cultural traditions, inherited tendencies, come down from generation to generation and distort a whole people's divine essence in a social, inaccurate mirror. This was the position of the Book of Mormon Lamanites prior to their conversion to the gospel. The innocent suffer with the guilty in such a case. They are sincerely wrong. And Christ, who was the innocent one, the one most pure and holy above all else, atoned for the sins of both.

Christ alone could perform the atoning sacrifice, because he alone lived a pure and sinless life yet understood sin in its fulness. He understood how it distorts all realities, destroys wisdom, and limits potential. Only through Christ can "transition figures" derive the power to stop the transmission of "sick" tendencies and distorted perspectives from one generation to another and thus help us to be free from the blood and sins of our generation. Only through Christ and the way he gave can transition figures change the maps their families or their people are following and bring them to "the way, the truth, and the life." Because the Savior provided the escape from that pernicious process of distortion for the whole human race, we must draw upon that power if we want to stop the process in our own lives and for our posterity.

THE INTERGENERATIONAL FAMILY

This work begins inside the family. By this I don't mean the nuclear family—just father, mother, and children. I mean the intergenerational family. The nuclear family is a secular concept. It is traditionally and culturally imposed upon us, but we do not have to receive it, because it reflects an inaccurate map. The heavy dependence which we have upon the government has to a large degree destroyed the intergenerational family and is even making undermining inroads into the nuclear family and its first extension, the two-generational family, in that many children are no longer feeling responsible for their parents; and in fact many parents no longer feel responsible for their children. Through enough citizens defaulting or being indifferent, these responsibilities are being transferred to the government. This is not only spiritually reprehensible but is also inadequate, since the government is not really capable of discharging these responsibilities.

The true concept of family in God's plan is the intergenerational family, the extended family. Ultimately, in the fullest sense, it embraces the entire family of God, but in the more specific sense it represents several generations—at least four. We speak about the four-generation program as illustrative of our responsibility in this matter, though we should ensure that the ordinances are done also for as far back as possible beyond these four generations.

NEUTRALIZING THE EFFECTS OF ANCESTRAL SINS

In a sense, too, perhaps the four-generation concept ties in with the scriptural statement that the sins of the parents may be transmitted to the third and fourth generations (Exodus 20:5). This might suggest we have a responsibility to all our brothers and sisters, cousins, aunts and uncles, and direct ancestors, living or dead. We should be concerned about both the temporal and the spiritual welfare of all of the living relatives. We should be concerned that our deceased relatives have the opportunity to continue to progress through our proxy temple work for them, and that we live lives righteous enough to stop the transmission of any unworthy tendencies of theirs into our generation. In this way we become saviors on Mount Zion and transition persons. We can gear ourselves so fully to the Lord and his work that any undesirable tendencies we have inherited through genetic or cultural forces for which our ancestors are responsible are eliminated or neutralized, stopped short at our own generation. In this way we remove the effects of their sins on future generations. Of course, Christ was the model for this, in that he took upon himself the sins of the world, one effect of this being that when we receive him in the full sense we will free ourselves of the transmission of sins over the generations.

I know of no more inspiring, motivating, and lofty concept than the realization that exaltation is a family affair. We cannot be saved and exalted without giving the same opportunity to our deceased ancestors. There is an eternal interdependence, and our present generation can literally work to save prior generations as well as the generations that follow. The whole key is to become God/Christ-centered in the full restored gospel sense.

All of us, I'm sure, can see some of our own unworthy tendencies going on to the next generation. Perhaps we could trace some of those to an earlier generation. It is understandable that our ancestors in the spirit world could be very concerned about these effects or consequences of their own transgressions that they initiated and that are transmitted because of this heavy social, cultural, and genetic programming.

Nevertheless, every person is responsible for his own sins and can choose his response to this "programming" or conditioning. We are uniquely endowed with the ability to be aware of it. We are the programmers, not the program. We each can stand aside from the self and observe what is happening. We can sense these tendencies within us and compare them against gospel standards and principles, and if we find them unworthy of us we can begin a process through obedience to the commandments so that we transcend them. We then rise above them; they no longer have any place within us.

When I spoke on one occasion on the subject of becoming a transition person, I had a dear friend tell me that his wife was such a person. Along with her brothers and sisters she had been culturally and socially programmed to think critically about certain Church leaders. But you simply can't think critically about Church leaders without starting to feel a lessening of faith in the Church itself, and this is what took place.

My friend's wife stopped it at her generation, however. She became totally devoted to the Lord, and while she was not naive about people's weaknesses, she never associated them with the Church or the gospel in any way. Her faith actually increased by her devoted approach, and she looked on others with compassion and understanding and a desire to bless and help, rather than with accusation and with criticism of their weaknesses. Consequently she became a change catalyst in her family; she began to influence her brothers and sisters and her mother in the same direction (her father had already passed on), and she completely stopped the transmission of these tendencies into her own children. Whenever they would go to three- or four-generation family reunions or gatherings, there was a clear separation evident between her children, who had a simple and beautiful faith in the Church and the gospel, and many of the cousins who had been powerfully programmed and influenced with a kind of cynicism and bitterness.

My friend said to me, "I can't describe how magnificent I think my wife is, in that she has fully given herself to the Lord, and the effect of all of the earlier transgressions has been neutralized or nullified. She is actually reversing the process and blessing the earlier generations." I am certain also that her father and others who had passed on before him must be very grateful for her faithfulness. I am enormously impressed with the thought that we not only do ordinances for those who have passed on but that perhaps we can help them by, so to speak, fostering the restitution process—that is, by leading worthy, service-oriented lives so that the effects of the sins which began in earlier generations are not transmitted into this one or into later ones.

MOSES' SUBLIME EXPERIENCE

Think of the case of Moses, that great transition person of antiquity. He was reared in the Egyptian court and therefore probably acquired a distorted map of man and God and the universe and the purpose of it all. His mother, however, had nursed him and helped rear him in his early infancy, and she may have given to him, consciously or unconsciously, some ideas, feelings, or attitudes which caused him to recoil when he viewed the injustices perpetrated against the Hebrew slaves, who were really his own people. These feelings eventually led him to the mount. There the Lord gave him a correct map.

The accurate account of that visit with the Lord on the mount was once contained in the Old Testament record but was taken from it through apostasy. In the present dispensation, the visions of Moses were again restored to the earth through the Prophet Joseph Smith.

Study carefully Moses chapter 1, thinking in terms of how the Lord is giving a correct map to one of his sons and servants and future prophets. The first thing God tells Moses is who He, the great God, is. "Behold, I am the Lord God Almighty." The next thing is to tell him who he, Moses, is. "And, behold, thou art my son." The third thing is to describe His mighty works and Moses' place in them. "And I will show thee the workmanship of mine hands. . . . And I have a work for thee, Moses, my son." Then, the Lord tells Moses about Christ. "Thou art in the similitude of mine Only Begotten; and mine Only Begotten is and shall be the Savior, for he is full of grace and truth." Then Moses is allowed to behold the world upon which he was created and to see all of the children of men that are and were created. (Moses 1:1, 3, 4, 6, 8.)

God then withdrew his presence from Moses so that Moses could come to understand that his very life-energy and strength came from God, and that without God he would be nothing. Moses fell to the earth, and for the space of many hours he experienced the contrast of being without God's sustenance. "Now, for this cause, I know that man is nothing, which thing I never had supposed," he cried. (Moses 1:9-10.)

The term *nothing*, in this context, does not mean worthless or valueless, for Moses' infinite worth and value had already been magnificently communicated to him in ways which far transcended anything he had ever experienced or visualized. *Nothing* meant powerless. And it will come to pass that all people, even those who decry God or who quietly disbelieve in him, will come to acknowledge that Jesus is the Christ, that he is the source of their power and strength, even their natural strength. As President Spencer W. Kimball put it to the BYU congregation at an opening school devotional in 1977, "It is not a matter of if man will surrender, but only when."

After Moses' great dialogue with the Eternal God, he was permitted to experience another power source: Satan. This being came to tempt Moses to worship him. But the prophet's profound prior experiences gave him courage to confront Satan. "Who art thou?" he asked.

> For behold, I am a son of God, in the similitude of his Only Begotten; and where is thy glory, that I should worship thee?
>
> For behold, I could not look upon God, except his glory should come upon me, and I were transfigured before him. But I can look upon thee in the natural man. Is it not so, surely?
>
> Blessed be the name of my God, for his Spirit hath not altogether withdrawn from me, or else where is thy glory, for it is darkness unto me? And I can judge between thee and God; for God said unto me: Worship God, for him only shalt thou serve.
>
> Get thee hence, Satan; deceive me not; for God said unto me: Thou art after the similitude of mine Only Begotten.
>
> And he also gave me commandments, when he called unto me out of the burning bush, saying: Call upon God in the name of mine Only Begotten, and worship me.
>
> . . . I will not cease to call upon God, I have other things to inquire of him: for his glory has been upon me, wherefore I can judge between him and thee. Depart hence, Satan. (Moses 1:13-18.)

Satan attempted to distort this divine map by exerting all the power at his command. He "ranted upon the earth" and commanded Moses, saying, "I am the Only Begotten, worship me." The angry demands of the evil one instilled fear in Moses as he saw the bitterness of hell. But he continued to call upon God and, receiving strength, commanded the father of lies, "Depart from me, Satan, for this one God only will I worship, which is

> **Any effort to use a secular frame of reference or map to evaluate the eternal/celestial one would be comparable to holding a flashlight up to get a better view of the sun.**

the God of glory." Satan began to tremble, and the earth shook, and Moses commanded Satan in the name of Christ to depart. "And it came to pass that Satan cried with a loud voice, with weeping, and wailing, and gnashing of teeth; and he departed hence, even from the presence of Moses, that he beheld him not." (Moses 1:19-22.)

Moses then returned to calling upon God, who now blessed him for his faithfulness. "Blessed art thou, Moses, for I, the Almighty, have chosen thee, and thou shalt be made stronger than many waters; for they shall obey thy command as if thou wert God. And lo, I am with thee, even unto the end of thy days; for thou shalt deliver my people from bondage, even Israel my chosen." (Moses 1:25-26.)

Here God announced the mission of Moses. It was a mission which no person nor thing could frustrate but Moses himself. It is so with each of us. Each one of us is uniquely valuable in his or her own right and has a unique mission in mortality. Only you can frustrate your mission; only I, mine. We have no call to compare ourselves with others, for those comparison tendencies come from the social mirror and only warp and distort our maps. On the other hand, when we look into the perfect law of liberty, that is, the gospel of Jesus Christ, and continue faithfully therein, we each have a correct understanding of our map and will be enabled to fulfill our mission and receive the fulness of the Lord's blessings.

After hearing the great declaration of his mission, Moses was permitted to discern the world and every inhabitant of it. God told him that, though He had created worlds without number, He would now give Moses only an account of this world and the inhabitants of it, beginning with Adam. Then Moses was allowed to hear and bear witness of the Lord's statement of His own mission and purpose: "For behold, this is my work and my glory —to bring to pass the immortality and eternal life of man" (Moses 1:39). This is the most simple yet comprehensive description of the Lord's purpose given anywhere in all the scriptures.

Now, in light of this record of Moses' experience on the mount, consider how God/Christ-centeredness becomes such a source of personal security, guidance, wisdom, and power. It becomes virtually self-evident how any other alternative center or frame of mind falls pitifully short in all four areas.

THE TEMPLE: TEACHER, MODEL HOME

It seems to me that the temple endowment experience is akin to Moses' experience. I see it as one of the Lord's great efforts to give man a correct map of himself and of his purpose in mortality, for it teaches of his origin and his eventual destiny and gives light and knowledge which is received by covenant.

There are four stages to the temple endowment: the preparatory ordinances, the visual lecture presentations, the covenants, and the tests of knowledge. The instruction given in the preparatory work prepares the participant for further light and knowledge regarding the creation of the world, the creation and nature of man, the Fall, the Atonement, and the divine process of receiving the Atonement in order to be redeemed from the Fall. The person accepts the light and knowledge communicated to him by binding himself in covenants. Then, through faithfulness to these covenants, he receives still more light and knowledge. (See "Temple Worship," lecture delivered by Elder John A. Widtsoe in the Assembly Hall, Temple Square in Salt Lake City, October 12, 1920.)

The divine mirror of the temple endowment gives an accurate map of man's true nature, and through his faithfulness it can subordinate, eclipse, or completely erase the distorted maps coming from the social mirror. These celestial principles and goals are as different from the best principles and goals which modern philosophy or psychology can suggest to man as the sun is from the moon. Any effort to use a secular frame of reference or map to evaluate the eternal/celestial one would be comparable to holding a flashlight up to get a better view of the sun.

The temple is also a model home that the Lord wants us to experience and use as a model for our own homes. In it, virtually every principle of the gospel is magnificently taught, either implicitly or explicitly. The Lord's home is purposeful, orderly, and reverent in every facet. Everyone knows exactly what he is doing and where he is going. If someone is temporarily confused or uncertain, he receives help and direction at once. Everything is done in proper sequence. No one can shortcut the processes. Regardless of their time pressures and personal deadlines, all accommodate the timetable and sequence of the Lord. No one yells at or belittles or condemns someone else. Cheerfulness and kindliness permeate the atmosphere, and any exception to this is exactly that—an exception, and offensive to the Spirit. The temple conforms to the Lord's expression in the dedicatory prayer for the first temple of this dispensation, the Kirtland Temple—"a house of prayer, a house of fasting, a house of faith, a house of learning, a house of glory, a house of order, a house of God" (D&C 109:8).

We all need models, and in the temple we have a model home. But we must return frequently and refresh ourselves deeply, through meditation and concentration and true temple worship and service, in order to centralize these significant eternal truths and their author and source, our Heavenly Father.

GOD THE ONLY SECURE CENTER

When we are anchored to social mirrors and models, however, we empower circumstances to guide and control us. We become reactive rather than proactive; we reflect what happens to us, we respond to external conditions and stimuli rather than choose our own responses or to cause things to happen. The latter is the course that is in line with the scriptures, which teach us that we were made to act and not to be acted upon. (See 2 Nephi 2:14; D&C 93:30.)

Because of a lack of wisdom (of accurate maps), our reactions will often tend to be either overreactive or underreactive instead of appropriately proactive. A proactive stance means that we act on the basis of our own decisions and values and not of our external conditions or internal moods. To put it in another way, we subordinate feeling to values (i. e., to higher feelings, to commitments).

One very common reactive pattern is to live in compartments. In that case one's behavior is based largely on the role expectations in each compartment — father, mother, leader, teacher, Church worker, lawyer, doctor, public official, carpenter, salesman, assembly-line worker, upholsterer, researcher, and so on. But each of these compartments carries its own value system, in which case the person may find himself meeting different expectations and living by differing values based on the role or the environment he is in at any particular time.

A life centered on God, on the other hand, brings him permanently into one's life with his unchanging value system and the guidance of the Holy Spirit. This approach makes all of life sacred. It is like a spiritual umbrella which integrates and fuses every compartment of life into a unified whole. Even so-called secular activities, when viewed in this way, are made sacred. No other center is capable of forming a solid security base through a true map of one's worth. No other center is constantly present to guide us to true wisdom and ultimate power.

After Nephi, the son of Helaman, had thoroughly proved himself trustworthy, the Lord assured the prophet of His unconditional trust in him in the following powerful language:

> Blessed art thou, Nephi, for those things which thou hast done; for I have beheld how thou hast with unwearyingness declared the word, which I have given unto thee, unto this people. And thou hast not feared them, and hast not sought thine own life, but hast sought my will, and to keep my commandments.
>
> And now, because thou hast done this with such unwearyingness, behold, I will bless thee forever; and I will make thee mighty in word and in deed, in faith and in works; yea, even that all

things shall be done unto thee according to thy word, for thou shalt not ask that which is contrary to my will.

Behold, thou art Nephi, and I am God. Behold, I declare it unto thee in the presence of mine angels, that ye shall have power over this people, and shall smite the earth with famine, and with pestilence, and destruction, according to the wickedness of this people.

Behold, I give unto you power, that whatsoever ye shall seal on earth shall be sealed in heaven; and whatsoever ye shall loose on earth shall be loosed in heaven; and thus shall ye have power among this people. (Helaman 10:4-7.)

What security, guidance, wisdom, power!

The Upward Spiral

> *Yea, come unto Christ, and be perfected in him, and deny yourselves of all ungodliness; and if ye shall deny yourselves of all ungodliness and love God with all your might, mind and strength, then is his grace sufficient for you, that by his grace ye may be perfect in Christ; and if by the grace of God ye are perfect in Christ, ye can in nowise deny the power of God. (Moroni 10:32.)*

We have thus far said a good deal about having God as the center or frame of reference to our lives, but little about how to do so. Clearly we cannot be God/Christ-centered merely as an exercise of the mind. It must be of mind, heart, soul, and behavior, an earnest striving for godliness. Jesus said to his twelve disciples, "What manner of men ought ye to be? Verily I say unto you, even as I am" (3 Nephi 27:27). Christ, our model, is perfect (3 Nephi 12:48). He became so by doing his Father's will. We similarly can achieve perfection by following Christ. God/Christ-centeredness, then, is the key to perfection.

Throughout the scriptures, the Lord uses different means of describing the *process* of achieving perfection. In several instances he describes it as just that—a process; line upon line; precept upon precept, here a little, there a little. (See 2 Nephi 28:30; D&C 98:12; etc.) As indicated in chapter 4, section 93 of the Doctrine and Covenants speaks of the process as going from grace *to* grace in the same way that the Savior went from grace *to* grace, and of our receiving grace *for* grace, perhaps implying that we receive grace, or divine goodness and power, as we give others grace, or kindness and forgiveness. There is simply no shortcut, no piecemeal approach, no faking or pretending genuine character growth (as distinct from temporary setbacks to serious efforts). It takes place only to the degree that we follow his Spirit and keep his commandments.

In other places in the scriptures (e.g., 1 Nephi 10:19; D&C 3:2) the Lord speaks of his course as being "one eternal round" —an ever-expanding, enlarging, upward-spiraling process of movement.

I suggest that the steady course to achieve perfection involves four processes that are independent yet interfused and are continually moving on this upward-spiraling course. The scriptures use different words to describe these four interlocking processes, but the most common ones used are: 1) learning; 2) listening or hearing; 3) covenanting; 4) obeying or doing.

EDUCATING THE CONSCIENCE

I choose to call the first, the learning process, the *education of the conscience*. I suggest that it comes first and is basic and fundamental.

The conscience is the internal voice, our sensitivity or awareness, our sense of right and wrong. It is the Spirit of Jesus Christ, which is given to every person who comes into the world (D&C 84:45-46). Through the conscience the Holy Ghost speaks to us. President David O. McKay taught, "To all faithful members of the Church who are in the line of their duty the Holy Ghost normally speaks through their conscience." By studying Moroni chapter 10 we come to understand that the gifts of the Holy Ghost come through the Spirit of Christ, the agency through which the Holy Ghost operates. Referring to the latter days, the Lord said: "I will put my law in their inward parts, and write it in their hearts; and will be their God, and they shall be my people. And they shall teach no more every man his neighbor, and every man his brother, saying, Know the Lord: for they shall all know me, from the least of them unto the greatest of them. . . ." (Jeremiah 31:33-34.)

Proper use of the divine conscience brings us to God (D&C 84:47). The conscience is the repository of divine knowledge, truth, conviction, and spirituality, which are thereby built into the fiber of the person's soul and nature.

To use again the computer analogy (see chapter 4), the conscience is the basic software program. It directs and controls and guides the processing, storage, and retrieval of information. In a general conference priesthood session, President Spencer W. Kimball referred to the conscience as a "Liahona" that every person possesses: the instrument of guidance. And *whatever is at the center of a person's life* forms the fabric of his conscience.

The conscience must be educated from divine sources in order for it to be keen and sharp, responsive and sensitive to the Spirit of the Lord.

LISTENING TO THE CONSCIENCE

In a previous book, *Spiritual Roots of Human Relations* (Deseret Book Co., 1970), I related a profound earlier experience with this idea that I feel merits repetition here. In an Arizona university at a "Religion of Life" week, I was invited to be a representative of our church, along with representatives of other churches. The second evening there I was asked to speak to a sorority/fraternity exchange at the Chi Omega House on the subject of the New Morality. Basically I gave the Church's approach to it: that chastity is an eternal law, that the new morality is really the old immorality, and so forth. But the feelings and views of the audience seemed to be against this, and I felt very alone. Two young men in particular were extremely articulate in expressing their opposition to my position. One on the front row said, basically, "Well, it seems to me that true, mature love gives more freedom than you're allowing."

I tried to reason with them, suggesting that chastity is an eternal principle—a law, a natural law, just as gravity is. I indicated that if you were to take poison unaware, its effects would nevertheless proceed, and that likewise unchastity would bring many negative consequences, personal and social, regardless of awareness. The front row young man argued against this, again from the viewpoint that this didn't give the kind of freedom a careful, mature, responsible love would give. Several others spoke against my position. One said I had no right to judge right or wrong for others.

Finally I asked the audience, "Would you listen for just a minute, and if you don't inwardly sense this principle to be true, I'll leave and not waste more of your time. I'll ask a question, then let's be still and listen—and I assure you that you'll inwardly sense that what I've been saying about chastity is true."

They became quite still. Some of them were looking around to see who was going to take my request seriously. I pressed the point: "Just listen for one minute."

At the beginning of that quiet minute, I asked the question: "Is chastity, as I have explained it, a true principle or not?" I paused. At the end of a full minute I turned to the fellow in the front and asked, "My friend, in all honesty, what did you feel? What did you hear?"

He replied, "What I heard is not what I've been saying."

I asked another, "What did you hear?"

"I don't know," he said. "I just don't know anymore."

Independently and spontaneously, a young man at the back stood and said, "I want to say something to my fraternity brothers I've never said before. I believe in God." And he sat down.

A completely different spirit was now present. It softened everybody. From then on it was easy to teach and testify. Many were very interested in the restored gospel and the Book of Mormon. We invited many to the institute of religion and gave several books out.

In that one moment, those who had really listened had heard (felt) the still, small voice, which cultural and social conditioning or programming had tried to silence through sophisticated and impressive orchestration. From then on it was up to them which voice they would listen to, which education they would accept.

LEARNING AND PRACTICING

For we must educate our consciences with at least as much discipline and diligence as we educate our bodies and minds. We educate our bodies to perform a particular skill, such as a sport —skiing, golf, or tennis—through learning, practicing, relearning, more practicing, learning again, and practicing on a higher level of ability, until there is a close body-mind coordination, until the body has a kind of second memory built into it. We often call it second nature—in other words, learned. The skill we have practiced becomes an automatic response. The person can then perform that skill without any conscious attention to it.

We educate our minds by our educational endeavors—by great concentration, by practicing mental discipline in analytical and creative thought processes, by problem solving, by abstract thinking, by penetrating the issues, by learning to communicate clearly, persuasively, both in writing and in speaking. Little by little our minds become honed, refined, capable of handling abstract material or penetrating so-called complex issues to their fundamentals, tackling complicated problems, and separating the wheat from the chaff, the important from the unimportant, the causal factors from their effects. We become skilled in selecting objectives and establishing their priorities and in identifying and evaluating alternatives and their consequences.

The process of educating the conscience is not unlike these physical or mental processes of self-discipline: learning, listening, committing, doing, listening again, recommitting, practicing, learning again, practicing again, and so on.

Imagine five sets of hands. All you can see are these five sets of hands. Behind the screen are the bodies and the heads to which these hands are attached. One set of hands belongs to a great concert pianist, who can enthrall audiences with his renditions. Another pair are the hands of a skilled surgeon, who can perform delicate operations on the eye or the brain that can save lives and eyes and thinking processes. Another set of hands belongs to a great golfer, who wins tournament after tournament by coming through in the clutches, and under tremendous

> We are instructed not merely to read the scriptures but to treasure them, ponder them, meditate on them, feast upon them, store them up, thirst for them, hunger for them, and delight in them.

pressure, with brilliant shots and putts. Another set of hands belongs to a blind man, who can read at incredible speeds by touching the raised markings on a page. And the fifth set of hands is owned by a great sculptor, who can make a beautiful art object out of a solid block of marble or granite. Each set of hands is limited to its own specialty. The sculptor cannot play golf. The surgeon cannot read braille. The blind man cannot play the piano. In each case the hands are simply not trained to do anything except the one thing that has claimed their exclusive, focused concentration through years of discipline and practice.

A highly educated or honed conscience is much like any of those sets of hands. A great price has been paid to educate it: Sacrifices have been made and obstacles overcome. Persistence and perseverance have paid off, and the result is a highly refined, sensitive, and tuned instrument—a soul instrument, a mind-body-spirit instrument, a heart instrument, a spiritual instrument called a conscience. It has taken as great an effort to educate this conscience as it takes to become a great sculptor, golfer, surgeon, braille reader, or concert pianist. But this is a far greater achievement, because developing an educated conscience requires a systematic, balanced approach throughout a person's entire life. He who educates his conscience develops character, not just a disciplined skill. A disciplined character, a complete person, has learned to sacrifice, to subordinate feelings to values, to achieve a beautiful balance over all the various forces of life.

Exactly how is a conscience educated? Naturally it begins in the family in one's earliest months and years, and the process is carried on there indefinitely by parental example and precept in both formal and informal settings. But when a person becomes converted to the need, he seeks to advance that education himself. He then finds that it takes a great deal of learning in the school of the Lord, his church. One must attend Church meetings on a continuous basis to hear the words of the Lord, to understand his ways, his standards, his requirements, his expectations, the history of his children and their relations with him, and the methods of solving problems using his frame of reference. It means paying close attention to the lessons taught in priesthood quorums, auxiliary meetings, and sacrament meetings.

STUDYING THE SCRIPTURES

To educate the conscience we must also privately study the word of the Lord with diligence and devotion. We are instructed not merely to read the scriptures but to treasure them, ponder them, meditate on them, feast upon them, store them up, thirst for them, hunger for them, and delight in them.

Many wonder "How can I make the scriptures alive in my life?" Many do not regularly read them because the scriptures simply are not alive within them. Others occasionally read them, out of habit or duty only, but obtain little from them. The solution lies in knowing how to study them. In part this means how to liken them to ourselves (1 Nephi 19:23) and then do what they advise. (Study 1 Nephi 19.) In seeking to make the scriptures alive in my life I have found the following ideas helpful.

Realize Importance of Scriptures

The scriptures are of supreme importance in our lives. They help to make us "whole." Most of us live in compartments. We speak and think in terms of "my family life," "my church job," "my work in the shop" or "at the office," "my political convictions," "my personal life," and so forth. Our Sunday mentality often differs from our weekday mentality. We may bring the sinner back into activity but may speak condescendingly and critically behind his back.

Some of the material under the heading "Studying the Scriptures" was contained in an article by the author that was first published in the *Ensign*, and is used by permission.

But there is no integrity in compartmentalizing. Integrity means wholeness, unity, harmony. It means the principles and the spirit. Those principles we covenant to obey are actual guidelines for our behavior in every area of our life.

We are exhausted far more from the tension of internal disharmony—not doing what we know we should—than from hard, unremitting work. And, naturally, the very effort to escape such tension—pleasure seeking, self-indulgence, escapism—produces more tension.

The absence of a fundamental core within us that unifies and integrates our spiritual, intellectual, social, and working lives also leaves us confused. We wonder how to tell the difference between the Lord's voice to us and other voices, from within or without. One put it in this way: "How do I distinguish between God's answers to my prayers and my own wants and psychological needs. This warm feeling I have—is it his answer or is it my own wish and longing projected onto him?"

How do we handle such tension and confusion? Mostly we tell ourselves "rational lies"—that is, we rationalize. We mentally explain the problem away as "the way things are." We then have to compartmentalize even more. But down deep we're torn, truncated, unfulfilled. We may be active in the Church (one of the compartments) but not active in the gospel (the unifying core which should thread through and unify the compartments). And unless we achieve such unity with self, we will continue to "repent" of the same sins again and again but not develop the capacity to repent of our sinning.

Grasping and holding on to the rod of iron (the word of God) is that discipline which will gradually bring unity and integrity to our lives. It will unravel confusion and replace the exhausting kind of tension with a healthy tension in the form of worthy goals to strive for. (Study Lehi's dream in 1 Nephi 8 and 11.)

You may ask "How does such a small activity as scripture study produce such large results?" It does so in two significant ways.

Regular and prayerful scripture study is like putting on the glasses of the Lord. It will influence you in all you look at, see, and do.

First, remember the metaphor of the map or the pair of glasses. Regular and prayerful scripture study is like putting on the glasses of the Lord. It will influence all you look at, see, and do. When you study how he deals with his children, you will better understand how he deals with you. For example, since his objective is the divine growth of his children, immortality and eternal life (Moses 1:39), he deals with us in terms of our growth needs, not our wants. This also gives us one of the keys to prayer: pray in terms of needs, not of wants. The lens also influences our hopes or expectations, over which we have control, which in turn influences our satisfactions as much as our realizations, over which we have much less control.

Scripture study also shows that the Lord does not do for his children what they can do for themselves, and when he does "do" for them he always "does" it in a way which maximizes their growth and learning.

With a little thought you can see how immensely helpful it would be to "put on" the Lord's glasses. It would affect for good everything we do, everything we think, everything we say. Such a lens would fortify us against temptation. It would foster inward anchorage and security so we could love unconditionally, freely, spontaneously, without fearing or demanding another's reason.

Second, I suggest that prayerful scripture study is the key to being given personal revelation. Jesus taught that the Holy Ghost does not "speak of himself" (John 16:13) and that he will "bring all things to your remembrance, whatsoever I have said unto you" (John 14:26).

Nephi taught that the Holy Ghost speaks the words of Christ and that if we will feast on the words of Christ we will be told all things that we should do. (Study 2 Nephi 31:18-21; 32:1-5.) In other words, we will be given guidance or revelation from the Holy Ghost. Whether we will receive the revelations given is another matter, for this will depend on our faith and on our obedience to the light already given. However the verb *feast* is most interesting and instructive. It implies savoring, believing, loving, pondering, meditating, relishing, all of which bespeak a spirit of faith and obedience.

Therefore, when we regularly feast on the words of Christ (prayerfully and meditatively study the scriptures) they become planted in our hearts ("I will put my law in their inward parts, and write it in their hearts" — Jeremiah 31:33) and then the Holy Ghost will bring them to our remembrance or consciousness as required by the demands of each occasion — perhaps somewhat as a computer would draw on its data bank to solve a problem.

After conferring the gift of the Holy Ghost on my eight-year-old son, over the months I counseled him to prayerfully study the scriptures so that the Holy Ghost would have Christ's words to draw upon in giving him guidance. We can't draw water from an empty well. The very words used in conferring the gift of the Holy Ghost are in the form of an instruction, "Receive the Holy Ghost," and this would certainly embody such counsel as "Prayerfully study the scriptures and be true to the light given and you will be given more light."

I believe that the habit of prayerfully searching and pondering the scriptures (feasting) is the single most vital spiritual discipline in life. What food is to the body, prayerful scripture study is to the spirit. We physically die without food, and we spiritually die without the Spirit and word of God.

Recognize Three Realities

There are three realities, the eternal, the situational, and the personal, and all three must be dealt with to effectively liken scriptures unto yourself. In other words, you work with yourself (personally) to view your problems and challenges (situation) through an external lens or frame of reference (eternal).

Eternal reality comprises the facts or truths of eternity. Some are descriptive: God lives; he is the father of our spirits; Christ lives with a resurrected body; we will all be resurrected; there are three kingdoms of glory; and so on. Some are prescriptive: we should seek the Spirit; we should treat others with love and respect; we should teach the gospel to our children; and so on.

Situational reality incorporates the facts of the situation you live in and the problems and opportunities you face. For instance, your oldest child is rebelling against Church and family standards. He breaks the Word of Wisdom and refuses to attend church or family home evenings.

Personal reality includes your own desire and capacity to deal with both of the other realities.

To illustrate, take the problem with the rebellious son. One father whose religion has only a vertical dimension (that is, between him and God) may approach the son in an involving, judging, rejecting manner, using his well-worn scriptures as his ammunition — valuing them more than he does his son. The boy may then rebel further, while the father continues to justify himself, thinking he has taught his son the gospel.

Another father, whose religion lies in a horizontal dimension (that is, between him and others), may compromise himself by joining his son in worldly Sabbath activities in order to placate and appease him.

The first father focused on the eternal reality, ignoring the present situation. The second father focused on the present and ignored the eternal. Neither was aware that the real problem lay within himself. We feel neither the pulse of God nor the pulse of his children unless we feel both. We can't serve God and ignore or mistreat his children. Neither can we serve his children and ignore our common Father.

A true understanding and achievement of brotherhood can come only through an understanding of fatherhood. True religion simultaneously embodies and synthesizes both the vertical and the horizontal dimensions.

To sum up this idea, we need also to study life and ourselves in order to understand the scriptures.

Obtain the Spirit's Aid

We need the Holy Spirit to properly translate the scriptures into our lives, to synthesize eternal and situational realities. The scriptures were given by revelation and can only be truly understood by revelation. The things of God can only be known by the Spirit of God. (Study 1 Corinthians 2.)

There are laws governing the operation of the Spirit which need to be obeyed. Consider four laws or principles, obedience to which will unlock our capacity to truly profit from the scriptures.

1. *Purify your motive.* The highest motive in searching the scriptures is to come to Christ, in order to have eternal life.

Ponder these two verses: "Search the scriptures; for in them ye think ye have eternal life: and they are they which testify of me. *And ye will not come to me,* that ye might have life." (John 5:39-40.)

Anciently the Jews studied the scriptures with the intent of justifying themselves. Working without the Spirit, they misunderstood the scriptures. They thought eternal life was in the scriptures, but the Savior taught them that eternal life was only in coming to him, of whom the scriptures testified.

We must try to search the scriptures with the real intent of coming to him. We may need to do some repenting, manifested by confessing and forsaking our sins. (You can't put new wine into old bottles.)

2. *Pray.* Whenever you study the scriptures sincerely, ask your Father in Heaven for his Spirit—the spirit of understanding—in applying them. Ask in a believing attitude and in the name of Jesus Christ, and if you are truly trying to keep his commandments, he will answer your prayers.

3. *Ponder.* When you read and pray, take time to think, to meditate, to feast, to truly weigh and ponder. (Use your Topical Guide and Index, and you'll find a world of scriptural references on these subjects.)

As with any true communication, true prayer is two way. You speak, then you listen. You then speak with an awareness of

> **We live too much out of our memories, too little out of our imaginations. The spiritual (mental) creation precedes the physical creation in all things. Always begin with the end in mind.**

what you heard. This is a dialogue. Monologues are boring, unfulfilling, self-deceiving.

Pondering and meditating are forms of listening to the still, small voice. Our prophets have often taught the importance of meditating and listening. President David O. McKay taught that "meditation is the secret, sacred door through which one enters into the presence of God, the conscientious moments of which are called prayer."

4. *Visualize.* This means to see in your mind's eye the characters and events portrayed in the scriptures. Such an empathetic effort will help you understand the situation which produced the teaching. Then you can relate that situation to your own and distill the universal principle which may apply in both.

When you visualize, you're exercising faith — not in what you see, but in what you don't see but believe. To ignore unseen realities is as unrealistic as to ignore seen realities.

Visualizing is a powerful mortal process, one of man's unique endowments, involving both memory and imagination. Visualization is one of the most powerful forms of influence.

Consider the impact of well-directed movies or television shows, and of imagery in literature. Consider the power of examples and illustrations in teaching and speaking. Consider the parables.

Try it now. Visualize the Savior washing his disciples' feet (study John 13:1-17) and see in your mind's eye the Creator of the universe, girding himself with a towel and washing each disciple's feet in turn. See Peter protesting, Christ teaching, Peter overreacting, Christ teaching again. Now see yourself in a real situation, wherein someone is not giving you the treatment and

> **If we truly receive the Lord we draw our ego strength from our relationship with him and from his definition and lofty estimation of us rather than from other people's treatment and fickle opinions of us.**

appreciation you feel you deserve. See yourself responding in a humble, service-minded, Christlike way.

I believe that most of us horribly neglect this creative power within us. We live too much out of our memories, too little out of our imaginations. Realize it or not, control it or not, the spiritual (mental) creation precedes the physical creation in all things. Always begin with the end in mind. Most of life's battles are really lost in private, not in public.

To illustrate the power of spiritual creation in using the scriptures, I believe a person can resist and overcome temptation by creating a righteous response to temptation before it comes. This involves going through a four-step mind-making-up process. First, feast on the words of Christ to cultivate a desire to know and do his will. Second, ask the Lord in deep prayer to give you a heightened awareness and sensitivity to temptation and tempting environments whenever they arise. Third, commit to the Lord that the moment he gives you such an awareness you will immediately turn away and do some worthy thing—for example, inwardly singing a hymn such as "I Need Thee Every Hour" or "O My Father," or reviewing some memorized scriptures, or working on Church assignments. Then see yourself in your mind's eye, confronting temptation and replacing it with good. Fourth, keep the commitment.

Learn to Ask Good Questions

Questions serve as catalysts when meditating and pondering the scriptures. They spark off exciting meanings and applications. They bring focus and discipline to the mind. They can link the ideal with the real, the eternal with the present.

Missionaries today are counseled to encourage their investigators to both pray and ponder as they read the Book of Mormon, and in doing so to ask themselves over and over again, "Could any man have written this book?" Gradually, the consistently obvious "no" answer will help bring irresistible connection to the soul of the honest in heart.

One of the most helpful questions in likening scriptures to ourselves is: "What useful principle can I learn from these doings of the Lord?"

Read; ask; then ponder.

For instance, the scriptures teach that the Lord took six days or six periods of time to create the world. You read that, then ask the above question and ponder the answer.

To me, several principles are taught here: patience; things must be done in order or in correct sequence; there is no shortcut to solid accomplishment.

Consider another example. Read D&C 19:16-17: "For behold, I, God, have suffered these things for all, that they might not suffer if they would repent; but if they would not repent they must suffer even as I."

Ask the question. Now ponder. To me there are several meanings, one of which has helped me not to be offended by others. Since in his atonement the Lord suffered for all, this included any who would ever trespass against me. Why then should I suffer, since the Savior has already suffered? If I would repent and receive him, I would have the desire and power to return good for evil, to bless rather than to defend and judge. For in receiving him, I would make his goals and principles mine. I would become his agent or steward and refuse to take offenses personally. Instead I would see them as opportunities to show his love and power so that the offender too would be drawn to him.

In other words, if we truly receive him we draw our ego strength from our relationship with him and from his definition and lofty estimation of us rather than from other people's treatment and fickle opinions of us. In that case no one else can harm us — only ourselves.

We have the power within to choose our reaction to any

person or condition. This is man's last ultimate freedom, which can never be taken from him by another, but which can only be developed through Christ, who overcame all things.

Also, there are great spiritual lessons and meanings in the physical world (see Moses 6:63). And since the physical world is seen and experienced by all, it becomes a common referent in teaching. (Most of Christ's parables began with the seen physical world and ended with an explicit or implicit spiritual meaning.) For example, note the many similarities between the first and second birth processes: presence of water, blood, and spirit in both (study Moses 6:53-63); there are "labor pains" both before and after each birth; and people often abort both first and second births because of these labor pains. There are symbolic physical-spiritual lessons in sports, in farming, in physical health, in medicine, in education, in all we see around us.

Words too are symbols. They represent meanings. The temple ceremonies are highly symbolic, and the closer we are to the Spirit, the more the spiritual meanings underlying the physical and verbal symbols will be revealed to us. And my experience has been that, combined with spiritual insights, the temple experience offers practical helps and specific solutions to everyday problems and challenges.

For life-likening purposes, it's also interesting to substitute modern names and places for the ancient names and places specified in the scriptures. And try reading some of the revelations in the Doctrine and Covenants as if the Lord was giving these instructions right to you. There are many ways to liken scriptures to ourselves. We are limited only by our desires and by our imaginative approaches and questions.

Tailor Your Approach

The best scripture study approach is one which is tailored to your needs and interests and challenges. Too many take someone else's approach, lose interest rapidly, and give up. For instance, how many times have you read "I, Nephi, having been born of goodly parents. . . ."? But have you read the last chapter of the Book of Mormon more than once or twice?

194

Consider eight approaches to scripture study:

1. *From the beginning to the end.* Most books are read in this way, but I find that most people don't have the interest or the discipline to persist in reading the scriptures like this. For the motivated it does have the strong advantage of giving an overall perspective, since the scriptures are largely arranged in chronological sequence.

2. *Subject approach.* Here you would use the Topical Guide, an index, a concordance, cross-referencing footnotes. Using these tools you would really search the scriptures for an in-depth understanding of a particular subject, such as the Atonement, faith, prayer, baptism, family life. The subject approach is often the best one in preparing to speak or teach.

3. *Personal need or problem.* This approach starts with you, with the pressing need or problem facing you now, and leads you into God's word and ways for help. Such relevance is highly motivating, and it truly inspires the spirit of "searching the scriptures" for solutions. I particularly recommend this approach for those who are not in the habit of searching the scriptures. The inspiration and enlightenment obtained from the search will strongly reinforce the value of continuing it.

4. *Theme.* This approach focuses on a generic topic or general subject and again inspires the spirit of search, which turns the reading into an exciting adventure. For example, my mission president in the early 1950s counseled us new missionaries to read the Book of Mormon three times through fairly rapidly—first for history, second for references to Christ, and third for doctrine. We would use a different-colored marking pencil each time through. We would search and mark, search and mark. To this day I retain the indelible impressions of those three readings—the excitement of the story, the frequency and power of the Christ references, and the significance, simplicity, and profundity of the doctrines and teachings.

This approach gives a solid feeling of accomplishment, of discovery, and of testimony. It really becomes an exciting search.

5. *Church correlation.* This approach involves privately studying the scriptures and lessons which are to be discussed and

presented in the quorum and auxiliary classes or within the context of the missionary discussions, which are available to all Church members. Great wisdom, long-range planning, and inspiration are embodied in the correlated curriculum for all age groups.

This approach has three clear advantages: first, a sense of preparing for a specific assignment and contribution, making classroom experiences more meaningful; second, powerful reinforcement and internalization of principles and lessons through repetition and application to life; and third, a uniquely created opportunity for family discussions, involvements, and accountability.

6. *Scholarly.* This approach would lead the student into an in-depth intellectual understanding of the scriptures in their historical and situational context. It may lead him to search the writings and commentaries of the prophets and other Church leaders, as well as those of historians, linguists, archaeologists, anthropologists, and the like.

7. *Favorite stories, passages, and chapters.* With this approach you would develop a mental or written list of those scriptures which deeply move, edify, and inspire you or which have helped you help and inspire others. You would refer to these again and again and memorize many of them.

I have carried a very small New Testament with me every day for the last twenty years, and I frequently read one of the books or a favorite chapter when I am waiting for an appointment or meeting, when I am preparing for a talk, or when I feel down or fatigued or spiritually hungry. I find that spending a few minutes in a little prayerful reading just before I go into my home inspires me to take a more positive, happy approach in greeting and being with my wife and children.

An ordained patriarch blesses with his touch and his voice. A natural, unordained patriarch — a father — also blesses with his touch and his voice. I've found that the scriptures inspire me to be in control, to bless rather than to lose control in impatience, overreaction, and criticalness.

8. *Personal or eclectic.* Each situation, need, and mood is often best served by an individualized scripture approach or a combination of approaches. We need to learn to "read" ourselves, others, and situations, seeking the Spirit to adapt our responses accordingly.

Arrange and Manage Time

Time needs to be arranged and managed for scripture study so that, as Goethe put it, "things that matter most are not at the mercy of things that matter least."

Are you ever too busy driving to take time to get gas? too busy sawing to take time to sharpen the saw? We don't need more time. We have all the time there is. No one has more of it than each of us has. What we need is to put priorities on our goals and activities and to manage ourselves accordingly, instead of allowing conditions to manage us. We always have time and take time for things which are really important to us. We must make prayerful scripture study important. No other activity that takes such a little time can have quite the impact on your total life.

Cultivate the habit of reading the scriptures every day— perhaps just before retiring. It's better to go to sleep on Helaman or Moroni than on the latest TV talk show. Isn't it interesting that in the Bible the Lord called the evening and the morning the first day, the second day, and so on? Could it be that we are open to divine influences during our sleep if we are spiritually prepared to receive them? I believe so.

The early mornings are also a highly impressionable time for scripture work. Begin the day right—with God's word. Get up a little earlier. Plan and visualize your day as you meditate on the Savior's life and teachings.

Over the weeks, from time to time, block off a healthy chunk of time for an in-depth study of a particularly significant subject such as the Atonement. You will feel born again for the concentration. I can testify of this.

My wife enjoys listening to the scriptures on records (also

available on tape) as she does housework in the mornings. Inter-
ruptions don't annoy her — she simply plays the record again. As
a missionary, I heard Elder Spencer W. Kimball relate how much
he enjoyed reading the scriptures out loud to his wife as she did
the dishes.

As well as studying privately, try to involve your entire
family in the scriptures. Have each one bring his own copies to
family home evening. Refer to them; invite family members to
look up passages and read out loud. Memorize a new scripture
each month as a family, reviewing the ones memorized in the
past months.

Have scripture bees and scripture chases with your family.
One may quote a scripture while the others seek its source. Or
one may introduce a subject while the others chase down relevant supporting scriptures. Challenge the children to come up
with new games and variations. Make scriptures an enjoyable,
positive experience in addition to a serious one.

Try reading a scripture before family prayer or the family
dinner hour, passing around the opportunity to choose and read.

Consider a regular morning family devotional around scripture reading and discussion. It can be done in ten to fifteen
minutes. It creates a positive, spiritual, happy spirit for the entire
day's activities. Much can come from such a little effort.

Observe Special Helps and Cautions

Consider adopting special helps and techniques to reinforce
and support scripture reading habits, such as written goals or
checklists to accomplish so much by a certain date, and putting
the scripture to be memorized that month on a small card for
each to carry around and/or on a large poster placed in a con-
spicuous central place.

Physical surroundings also are important. As far as is practical, when studying the scriptures try to get free from distractions.
Go to a special room or place that is beautiful, uplifting, and
inspiring.

Three cautions need to be observed. *First*, avoid special
hobby-horse subjects on doctrines, and preoccupation with the

mysteries. Maintain overall perspective. See the relationship the principles have with one another. Realize that the power source resides more in the author of the principles than in the principles themselves. The word of God is not as great as God.

Second, be careful of private interpretation, of taking your understanding and opinion of a scriptural meaning and generalizing it into everyone else's life. Share it as your understanding, not as a fact. Look to the present prophet and Church leaders and official Church policies for the manifestation of the Lord's will and interpretations to the Church and world today. The inspired words of living prophets may be of greater worth to us than the words of the dead prophets. Their words also can be scripture.

> And this is the ensample unto them, that they shall speak as they are moved upon by the Holy Ghost.
> And whatsoever they shall speak when moved upon by the Holy Ghost shall be scripture, shall be the will of the Lord, shall be the mind of the Lord, shall be the word of the Lord, shall be the voice of the Lord, and the power of God unto salvation. (D&C 68:3-4.)

Therefore, also study the general conference reports.

Third, beware of the spirit of the scribes and the Pharisees, who used the scriptures to justify themselves and to judge and condemn others. Love is to be the ruling principle, and if our highest commitment is to the Lord, we will govern ourselves by that principle and spirit and the Lord's converting miracles will work through us. To teach celestial doctrine with a telestial spirit is not of God. (Study D&C 50.)

Love the Author

The story is told of a young woman who received a book as a gift, but after reading a chapter or two, she gave it up as dull and boring. It was consigned to gather dust on a shelf.

A year or so later she met a man she found initially attractive. As they came to know each other better, she found herself growing to love him. One day she discovered from a mutual friend that the young man had written a book, and on inquiring

> The way to really enjoy the scriptures is to truly love the Author. This will come about as we develop our highest purpose and motive for scripture study—to come to Christ, to get to know him, to be more like him, to put him and his Father at the center of our lives, and to have them bless others through us.

as to its title, she recognized it as the "dull" book she had received as a gift.

On arriving home that evening she quickly sought out the book and began reading it. To her surprise she rapidly became absorbed in it. It seemed to be all that a book should be—well-researched, creatively composed, brimming with imaginative ideas, written in a sparkling, vivid, style that kept her engrossed from the first to the last page.

The book had not changed, of course. The different response came about because now she knew and loved the author. It is that way in reading the scriptures. The way to really enjoy them is to truly love the Author. This will come about as we develop our highest purpose and motive for scripture study—to come to Christ, to get to know him, to be more like him, to put him and his Father at the center of our lives, and to have them bless others through us.

SERIOUS APPROACH IMPERATIVE

To become a regular part of one's daily life, this kind of study habit must be cultivated. It is not something that can be tampered with casually or indulged in only when occasion permits or when it is convenient, any more than the concert pianist could practice in such a desultory fashion and still expect to awe his audiences. It requires regular daily effort to seek an understanding of the word of the Lord, to memorize part of it, to ponder it in the heart and mind, to think deeply about it. The

Prophet Joseph Smith wrote: "The things of God are of deep import; and . . . careful and ponderous and solemn thoughts can only find them out" (*TPJS*, page 137).

NEW LATTER-DAY SAINT SCRIPTURES

At a Regional Representatives Seminar held on April 2, 1982, Elder Bruce R. McConkie said the new Latter-day Saint edition of the scriptures was one of the most important Church developments in this century. He gave the following explanation and exhortation:

> May I suggest, based on personal experience, that faith comes and revelations are received as a direct result of scriptural study. . . .
>
> Faith is . . . born of scriptural study. Those who study, ponder, and pray about the scriptures, seeking to understand their deep and hidden meanings, receive from time to time great outpourings of light and knowledge from the Holy Spirit. This is what happened to Joseph Smith and Sidney Rigdon when they received the vision of the degrees of glory.
>
> However talented men may be in administrative matters; however eloquent they may be in expressing their views; however learned they may be in worldly things — they will be denied the sweet whisperings of the Spirit that might have been theirs unless they pay the price of studying, pondering, and praying about the scriptures. . . .
>
> Never since the day of Joseph Smith; never since the translation of the Book of Mormon; never since the receipt of the revelations in the Doctrine and Covenants and the inspired writings in the Pearl of Great Price — never has there been such an opportunity to increase gospel scholarship as has now come to those who have our new English editions of the scriptures.
>
> This opportunity arises for two reasons: One is the new teaching aids that have been made a part of each one of the Standard Works. The other is the imperative need, because of textual and other corrections, for all concerned to re-read and re-mark for reference all of our four volumes of scripture as they are now constituted and in their new format. . . .
>
> May I suggest for you and your families and all those with whom you labor in the kingdom, the following:
>
> 1. Study the scriptures daily. Drink directly from Holy Writ. Learn the word as it is found in the scriptures.

2. Mark a new set of the Standard Works. Learn to use the footnotes and teaching aids in our new editions of the scriptures. Pay particular attention to the inspired changes made by the Prophet Joseph Smith in the Bible. Be sure any quotations you make include the new textual corrections.
3. Apply what you learn to your life and to your administrative assignments in the Church. Act and live as the scriptures decree.
4. Use the scriptures in all your sermons and teaching. Rely upon the scriptures. Quote the scriptures. Believe the scriptures. Choose your illustrations from them.
5. Ponder the revealed word in your hearts. Pray about its deep and hidden meanings. Let the things of eternity be your constant meditation.
6. Expound the scriptures. Explain their meanings. Let others know what you know. Raise your voice in testimony.
7. Get others to go and do likewise with reference to all these things.

LISTENING AND HEARING

The second process on our course toward perfection is that of *listening to and hearing* the word of the Lord. In other words, once the conscience has been trained and educated by divine sources, we need to pause, to wait on the Lord, to listen for the promptings of the Spirit, and to hear them when they come. These promptings may direct us to specific practices; or they may come in the form of a general impression of a basic law or commandment of God, which impression creates a framework for thinking, solving problems, making decisions, and taking action.

The Prophet Joseph Smith gives what I feel is the best description of the spirit of revelation that I have ever read:

A person may profit by noticing the first intimation of the spirit of revelation: for instance, when you feel pure intelligence flowing into you, it may give you sudden strokes of ideas . . . and thus by learning the Spirit of God and understanding it, you may grow into the principle of revelation, until you become perfect in Christ Jesus. (*TPJS,* page 151.)

NOT FOR "ELITE" ONLY

This is an important correct map. With it, we do not look "beyond the mark" (Jacob 4:14) and conclude that such intimations are not the spirit of revelation, that revelations are only for "the élite" and not for us, and that the process is simply too complicated, too mysterious, and too spiritual for the likes of us.

Missionaries find it essential to teach the true concept to investigators in order to remove the mystique surrounding revelation. They have to give them the assurance that it is a natural process, although spiritual, and is available to the investigators if they will only seek it—if they will pray with some faith and real intent. It is important also for parents, leaders, and teachers to identify the Spirit when it is present and to recognize the process.

Particularly it is important to emphasize the fact that personal revelation is available to any earnest, honest seeker. Indeed, we must "de-mystify" and "de-éliticize" the matter! I am convinced that in response to prayer or to deep questions and hungers, many have had answers in the form of inspiration, guidance, or revelation (whichever word best fits) and do not know it. Notice the Savior's words to the Nephites:

> And ye shall offer for a sacrifice unto me a broken heart and a contrite spirit. And whoso cometh unto me with a broken heart and a contrite spirit, him will I baptize with fire and with the Holy Ghost, even as the Lamanites, because of their faith in me at the time of their conversion, were baptized with fire and with the Holy Ghost, *and they knew it not.* (3 Nephi 9:20; italics added.)

Some may similarly not know they have received revelation. If they did know it they would be encouraged and would "do it" some more and "by learning the spirit of God and understanding it . . . may grow unto the principle of revelation."

Imagine how Satan would want to keep revelation a mystery, as something only for the élite! Just as he wants to keep God a mystery. What a map! And imagine how those whose security comes from being among the spiritually élite ("those of us who really know") might be threatened by "de-mystifying" and "de-éliticizing" spiritual communication!

SPIRITUAL COMMUNICATION

Elder Boyd K. Packer, speaking to missionaries, made the following comments relative to receiving spiritual communications:

> We cannot express spiritual knowledge in words alone. We can, however, with words, show another how to prepare for the reception of the Spirit.
>
> The Spirit itself will help. "For when a man speaketh by the power of the Holy Ghost, the power of the Holy Ghost carrieth it into the hearts of the children of men." (2 Nephi 33:1.)
>
> Then when they have a spiritual communication, they say within themselves, "This is it! This is what is meant by those words in the revelation." Thereafter, if they are carefully chosen, words are adequate for teaching about spiritual things.
>
> We do not have the words (even the scriptures do not have words) which perfectly describe the Spirit. The scriptures generally use the word *voice*, which does not exactly fit.
>
> These delicate, refined spiritual communications are not seen with our eyes, nor heard with our ears. And even though it is described as a voice, it is a voice that one feels more than one hears.
>
> Once I came to understand this, one verse in the Book of Mormon took on a profound meaning, and my testimony of the book increased immeasurably. It had to do with Laman and Lemuel, who rebelled against Nephi. Nephi rebuked them and said, "Ye have seen an angel, and he spake unto you; yea, ye have heard his voice from time to time; and he hath spoken unto you in a still small voice, but you were past *feeling*, that you could not *feel* his words. (1 Nephi 17:45; italics added.)
>
> Nephi, in a great profound sermon of instruction, explained that "angels speak by the power of the Holy Ghost; wherefore, they speak the words of Christ. Wherefore, I said unto you, feast upon the words of Christ; for behold, the words of Christ will tell you all things that ye should do." (2 Nephi 32:3.)
>
> Should an angel appear and converse with you, neither you nor he would be confined to corporeal sight or sound in order to communicate. For there *is* that spiritual process, described by the Prophet Joseph Smith, by which pure intelligence *can* flow into our minds and we can know what we need to know without either the drudgery of study or the passage of time, for it is revelation.
>
> And the Prophet said further: "All things whatsoever God in his infinite wisdom has seen fit and proper to reveal to us, while we are dwelling in mortality, in regard to our mortal bodies, are

revealed to us in the abstract, . . . revealed to our spirits precisely as though we had no mortal bodies at all: and those revelations which will save our spirits will save our bodies." (*TPJS*, page 355.)

The voice of the Spirit is described in the scripture as being "neither loud, nor harsh" (3 Nephi 11:3). "It was not a voice of thunder, neither was it a voice of a great tumultous noise," but rather, "still and small, of perfect mildness, as if it had been a whisper," and it can "pierce even to the very soul" (Helaman 5:30) and "cause the heart to burn" (3 Nephi 11:3, D&C 85:6-7). Remember Elijah found the voice of the Lord was not in the wind, nor the earthquake, nor the fire, but was a "still small voice" (1 Kings 19:12).

The Spirit does not get our attention by shouting or shaking us with a heavy hand. Rather, it whispers. It caresses so gently that if we are preoccupied we may not feel it at all. . . .

Occasionally it will press just firmly enough for us to pay heed. But most of the time, if we do not heed the gentle feeling, the Spirit will withdraw and wait until we come seeking and listening and say in our manner and expression, like Samuel of ancient times, "Speak, Lord, for Thy servant heareth." (1 Samuel 3:9-10.) (Seminar for New Mission Presidents, June 25, 1982.)

LISTENING IN PRAYER

Listening involves being open in prayer and taking counsel from the Lord. Too many prayers end up in what is essentially counsel to the Lord, directing where he should go, what he should do, whom he should bless, and when. Praying for blessings for other people is fine and necessary, as long as those prayers are dictated by the Spirit of the Lord. And we should seek first the spirit of prayer, so we will know what to pray for, for that which is wise or expedient in the Lord's eyes. Otherwise our prayers can be full of vain repetitions, or asking for things which are not wise, which are contrary to the Lord's will and ways, or which tend to shift the entire burden to the Lord. I'm certain these kinds of prayers are displeasing to our Father in Heaven, although (as D&C 88:65 suggests) he may answer them to our own condemnation. Again, I find that one key is to pray more in terms of our own needs than our wants, and to try to sense our needs from his point of view.

In this quiet moment of listening to the whisperings of the

Spirit we find a uniquely human characteristic. None other of his creations has the power of introspective thinking, of self-reflection, of self-awareness, of moral agency, of free will. It is the proper use of that free will that enlarges and develops these unique human powers and capacities. Angels are of a different degree of mind than man and possess higher powers and capacities than man does. God is of a significantly higher degree than angels and possesses even greater capacities and powers. Yet all of these ultimate powers are latent within man's own nature, simply because man is God's own child. Man, therefore, possesses in seed form all of the ultimate capabilities and powers God himself possesses.

The key to activating these capacities lies in becoming aware of them and using our freedom properly to develop and direct them. If we use our freedom properly the potentialities will develop and our freedom will expand. If we use our freedom improperly it will wither, and our potentialities will remain dormant and dysfunctional.

The still, small voice of the Spirit sparks the eternal seed of godhood that is in the most absolute sense "life-giving."

The Covenant Standard

Chapter 8

*And this shall be our covenant—that we
will walk in all the ordinances of the Lord.
(D&C 136:4.)*

In the previous chapter we discussed the constantly expanding,
upward-spiraling movement in the development of the human
soul that constitutes the road to perfection. Educating the conscience and learning to listen to the promptings of the Spirit were
shown as two of the four essential processes. We now move to
the remaining two.

COMMITTING AND COVENANTING

The third process in this ever-enlarging spiral of growth and
development is *committing and covenanting*. This is one of
the most vital steps. It is the unique way for man to make a
formal break with the past and take a new step into the future.
When we commit deeply within ourselves, we marshal and energize all of the forces within us. When we say, "I will," we visualize ourselves on a different level than that which we presently
occupy, going in a different direction than that which we are
now following, doing different things than those we are now
doing, breaking certain habits we now have and cultivating
habits of a more divine level.

But there is a basic difference between a commitment and a
covenant. A commitment is a one-way promise, a promise that a
man makes to himself, or to another, or perhaps even to God.
W. H. Murray attempts a description of the mysterious power of
commitment:

> Until one is committed there is hesitancy, the chance to draw
> back, always ineffectiveness. Concerning all acts of initiative (and

creation), there is one elementary truth, the ignorance of which kills countless ideas and splendid plans: that the moment one definitely commits oneself, then providence moves too.

All sorts of things occur to help one that would never otherwise have occurred. A whole stream of events issues from the decision, raising in one's favor all manner of unforeseen incidents and meetings and material assistance, which no man could have dreamt would have come his way.

I have learned a deep respect for one of Goethe's couplets:
Whatever you can do, or dream you can, begin it.
Boldness has genius, power and magic in it.

A covenant, on the other hand, is a two-way commitment or promise between man and God. If we covenant to do the things the Lord asks us to do, he enters into the process and commits himself to us. In covenanting we not only marshal and energize the powers within ourselves; we also release in our behalf the powers of the God of heaven. In such a covenant, heaven is moved and new energies are generated in the mortal covenant-maker.

TRANSCENDENT SIGNIFICANCE OF GOSPEL ORDINANCES

Many people are unaware of the transcendent significance of the ordinances of the gospel. Other than as an outward sign of an inward belief, they see no real, practical reason for them. They think them to be cultural, social, or religious rituals. Much of the Christian world believes this. But there is unusual power in covenant making—godly power. It has taken me years and many responsibilities to come to understand this. The adversary has clouded the concept and people have become entrapped in the idea that willpower alone is sufficient to make desired changes in character and personality. If Satan could remove the concept of covenant making, he could keep man from tapping this divine power source which can change man's nature and help him become a "partaker of the divine nature" (2 Peter 1:3-8). The lack of covenanting will always keep man far beneath his potential, for the *arm of flesh alone is incapable of developing godlike powers and capacities.*

"And this greater [Melchizedek] priesthood administereth the gospel. . . . And without the ordinances thereof, and the authority of the priesthood, the power of godliness is not manifest unto men in the flesh" (D&C 84:19, 21). This scripture tells us that the powers of godliness (powers of perfection) are transmitted to man's nature through ordinances (covenants) of the higher priesthood. These are the ordinances of the Melchizedek Priesthood wherein the Holy Ghost is the attendant agent and acts to seal them. The Holy Ghost, in his capacity as sealer and ratifier, is sometimes called the Holy Spirit of Promise, meaning God's promise to man. The covenant of the Melchizedek Priesthood is confirmed by the Father with an oath that he cannot break (see D&C 84:33-40), a situation that reflects the total and complete integrity that is part of God's nature.

Therefore, when we covenant under the influence of the Holy Spirit the Lord also covenants with us. Satan has no power to match the powers of heaven, and in its face he must stand aside and withdraw. The adversary cannot enter into the heart of a deeply committed covenant maker. However, if that covenant maker lets up and forgets or breaks his covenants, he no longer has that immunity from Satan.

ORDINANCE-COVENANTS FULFILL COMMANDMENTS

We may speak of the ordinances or covenants as "fulfilling the commandments." John the Baptist at first refused to baptize the Savior, saying in effect, "I am not worthy even to unlatch thy shoes." The Savior answered him, "Suffer it to be so now, for thus it becometh us to fulfill all righteousness." (Matthew 3:13-15.) I believe that when we enter into the waters of baptism, or when we conscientiously renew that basic covenant through partaking of the sacrament, we are, in a sense, fulfilling all righteousness. That is, we completely turn our backs on the lower road, the adversary's or our own way, and we totally commit ourselves to the Lord's way. He too has entered into that covenant. In this process, our repentance has reached its apex. Our minds are absolutely made up; our old sins and ways of thinking are no longer relevant nor comfortable. We have acquired new software. We have fulfilled the commandments.

The basic principles of the gospel are, first, faith in the Lord Jesus Christ, then repentance, and then covenant making in the waters of baptism, renewed each week by the partaking of the sacrament. The Lord then gives us the Holy Ghost, his covenant confirmer, his Holy Spirit of Promise; and this, if we live righteously, confirms, the Father's covenants with us, sanctifies us, purifies us, testifies to us, comforts us, and teaches us the process of perfection. If we then stay faithful and true, obeying the general and personal commandments given to us, if we live true to our covenants, we set ourselves firmly on the celestial path.

Entering into a covenant is equivalent to winning a private victory. President David O. McKay taught that the most important battle of life is the one we fight daily in the silent chambers of the soul. There are many references by President Spencer W. Kimball to the importance of making decisions early and once only about how we will respond to the various commandments of the Lord, such as attending our Church meetings, honoring the Word of Wisdom, and paying our tithing. Once the decision is wholeheartedly made on any such issue, we need not fight the battle anymore. Energies can then be expended in other directions and not wasted in internal strugglings whenever we find ourselves in tempting environments. It is a private victory, a winning within, which will lead to the inevitable public victories in life's arenas when great pressures and temptations descend upon us. It is important that each of us win these private victories, and win them not narrowly but definitively, lest we find ourselves uprooted by life's stresses and pressures.

FREQUENT RECOMMITTAL EXPERIENCES NEEDED

The Lord tells us, "Thy vows shall be offered up in righteousness on all days and at all times" (D&C 59:11). All of us need to carefully think through our covenants with the Lord and renew them in our personal prayers, through the sacrament prayer, when we are doing work for the dead in the temples, when the Spirit settles upon us in an inspirational moment in a meeting, when watching or listening to an inspiring person, or when we feel deeply grateful to the Lord for special blessings he has given to us, to our loved ones, or to any of his children.

My wife and I have found that one of the most humbling and inspiring and recommitting experiences we can have is, before praying, to carefully think through and even talk through the basic covenants we have made with the Lord. We find it sobers us and causes us to be mentally and emotionally open, humble, and grateful for his blessings. It causes us to want to take counsel from him rather than give counsel to him in our prayers; to want to be sensitive, alert, and open; to want to listen and to hear. It inspires us to want to obey and to do his will.

ORDINANCES AND REVELATION

Most covenants are associated with ordinances, and ordinances open the doors and windows of revelation. "Salvation cannot come without revelation," the Prophet Joseph declared (*TPJS*, page 60).

Without revelation, man's reasoning and best wisdom cannot "by searching find out God" (Job 11:7), for, as Jacob put it, "no man knoweth of his ways save it be revealed unto him" (Jacob 4:8). The Apostle Paul said it in this way:

> Which things also we speak, not in the words which man's wisdom teacheth, but which the Holy Ghost teacheth; comparing spiritual things with spiritual.
> But he that is spiritual judgeth all things, yet he himself is judged of no man. (1 Corinthians 2:13, 15.)

> For I neither received it of man, neither was I taught it, but by the revelation of Jesus Christ. (Galatians 1:12.)

Hugh Nibley writes: "The fundamental purpose of ordinances is to bridge the gap between the worlds (this world and the other one); all are in a sense 'rites of passage,' that is, amphibious by nature 'with a foot in either camp.' " ("What Is The Book of Breathings?" *BYU Studies*, Winter 1971, pages 186-87.)

The Prophet Joseph Smith taught: "Reading the experiences of others, on the revelations given to *them*, can never give *us* a comprehensive view of our condition and true relation to God. Knowledge of these things can only be obtained by experience through the ordinances of God set forth for that purpose." (*TPJS*, page 324.)

COVENANTS AND PERFECTION PROCESS

The first ordinance, of course, is baptism. Jesus taught Nicodemus of this. "Except a man be born of water and of the Spirit, he cannot enter into the kingdom of God" (John 3:5). This rebirth is of water and spirit. Alma soberly declared that everyone, "all mankind, . . . must be born again . . . changed from their carnal and fallen state, to a state of righteousness, being redeemed of God. . . . and unless they do this, they can in nowise inherit the kingdom of God." (Mosiah 27:25-27.)

The Lord understands us and the processes of repentance and perfection and gives us the opportunity every Sabbath day to renew these baptismal covenants, to once again take upon ourselves the name of Christ, to recommit ourselves to remembering him and keeping his commandments—all so that we might always have his Spirit to be with us.

It is vital that we bring the sacrifice of a broken heart and a contrite spirit to the sacrament table so that all the "old wine" is poured out before we attempt to put new wine in.

We are thus led from ordinance to ordinance until we receive the higher ordinances of the priesthood in the temple and increasingly become a partaker of the divine nature. The Prophet Joseph taught that "those who keep [God's] commandments shall grow up and from grace to grace, and become heirs of the heavenly kingdom, and joint heirs with Jesus Christ" (Lectures on Faith 5:2) and will thereby have done

the same as all gods have done before, . . . namely, by going from one small degree to another, and from a small capacity to a great one; from grace to grace, from exaltation to exaltation, until [they] attain to the resurrection of the dead, and are able to dwell in everlasting burnings, and to sit in glory, as do those who sit enthroned in everlasting power. (*TPJS*, pages 346-47.)

212

In connection with the temple ordinances, the Prophet Joseph Smith spoke of "all those plans and principles by which any one is enabled to secure the fullness of those blessings which have been prepared for the Church of the First Born, and come up and abide in the presence of Eloheim in the eternal worlds." (*History of the Church* 5:2.)

Brigham Young explained:

> Your endowment is to receive all those ordinances in the house of the Lord, which are necessary for you, after you have departed this life, to enable you to walk back to the presence of the Father, passing the angels who stand as sentinels, being enabled to give them the key words, the signs and tokens, pertaining to the Holy Priesthood, and gain your eternal exaltation in spite of earth and hell. (John A. Widtsoe, comp., *Discourses of Brigham Young,* Deseret Book Co., 1954, page 416.)

Paul wrote: "Eye hath not seen, nor ear heard, neither have entered into the heart of man, the things which God hath prepared for them that love him" (1 Corinthians 2:9). But I believe that those who recognize and use the ordinances as intended have a glimpse, or even more than a glimpse, of those wonderful things.

OBEYING

The fourth process in this upward spiraling growth is *obedience* to that which we have covenanted to obey; in others words, "doing" the word. Jesus said, "If any man will do his will, he shall know of the doctrine, whether it be of God, or whether I speak of myself" (John 7:17).

Obedience is the ultimate test of discipleship and the most powerful form of truly educating our conscience. The true disciple of the Lord puts his life on the line, keeps his commitment, honors his promise, fulfills his covenant, and does the Lord's will. This habit of obedience to God's will, this habit of doing and keeping the commandments, is the essence of a truly disciplined life, character, and soul. It is also the essence of true integrity, reflecting the value we place on ourselves.

Obedience is the ultimate test of discipleship and the most powerful form of truly educating our conscience.

NEW LIGHT DEPENDENT ON OBEDIENCE
TO FORMER LIGHT

Once a person is true to the light he has received, he is then capable of receiving more light and obeying it. Until he is true to the light already given, additional light would only condemn him, for he is capable neither of understanding it nor appreciating it. He would fall into the trap of being given a gift but being unable to receive it. The Lord gives to his children what they are able to receive and no more. If they are true to that, he will give them more.

This vital lesson is learned, often the hard way, by almost every missionary. A missionary often is trapped into taking the course of least resistance, of continuing to present more discussions, more light and knowledge to investigators who simply are not living up to the commitments they have made. If he takes this course, eventually the teaching process will deteriorate into one of intellectualization, if that is the bent of the contacts, or into one of socialization, if they are so inclined.

I remember working with a missionary who learned this principle the hard way out of his own life, but who learned it so deeply that he simply would not teach additional discussions until investigators had lived up to the commitments of the prior discussions. If he did continue to teach anything, it was on the point being made here—the importance of making and keeping commitments.

One time he and his companion kept a teaching appointment with a widow and she cordially invited them in as usual. She was several discussions along, was very friendly, and had been making good progress. On the doorstep the elder said, "Sister, did you keep the promise you made last week?"

She paused, then finally said, "Well, I did till last night, but then my parents came over and we felt pressured and so we smoked with them. Sorry, elders. Come on in."

The elder just stood there and wouldn't move. His companion said, "Elder Stewart, what's wrong? Let's go in." The elder continued to stand there. His companion nudged him forward, eventually getting him into the house. Once in there, Elder Stewart stayed solemn and glum. He sat down and said nothing. The other elder didn't know what to do. He was new in the mission field, and since this was before the days of the Missionary Training Center, he didn't know the discussions. Eventually the silence became so noisy that he turned to his companion and said, "Elder Stewart, I can't go on. I don't know what to do." He knew they had to have a prayer, so he prayed and then asked again, "What's wrong? Can I help you?"

Eventually Elder Stewart looked the lady in the eye and said, "Sister, you promised you would quit smoking. You broke your promise. We will not teach you any more until you keep that promise. Let's go, Elder." And he stood up and walked out.

She ran and grabbed them at the door and pleaded with them to come back. She recommitted herself to obey the Word of Wisdom so that he would come back and teach. She said, "You are the finest people that have ever come into this home. You must stay and teach." It was almost like the scene in which the Savior turned to his disciples and said, "Will ye also go away? Then Simon Peter answered him, Lord, to whom shall we go? thou hast the words of eternal life." (John 6:67-68.) This elder knew the power of making and keeping commitments, of educating the conscience sufficiently to be able to receive more light and knowledge and then to move to higher levels of commitment.

This is the clear pattern throughout the entire Church. Receipt of Aaronic Priesthood authority precedes that of Melchizedek Priesthood authority. Aaronic Priesthood ordinances precede Melchizedek Priesthood ordinances. In the temple endowment we receive certain light and knowledge and covenant to obey it and then move on to receive further light and knowledge and covenant to obey that.

> Doing actually changes the fiber of
> a person's nature—his soul, his conscience,
> his character. Doing changes his view
> of himself. A person's behavior is largely
> a product of such self-made fuel.

Observing our covenants may not always be easy, and it may require sacrifice. The Lord said: "Verily I say unto you, all among them who know their hearts are honest, and are broken, and their spirits contrite, and are willing to observe their covenants by sacrifice—yea, every sacrifice which I, the Lord, shall command—they are accepted of me." (D&C 97:8.)

One of the reasons why many never experience the power of covenants is that they have not repented before entering into them. You cannot make a new covenant with an old mental-emotional set. A person might try to do it, but it won't take. This is similar to the Prophet Joseph Smith's expression about the rights of the priesthood: that they may be conferred upon us, but they will have no efficacy except by obedience to the principles of righteousness. (See D&C 121:36-37.)

OBEDIENCE EQUATES VALUE AND HABIT SYSTEMS

When everything is ready for the takeoff, the astronauts say "All systems go." That says that everything is in proper balance and working order. They can have a launch-off from the launching pad, or they can make some significant maneuver in space, because everything is well coordinated, logistically harmonized, and prepared to move. "All systems go" might be a good expression for us too, to indicate that our value system and our habit system are in harmony with each other so that all systems can take us to the heights planned. When our habit system and value system are not synchronized we are subject to internal reservations, fears, doubts, and hesitancies. Then we need to bring them into harmony so that the mission does not fail.

Someone has said that repentance brings our conduct up to the level of our ideals, while rationalization brings our ideals down to the level of our conduct. A God / Christ-centered life is one that internalizes the values and ideals of Christ and strives to make the behavior a complete expression of these ideals and values.

Enoch and his city reached this level of perfection. They became a Zion culture, a culture of individuals who were not only pure in heart but who chose interaction with others who were pure in heart and ultimately developed an entire community akin to the celestial community. When they had passed their probationary period tests and had no reason to remain on earth longer, they and their city were taken. From that translated city have come many of those who have ministered to the inhabitants of the earth in various ways and served various divine purposes.

One of the most powerfully evident results of being a doer of the word and not a hearer only, of obeying that which one has committed to obey, is that such active behavior assists the education of the conscience and reinforces its knowledge in ways that no amount of church attending or studying can. *Doing* actually changes the fiber of a person's nature—his soul, his conscience, his character. *Doing* changes his view of himself. A person's behavior is largely a product of such self-made fuel.

THE FOUR PROCESSES IN ACTION

Consider again these four interlocking processes. First, educating the conscience; second, listening and hearing the promptings of the Spirit to the conscience; third, committing ourselves to obey the general commandments and the personal promptings; and fourth, obeying, fulfilling that commitment. Put these four processes on this ever-enlarging, spiraling path. An investigator of the gospel may be at the low end of the continuum, but he is undergoing the same process nevertheless. He is being taught the discussions by missionaries. In other words, his conscience is being educated. He listens and learns. He commits himself to do what the missionaries counsel him to do, and he does it. As he acts, his conscience is enlarged. It becomes more educated, more open, and susceptible to more learning, commitment, and obedience.

As we approach the other end of this continuum we find the spiritual giants. At the conclusion of a general conference, President Spencer W. Kimball, the prophet of God, expressed his delight at what he had heard at the conference and his desire to return to his own home and put the counsel into practice. Such an expression deeply touched the members of the Church, who recognized their prophet as nearly perfect as far as mortal possibilities are concerned. It reminded them that all the children of our Father in Heaven are still growing. They saw the true humility of their prophet. Joseph Smith said: "The nearer man approaches perfection, the clearer are his views, and the greater his enjoyments, till he has overcome the evils of his life and lost every desire for sin." (*TPJS*, page 51.)

Elder Neal A. Maxwell writes, "There is no such thing as a casual Christian" (*Wherefore Ye Must Press Forward*, Deseret Book Co., 1977, page 73). One of his favorite authors, C. S. Lewis, in the book *Mere Christianity*, gives a beautiful illustration of what happens when the Lord is able to take hold of someone—that he will not let him loose until he has perfected him. He tells of how as a little boy with a painful toothache he would not complain to his mother till he could not stand the pain any more. He knew she would take him to the dentist, who would not merely work on the offending tooth but also on any others he could see needed treatment, although they were not yet aching. Similarly, the author suggests, when we go to the Lord he gives us the "full treatment." This is a good illustration of what happens when we really begin to yield our hearts to the teachings and commandments of the Lord.

PRICE MUST BE PAID

Anyone who has made efforts at spiritual and character development will realize that attaining the upper reaches of this four-process continuum, though obviously intensely rewarding, is far from easy. I had occasion to explain this to an associate of mine who visited with me some years back regarding what he and his wife could do to get back together and have a unified and happy family life. He told me a long story which involved deep transgression followed by partial repentance, an ever-present and attractive temptation to sin, all mixed with much contention in the marriage, broken communication, occasional separation, spiritual and emotional alienation, strong accusations, and constant self-justification. I counseled him to see his bishop as the first steps to putting his life in order, and this he did. But because I had been his mission president while he was a missionary, he asked me for some general advice. I proceeded to teach him the importance of educating and obeying his conscience as the essential way of returning to the gospel path so that he and his wife might be worthy to receive the blessings they both desired.

Some time later I was visiting with them both about these matters, and the man said to his wife, "You know, honey, we really should do this. It makes a lot of sense. Why don't we resolve together, here and now, that every night before we retire we will spend some time in reading the scriptures, at least one chapter."

All I could say in response was, "My friend, you don't have the foggiest idea of what I am talking about. Do you know what my son does to get ready to be a pass receiver for BYU? Do you know the kind of price he pays every afternoon? the grueling workouts, the punishing practices? All so that he can catch a pass or two in a game. Every day they put him against the number one defense team, and he knows full well that the moment he catches the ball he will be smashed to the ground. One such hit, and my body would be dislocated for life. Do you have any idea the kind of price he has to pay to get ready to sustain those hits, one right after another, day after day after day?

"That, my friend, is the kind of price you have to pay, in the spiritual sense, if you really want to educate your conscience; if you want to some day be living the kind of life you know you must live to be worthy of eternal life; if you want immunity from all these worldly temptations; if you want full forgiveness of past sins. There is simply no quick fix in this area, no cheap-grace approach, no easy way to develop this kind of strength and character. You might as well expect your infant son's mind to do the work of genius. There is simply no shortcut. The price must be paid."

I quoted the words of Elder John A. Widtsoe, which the apostle offered in a talk at the University of Utah Institute of Religion: "It is a paradox that men will gladly devote time every day for many years to learn a science or art; yet . . . will expect to win a knowledge of the gospel, which comprehends all sciences and arts, through perfunctory glances at books or occasional listening to sermons."

Thomas Paine, the brilliant writer of American Revolution times, put the essence of the matter in these words: "What we obtain too cheap, we esteem too lightly; it is dearness only that gives everything its value. Heaven knows how to put a proper price upon its goods."

But it *can* be done, this price-paying, this pulling together of the various processes. A student of mine was successful in this way in making corrections in an important area of his life. At one point he said to me, "All my mature life I've had trouble with bad thoughts. Even during my mission. Whenever I was asked a question, 'Are you morally clean?' I answered yes because I was considering my practices, but I always had some plaguing feelings about my thoughts."

Time went by. Then one day, when we were walking into the final examination, this young man said, "Brother Covey, I can look you in the eye and say I am morally clean, right to my core."

What had he done? For a period of several months he had *feasted* upon the words of Christ, asked the Lord for a heightened awareness of temptation, turned immediately at the very first onset of that temptation and done worthy things. Faced by temptation, he had returned to his divine purposes and his work. Elder Boyd K. Packer had suggested, "Hum a hymn. Memorize a scripture." And he did it. And the Holy Ghost purged that other disposition out of his nature.

TACTICS OF THE ADVERSARY

The adversary could destroy this upward spiraling growth movement by undermining any one of the four processes. For instance, he could move in on the process of educating our conscience by inspiring us to become so involved in busy work and various activities that we would have no time to contemplate the word of the Lord, to study the scriptures, or to think on sacred things. Were a person to yield to such a strategy, his conscience would become desensitized, unrefined, and unresponsive. This dullness would cause him to be less open, less willing to listen during his prayers. It would result in his praying mechanically, repetitively, as if going down a checklist, saying all the right words and phrases but having little awareness of meaning and little openness to the Spirit. His situation would become similar to that described by Alma:

> But if ye neglect the tree, and take no thought for its nourishment, behold it will not get any root; and when the heat of the sun cometh and scorcheth it, because it hath no root it withers away, and ye pluck it up and cast it out.
>
> Now, this is not because the seed was not good, neither is it because the fruit thereof would not be desirable; but it is because your ground is barren, and ye will not nourish the tree, therefore ye cannot have the fruit thereof. (Alma 32:38-39.)

Similarly, Satan could tempt us to lose faith in the power of making covenants in the ordinances and in our prayers. He could seduce us into thinking, "I have broken them before — why make them again?" He could cause us to make covenants superficially, before we had repented and cleared ourselves of the worldly, selfish, and sensual desires of the flesh. (Frequently people who covenant without repenting find that they cannot keep their covenants, for the Lord does not covenant with an unrepentant person. Such a person is left to the power of his own commitment, which will falter under pressure.)

Above all, Satan would like to thwart the process of obedience — the doing the work of the Lord.

If a person makes a covenant but does not fulfill that cove-

> If a person makes a covenant but does not fulfill that covenant, there is danger of a basic breakdown taking place in his character. His sense of honor and integrity is threatened, even weakened. His self-esteem tends to diminish. He tends gradually to cultivate a different picture of himself than the divine one, in which case his behavior then conforms to that picture.

nant, there is danger of a basic breakdown taking place in his character. His sense of honor and integrity is threatened, even weakened. His self-esteem tends to diminish. He tends gradually to cultivate a different picture of himself than the divine one, in which case his behavior then conforms to that picture. He experiences a stagnation of the growth process. If he does not perceive what has happened and mend his ways through sincere repentance and new covenant making which is consummated in obedience, he is likely to fall under the influence of the adversary and gradually lose his freedom. This could put him in line to be programmed by Satan, the father of all lies, who seeks to make all men miserable like himself (see 2 Nephi 2:27). Fortunately the situation need not deteriorate that far, since the repentance road is always open.

CHALLENGES ALL THE WAY

We must never deceive ourselves into thinking that the growth processes are easy. At each new level there will be entirely new challenges. The understanding and covenanting at an earlier level may simply not be sufficient to deal with the challenges of a later level. That's when temptations come of entirely different kinds, kinds which perhaps we could never have endured earlier. But the Lord is faithful and will not allow his children to be tempted beyond their capacity to endure (1 Corinthians 10:13); and as they deal with each new challenge or temptation and overcome it, they unleash within themselves a new kind of freedom or power or capacity to soar to heights previously undreamed of.

One of the main repentance challenges we confront is that of *forgiving others*—those who have offended us or have dealt with one of our loved ones unjustly.

Another major challenge in repentance is the *confession* of our sins to the Lord and to any whom we may have offended. Unless we draw close to the Lord and internalize an awareness of the great atoning sacrifice, we may not develop a broken heart and a contrite spirit capable of making full and deep confession. But unless we make such a confession, "old wine" is still in us (Matthew 9:17), and we feel ourselves to be lacking the necessary divine energy and power to handle more of the subtle and insidious temptations of life. It takes a deep awareness of the depth and height of the Lord's love, as manifested in the atoning sacrifice of Christ, to cultivate the capacity to experience godly sorrow (see 2 Corinthians 4:9-11) and thereby the strength and courage to make proper confession.

Another major challenge of life is that of *service*. We could halt the necessary growth process by achieving a certain level of righteousness in keeping the general commandments and leaving it at that. Because the culture would sufficiently reward such persons for their faithfulness, they might be tempted not to continually educate their conscience to receive personal commandments regarding the innumerable opportunities to serve which may be outside of the job definitions of their present duties, within either the family, the Church, or the world.

THE TESTS ARE PERSONAL

A missionary once asked President Harold B. Lee, "What is the most important commandment in the gospel?" President Lee thought for a moment and then gave this profound, personalized response to the missionary. "Elder, the most important commandment of all is the one you're having the greatest difficulty in living."

Such a response is applicable to any person at any level of

growth. Although you may have passed many of the tests which other people are yet struggling with, you have new tests still to pass. No one else may be aware of the test you are meeting, because it is not visible. It is clearly at a level that the culture itself does not deal with. Most people would not even be aware of it if you failed. It is a private test, a private struggle, perhaps the greatest battle of life, and it is taking place right there, today.

President Lee once defined courage as "the quality of every quality at its highest testing point." Such a statement is deeply motivating and inspiring, for each of us is aware of his own testing points and the great courage required to endure them in faithfulness.

For some members, the great test is simply that of staying true to the Church. Changing practices and policies affect people differently (according to their map or life center, of course), and some find in them the stimulus to question and challenge. Others, having delved deeply to make historical and doctrinal comparisons and evaluations, think they find the modern Church lacking. Inspired by the wrong spirit yet convinced they are right, they often end up in apostasy. This is not a new development. Many of the apostates from the Church in this and other dispensations left it actually thinking they were being guided by God. Many claimed that the Church deserted them rather than the other way around, that the prophet was a fallen prophet, and that they were following the Lord.

RELY ON THE PROPHET

But there is a marvelous check and balance system in the Lord's program. The Church of Jesus Christ of Latter-day Saints is literally God's church, and the President of the Church is truly God's prophet. God will never allow his prophet to lead the Church astray. To quote President Wilford Woodruff: "I say to Israel, the Lord will never permit me or any other man who stands as president of this Church to lead you astray. It is not in the program. It is not in the mind of God. If I were to attempt that the Lord would remove me out of my place, and so he will any other man who attempts to lead the children of men astray from the oracles of God and from their duty." (*The Discourses of Wilford Woodruff*, G. Homer Durham, compiler, Bookcraft, 1946, pages 212-13.)

It follows that any individual who is in opposition to the Lord's anointed prophet is also in opposition to the Lord, no matter how strongly he may feel he is directed and guided by the Lord. What is actually happening to the apostate is that he is being guided by another spirit. He is in violation of general commandments of the Lord. I am convinced that careful examination of his life will reveal transgression of one kind or another of these general commandments. In this situation, his personal commandments are being received not from the Lord but from some other source: the adversary. It is he who leads us to seek our own glory, who bloats our hungry souls with pride, revenge, hatred, strife, or jealousy.

WHAT VOICE DO YOU FOLLOW?

There is an excellent test to determine whether or not a person is on the right track to God/Christ-centeredness: Does he keep the general commandments, and is he consecrated to The Church of Jesus Christ of Latter-day Saints and submissive to its appointed apostles and prophets? This is not to say that any person, regardless of his calling, is infallible. It *is* to say that the Lord will not allow his church to be led astray. A good criterion for measuring our faithfulness and our desire for harmony with the Father and the Son is our level of obedience to Church authorities and gospel principles.

But many individuals are in harmony with the general commandments and teachings of the leaders of the Church and yet are not God-centered. The questions every individual must ask himself are: "What voice do I follow? What controls me? What directs me?" The answers to these questions will indicate what is at the center of that person's life.

For instance, say it is fast Sunday and you can feel hunger pains. Through your conscience the Lord directs you to fast.

AN EXAMPLE ILLUSTRATING
THE FOUR INTERLOCKING PROCESSES
IN BECOMING DIVINELY CENTERED

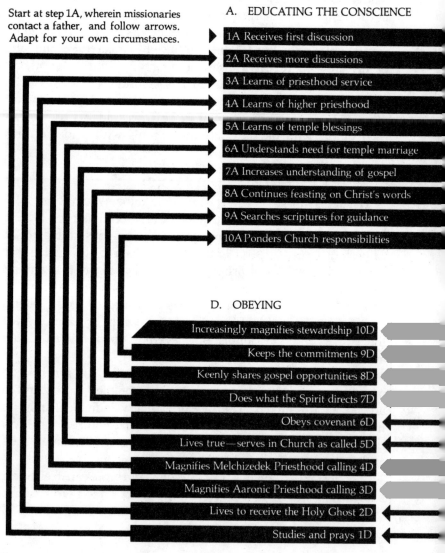

Start at step 1A, wherein missionaries contact a father, and follow arrows. Adapt for your own circumstances.

A. EDUCATING THE CONSCIENCE

1A Receives first discussion
2A Receives more discussions
3A Learns of priesthood service
4A Learns of higher priesthood
5A Learns of temple blessings
6A Understands need for temple marriage
7A Increases understanding of gospel
8A Continues feasting on Christ's words
9A Searches scriptures for guidance
10A Ponders Church responsibilities

D. OBEYING

Increasingly magnifies stewardship 10D
Keeps the commitments 9D
Keenly shares gospel opportunities 8D
Does what the Spirit directs 7D
Obeys covenant 6D
Lives true—serves in Church as called 5D
Magnifies Melchizedek Priesthood calling 4D
Magnifies Aaronic Priesthood calling 3D
Lives to receive the Holy Ghost 2D
Studies and prays 1D

"For behold, thus saith the Lord God: I will give unto the children of men line upon line, precept upon precept, here a little and there a little; and blessed are those who hearken unto my precepts, and lend an ear unto my counsel, for they shall learn wisdom; for unto him that receiveth I will give more; and from them that shall say, We have enough, from them shall be taken away even that which they have."

2 Nephi 28:30

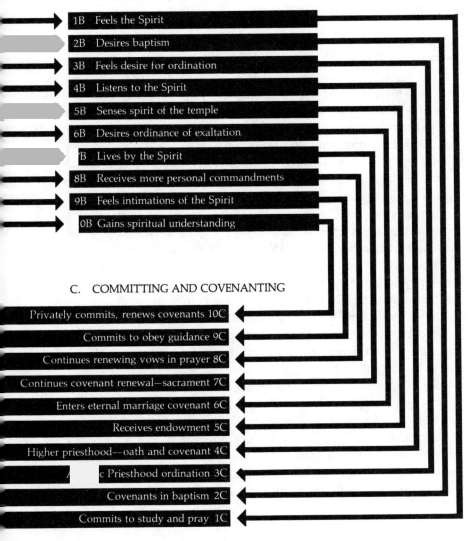

B. LISTENING AND HEARING

1B Feels the Spirit

2B Desires baptism

3B Feels desire for ordination

4B Listens to the Spirit

5B Senses spirit of the temple

6B Desires ordinance of exaltation

'B Lives by the Spirit

8B Receives more personal commandments

9B Feels intimations of the Spirit

0B Gains spiritual understanding

C. COMMITTING AND COVENANTING

Privately commits, renews covenants 10C

Commits to obey guidance 9C

Continues renewing vows in prayer 8C

Continues covenant renewal—sacrament 7C

Enters eternal marriage covenant 6C

Receives endowment 5C

Higher priesthood—oath and covenant 4C

c Priesthood ordination 3C

Covenants in baptism 2C

Commits to study and pray 1C

> We simply can't repent of our sins unless we repent of sinning. Unless we change our life-style by rooting out of our nature these deeply embedded habits and dispositions, we will continue on in a self-deceiving circular process of making and breaking resolutions to change and improve.

Your stomach directs you to eat. Which voice do you follow?

Take another example. It is late at night and you are very tired and fatigued, but the Lord, through your conscience, directs you to have meaningful prayer. Your body directs you to ration-alize away the need for meaningful prayer and just go to sleep. Again, which prompting do you follow?

Take a situation in which your curiosity directs you to go to a movie which is not appropriate for a Latter-day Saint. Which voice do you follow? What controls you?

Or let's say that someone behaves offensively toward you. Your pride directs you to return evil for evil, to defend yourself and offend the other person. Which voice do you follow?

You are a parent. One of your children is disobedient, causing you great embarrassment in public. Your pride directs you to "cut the child low," to overpower him through embar-rassment, belittlement, and intimidation. Your conscience directs you to be patient and understanding, to calmly carry out the agreed-upon consequences in a kind but firm manner. Which voice do you follow?

Suppose you followed the voice of pride and overreacted against your child. Your pride would then guide you to defend yourself and to justify yourself in the name of the child's dis-obedience. Or your conscience might direct you to acknowledge your overreaction and apologize for it. Suppose you again follow your pride and justify your overreaction, refusing to apologize; but you confess your own sin just before taking the sacrament.

You sense that you should make reconciliation with your child in the spirit of humility and contrition before you partake of the emblems, but your social pride inspires you to partake regardless of your need for repentance.

Do you give the same time and effort to preparing your family home evening as you do to preparing your priesthood, Relief Society, or Sunday School lesson?

This kind of analysis can go on and on. All of us are confronted daily with temptations to follow voices other than the voice of conscience. That voice is really an "upward temptation" — the "enticings of the Holy Spirit" (Mosiah 3:19).

THE POWER OF FASTING

We all face particularly stubborn problems or habits so deeply embedded that our usually successful approaches, such as prayer and willpower alone, simply don't budge them. "This kind goeth not out but by prayer and fasting" (Matthew 17:21). These were the Savior's words to his disciples who wondered why they could not cast an evil spirit out of a child. They had previously been given the necessary authority, but they could not evoke the necessary power on this occasion.

As an example of intractable habits, we may be lazy or selfish or cowardly or prideful or bad tempered or impure or irreverent or whatever, and from time to time temporarily feel sorry and repentant over the unhappy consequences that follow, but these habits and tendencies may still persist.

Unless we change our life-style by rooting out of our nature these deeply embedded habits and dispositions, we will continue on in a self-deceiving circular process of making and breaking resolutions to change and improve. In other words, *we need to change our method of changing ourselves.* We need a power source to help us, one which is stronger and more penetrating than the strength and depth of these habits.

Some of the material under the heading "The Power of Fasting" was contained in an article by the author that was first published in the *Ensign,* and is used by permission.

God is that power source, and fasting is one practice that, as I have found for myself, helps immeasurably to open up and release those divine powers within our nature. As was said of the people of Nephi:

> Nevertheless they did fast and pray oft, and did wax stronger and stronger in their humility, and firmer and firmer in the faith of Christ, unto the filling their souls with joy and consolation, yea, even to the purifying and the sanctification of their hearts, which sanctification cometh because of their yielding their hearts unto God. (Helaman 3:35.)

THREE WAYS FASTING HELPS

I see this as happening in three ways. *First,* voluntarily going without food and water is a very physical, very concrete practice. It represents a break in an eating life-style itself. In this way we take charge of our own appetites, which in my opinion is a first step in mastering our passions and in placing our own spirit under the direct influence of the Holy Spirit. (After forty days of fasting, the first temptation Christ received from Satan was to an appetite.) The body is a good servant but a bad master. President David O. McKay continually taught self-mastery as a characteristic of true spirituality — "Spirituality is a consciousness of victory over self. . . ."

Second, fasting humbles and subdues the spirit. It makes us aware of our limitations, of our dependency on the Creator and his creations (food) for life itself. As the Holy Spirit works on us, we become more sensitive to the unseen realities; our awareness of our shortcomings and true spiritual nature enlarges; our sense of need for a Savior and faith in Christ as our Savior increases; our desire and ability to fully confess and repent deepens.

Third, these spiritual endeavors will focus and unify our thinking and feeling so that we can renew our covenant relationship with the Lord. When our mind is truly made up, we keep the promises we make. The sacrament is the ordained divine channel to express these promises and commitments — to renew our covenants. We witness or promise to take upon ourselves his name and to keep his commandments, which would include both his general commandments given through his prophets, ancient and modern, and his personal commandments given through his Holy Spirit to our conscience.

As we promise or covenant, he covenants. He promises us his Spirit, which is the key to every good thing in time and in eternity. Such a releasing of the powers of godliness into our lives through faith in Christ, repentance through his power, and covenant making with him enables us to overcome deeply embedded habits and dispositions and to gradually become a partaker of the divine nature. I believe that just as the Lord told his disciples that certain spiritual blessings can only come by a faith born of both prayer and fasting, so also certain malignant sinful dispositions and cancerous habit patterns can only be broken by a faith and faithfulness inspired by prayer and fasting.

HOW TO FAST

Just as we can be, in one sense, active in the Church without being active in the gospel, so also can we fast and not receive the above-mentioned benefits. I offer four suggestions regarding how to fast.

1. *With divine purpose and spirit.* Prepare to fast. Pray for the true spirit of fasting. Think about your spiritual needs and/or about others' physical and spiritual needs. Fast in order to come unto Christ; to be more like him. Fast from worldliness as well as food, from anything which causes static in your spirit.

2. *With prayer.* Prayer is two-way communication. Listen as well as express. Be very open and receptive to the still, small voice. Conduct a dialogue. Don't counsel the Lord how to bless you as much as desire to take counsel from him.

3. *Feast.* Feast (savor, treasure, meditate, adore, worship) on his love and his word. Prayerfully ponder the scriptures when you otherwise would be eating, or at other appropriate times.

4. *Serve.* In various ways get outside yourself in love. (Study Isaiah 58.) Give of yourself. Pay a generous fast offering to the poor through the Lord's priesthood channel. Bear testimony at the fast and testimony meeting. Express love and appreciation to your loved ones, leaders, and teachers. Forgive. Make reconciliation with any offended or offenders.

Remember—getting bogged down in a lot of introspective self-analysis will serve to undermine the spirit of resolute and devoted service.

SOME CAUTIONS

There are one or two cautions to be observed. First, *avoid extremism in fasting.* Sometimes it's easier to fast than to eat wisely and moderately—we fill up with a spirit of martyrdom. Sometimes it's easier to try to work on our relationship with God through fasting, prayer, and scripture study than to love and serve his other children or to repair broken human relations. Just as we can sometimes avoid confronting our real spiritual need to change and repent by intellectualizing about gospel principles, so also can we escape dealing with pulsating spiritual needs and service hungers by theatrical and/or excessive fasting. Unless otherwise directed by the Spirit to fast more frequently, we can gain the blessings of fasting by following the Church practice of fasting for twenty-four hours a month on the designated fast Sunday.

Second, *don't take fasting lightly.* Fasting and prayer with the Spirit can literally release the powers of heaven in our lives. We shouldn't toy and play games with it or it will turn to our condemnation and then we will harden to the principle.

When we really want to change or to undertake any worthy project requiring fasting and prayer to obtain God's help, we had better be prepared for things to happen according to our needs and his will in his time rather than to our wants and our will in our time. We may be given very difficult and trying experiences, but if we will stay true and faithful, all things will work together for our good, and we will come to a divine perspective and see how the Lord has been fashioning us to his service, has been making us "fishers of men."

Finally, let us remember that anytime we break our addiction to anything, whether it be drugs, certain foods, or habits, we will go through a painful withdrawal process. For instance, when we fast, we may experience headaches caused by withdrawing from certain foods to which we have become addicted. We then may become edgy and irritable and lose the whole spirit of the fast. But if we are aware of the forces at play and "stick with it," we can experience a degree of physical cleansing and breaking of the food addiction in addition to conquering a natural bad temper.

In my opinion, these physical illustrations have many spiritual parallels. We should never abort second-birth processes because of the labor pains.

THE POWER OF TESTIMONY

I have cause to believe that there is one gospel activity in life which both integrates and expresses all four processes discussed in this chapter and the previous one—learning, listening, covenanting, and doing. That activity is testifying. Elder Boyd K. Packer said: "The spirit and testimony of Christ will come to you for the most part *when*, and remain with you only *if*, you share it. In that process is the very essence of the gospel. . . . It is by giving it away freely that it becomes yours." (Seminar for New Mission Presidents, June 25, 1982.)

The very act of sincerely bearing a testimony under the influence of the Holy Spirit accelerates the education of the conscience and recommits us to the truths testified of. When we testify we bear witness. When we witness we promise. When we promise we commit or covenant. The words, as well as the processes, are almost interchangeable, almost synonymous in a spiritual sense—testify, witness, promise, commit, covenant; fulfilling the commandments.

Sometimes I am shocked by the power of a testimony. After all, it's only a few more words—or so it seems. But the power of those words!

I remember speaking on communication to a large group of students and faculty at a college in Toronto, Canada, and near

---

Some of the material under the heading "The Power of Testimony" was contained in an article by the author that was first published in the *Ensign*, and is used by permission.

> **When we are anchored and invulnerable down deep, we can be open and vulnerable on the surface of our lives by flowing with changes, loving unconditionally, and viewing life as a marvelously exciting adventure.**

the end of my speech I felt impressed to bear testimony of the principle of ultimate justice. Several came up afterwards, visibly shaken, expressing both the hope to believe and the fear of being so vulnerable in such a belief. They wanted further explanation. I was stunned by the reaction to one sentence of certain conviction. "Faith cometh by hearing. . . ." (Romans 10:17.)

Another time, speaking to the missionaries at the Missionary Training Center, I suddenly felt impressed to testify of the intrinsic worth of each person there; that there was no need for anyone to compare himself with another, that the Lord knew and loved each one as a separate person and had special guidance and power to give in helping each one move on to the next step, and so on. Afterwards, several asked me to bear that exact testimony again and to give more explanation, almost as if they desperately wanted to believe it. One of them was almost overcome with a feeling of relief and joy.

I remember many times—after teaching the gospel to investigators in the mission field, or to members in church meetings, or to counselees in my office, or to strangers on planes—feeling impressed to witness of the reality and power of the Savior, and on doing so, feeling like a conduit of light and love and power. Though it seems so right and normal at the time, afterwards I am often amazed at the almost miraculous effect of one soul bearing testimony to another through the Spirit.

The testimonies of others have a similar effect on me. I remember one time determining to break a selfish pattern of living—feeling active in the Church but inactive in the gospel—by deeply covenanting with the Lord at the very time President Harold B. Lee bore his testimony of the Redeemer of the world at the funeral of a dear friend. His testimony opened up the deepest recesses of my soul, almost as rapid speed photography pictures a rose unfolding, and "without compulsory means" (straining or even willing), I could feel the power and efficacy of that covenant for many weeks.

COMMUNICATION, AWARENESS, ANCHORAGE

Why is testimony bearing so powerful, so needful? At least three reasons come to mind. *First*, testifying is the purest form of human communication. The deepest meaning, the deepest conviction of one's soul, is being given to another through the medium of the Holy Spirit. "Wherefore, he that preacheth and he that receiveth, understand one another, and both are edified and rejoice together" (D&C 50:22). The Lord wants his children to hear and receive divine truths so that they might live by them and receive more.

Second, testimony bearing helps us to feel less of a "stranger here." Undoubtedly, we knew many eternal truths before coming here, and "pure testimony" thins the veil sufficiently to remind and recover, to plant premortal spirit knowledge into our flesh, to penetrate the mortal overlay with eternal awareness. To a degree, we feel "home."

President Joseph F. Smith taught: "All those salient truths which come home so forcibly to the head and heart seem but the awakening of the memories of the spirit." He then asked: "Can we know anything here that we did not know before we came?" (*Gospel Doctrine*, Deseret Book Co., 1966, page 13.)

Third, people hunger for something fixed and certain in the universe; something they can deeply believe in and depend on. Perhaps this is true more now than ever before, because virtually everything in the world is changing, including the speed of change itself. There *must* be something changeless that is true! When we are anchored and invulnerable down deep, we can be open and vulnerable on the surface of our lives by flowing with changes, loving unconditionally, and viewing life as a marvelously exciting adventure. Otherwise, without such anchorage, without a changeless invulnerability down deep, we need to fabricate some idea of reality for a modicum of security to keep us from being vulnerable to all the unpredictable forces which play upon our lives.

Such mental-emotional defenses take many forms, including (1) categorizing and prejudging people, places, and ideas, so as to be protected from the new and unexpected (prejudice); (2) expecting nothing, so as to not be disappointed (hopelessness); (3) believing nothing, so as to not be responsible (cynicism); (4) communicating in sarcasm and cutting humor, so as not to be emotionally exposed and vulnerable (lightminded, guileful); (5) waiting on others to love us first, and even then inpugning the motive of one taking such initiative (doubting, fearing). On the other hand, a genuine testimony provides its own armor, making such defenses unnecessary. (Study D&C 27:15-18.)

WAYS TO BEAR TESTIMONY

There are probably as many answers to the question "How shall we bear testimony?" as there are people. But there are some underlying ideas which may have general value. Consider ten guidelines.

1. *Bear testimony by and through the Spirit.* Timing is often critical. By cultivating the gift of the Spirit called discernment, by praying specifically for the spirit of a testimony, and by being open and receptive, we will come to know when and how to bear testimony. I feel it is generally inappropriate, even destructive, to bear testimony when the Spirit is not present, when love is not felt, when the teaching has been vague and confusing, and when our personal lives clearly do not comport with our words.

"And the Spirit shall be given unto you by the prayer of faith; and if ye receive not the Spirit ye shall not teach" (D&C 42:14). "Ye shall not teach" is as descriptive as it is prescriptive.

Wise member-missionary friendshipping and teaching shows an inspired balance between formal and informal testimony as well as between the mind (intellect), the heart (feeling), and the soul. While a testimony certainly contains emotions, it is more than emotions and we need to guard against unsuitable and excessive emotionalism, which can be self-seeking and affected. A testimony confirms and puts the capstone on our teachings. It doesn't substitute for them.

Neither, I suggest, should we overdo formal testimony by saying "I know," "I know," every few minutes. This too can gradually lose its impact.

We bear our testimony informally by the tone of belief in our gospel principle explanations and in the amount of respect we show to others, particularly when things get rough. In this connection, consider John 13:34-35.

Someone wisely observed, "He that is good with a hammer tends to think everything is a nail." In testimony bearing in particular we must not suffer this illusion.

2. *Testify when you feel full of love.* Showing love when teaching gospel truths is a form of testimony in itself. People often cannot receive more light and truth except on condition of their being loved in various ways, including our teaching and testifying, praying with and for them, encouraging and affirming them, empathizing with and understanding them, and walking with and sacrificing for them. Many parents, teachers, and member missionaries who do the first three and not the last two would be amazed at the power of all five together.

In working with students, I find that many who have experienced human abuse, hypocrisy, exploitation and manipulation by "active" testifying fathers and various authority persons come to distrust testimony altogether. In such a situation, testifiers become "guilty by association." One student protected himself from further wounding by labeling formal testimony-bearing as prime evidence of weakness, self-deceiving emotionalism, and meaningless social ritual.

Righteous use of authority comes from character, not position. A testimony from an authority person who uses persuasion, kindness, gentleness, love unfeigned, is many times more powerful and influential than from one who, lacking strength inside, borrows it from his position.

3. *Testify to people, not at them.* The purpose is to bless people, not to blast them. Even in those instances in scriptural

> **Testimony of the true identity, worth, potential, and agency of another serves in one sense like a patriarchal blessing or an ordinance: it gives a person a divine definition of himself. Such a self-view energizes hope and courage in contrast to the fear and insecurity and self-doubting which naturally flow from a social or cultural self-definition.**

history in which pure testimony was being borne against people (see Alma 4:19), the ultimate motive was to call (shake) to repentance and to bless, not to condemn.

4. Occasionally, as moved by the Spirit, *testify of the identity and worth of the other person* and of his or her ability, with God's help, to accept and obey the truth given and of the power or freedom to choose to obey. As a mission president, I wrote a letter to each new convert asking for a letter in return outlining the conversion process, including the problems and obstacles confronted. About half of the responses indicated that from the beginning they never doubted the truth of the message. Rather, they doubted themselves. They doubted their worth or their ability to live the truth.

When people become aware of their own eternal identity, however, of their godly potential and of their agency or power to choose their response to any set of circumstances, a vital something is unlocked and released. This happened to Moses on the Mount, as discussed in chapter 6.

Testimony of the true identity, worth, potential, and agency of another serves in one sense like a patriarchal blessing or an ordinance: it gives a person a divine definition of himself. Such a self-view energizes hope and courage in contrast to the fear and insecurity of self-doubting which naturally flow from a social or cultural self-definition.

5. *Testify, as impressed, of how testimony comes.* Testimony comes from the Holy Ghost to one who is open and seeking and

who is *trying to be true to the truth already given*. If they are not informed to the contrary, many people carry the cultural notion that the way to truth is intellectual, which is part of it but certainly not the important part. People will come to know the truth to the degree that they are true to the truth. To find truth, we must set out to *be true*. I remember many times teaching people who claimed to be doubting the Joseph Smith story but who were really having problems with tobacco or tea or some other practice. I told them that if they would live the Word of Wisdom (or whatever the Spirit indicated was the problem) they would receive a hidden treasure of knowledge, including a testimony of the prophetic calling of Joseph Smith. ("Ye receive no witness until after the trial of your faith" — Ether 12:6.) Many of them immediately acknowledged the real problem, then later conquered the habit and experienced a fulfillment of the promise.

6. Occasionally, *identify the Spirit when you sense it and feel others sense it also*. Otherwise, many get a wrong idea of what to expect and will continue looking through a false expectation lens for the more dramatic and mystical, all the while "looking beyond the mark" (Jacob 4:14), discounting the sweetness, the mind-heart harmony and the quiet reassuring peace of the still, small voice. You can say something like, "My friend, the sweet, peaceful spirit you and I both feel right now is the same spirit you will feel when you prayerfully ponder the Book of Mormon."

7. *Learn to pause as you testify*, to give time for the other person to think and to feel. Sometimes we need to stop our restless minds, to jump off the rushing, almost hypnotizing treadmill of life, to pause for breath and perspective and to get our bearings. I remember watching Elder Boyd K. Packer, as president of the New England Mission, train his missionaries to slow down their presentations, and particularly to pause when testifying, in order to give room for the Spirit to work its matchless converting miracle. He said: "Be calm. Be believing. Look them in the eye. Then testify."

"Be still and know that I am God" (D&C 101:16).

8. *Use testifying words and expressions which can be under-*

stood by the hearers. This is especially important when speaking to nonmembers. So many communication obstacles are unnecessarily created by Mormon jargon—common Church vocabulary that others might not understand. Just as we wouldn't hesitate to learn another language, we shouldn't hesitate to work within the vocabularies of others to communicate our meanings. I have found in speaking to various non-LDS groups in different cultures that we can teach and testify of many gospel principles if we are careful in selecting words which carry our meaning but come from their experience and frame of mind. I suggest that the communication problem is more often one of different word definitions than one of genuine disagreement. In parabolic teaching and plain speaking, the Savior is the perfect model for us here.

"For my soul delighteth in plainness; for after this manner doth the Lord God work among the children of men. For the Lord God giveth light unto the understanding; for he speaketh unto men according to their language, unto their understanding." (2 Nephi 31:3.) If there is any obstacle, it should be in another's spirit, not in ours, or in our language.

9. *Prepare to testify.* Specifically pray for the spirit of testimony. Pray for courage to express testimony. Humble yourself in fasting and repentance. It is instructive that the monthly fast and testimony meeting is *preceded* by fasting and renewing our covenants. Also, bearing testimony in such a meeting is more than expressing appreciation, as beautiful and appropriate as that may be. It involves taking a stand, declaring one's position, expressing the soul's deepest convictions born of the Spirit regarding the divine sonship of Jesus Christ, the prophetic calling of Joseph Smith and his successors, and the divinity of the Church.

The way we live, particularly under strain and threat, is our clearest testimony. Over time it reflects what we really believe. If it is in harmony with what we say we believe, the Lord will use us and bear testimony through us in some way to every person we meet.

10. *Testify.* Testify often. Monthly. Weekly. Daily. Both formally and informally. Like a muscle, testimony will grow through sincere use. "Use it or lose it."

Relatively few of the children of our Father in Heaven possess testimonies of those precious truths and powers which alone can heal individuals and families and even nations. If the leavening influence of these few is compromised because of impurity or the fear of men, how will the Lord do his vital work? "But if the salt shall lose its savor, wherewith shall the earth be salted?" (3 Nephi 12:13.)

> But with some I am not well pleased, for they will not open their mouths, but they hide the talent which I have given unto them, because of the fear of man. Wo unto such, for mine anger is kindled against them.
>
> And it shall come to pass if they are not more faithful unto me, it shall be taken away, even that which they have. (D&C 60:2-3.)

A LIFE-CHANGING EXPERIENCE

In the spirit of testimony and in the hope that it may help others, I now want to share in its outlines a personal experience that went deeper than I can express it and is very sacred to me.

During my second mission I came to realize, more than ever before, the transcendent importance of the Atonement. I could see how this supreme sacrifice gave power and efficacy to every gospel principle, teaching, law, and ordinance.

I desired to increase my understanding of it, particularly to more fully understand the nature, depth, and extent of the divine love, in both the Father and the Son, that motivated it. For several months I prayerfully studied the scriptures on this matter. Not expecting any big or unusual thing, I found increased enlightenment and understanding and my soul was satisfied. But I persisted in my study and pondering and asking, finding that the more I knew and felt the more light I desired.

After touring the mission for a few days on one occasion, I was returning from Portadown to the mission home in Belfast in the early evening. I was most anxious to get home as soon as possible so that I could see my two little daughters Cynthia and Maria before they went to bed.

I parked the car, and without unpacking it I anxiously dashed upstairs to their bedroom and found them fast asleep. My wife had stepped out for a few minutes, and I was alone with my thoughts and feelings. I was surprised to sense that I was not disappointed after such an effort, but rather felt full of spiritual desire. Even now I can't describe the nature of this desire, except to say I enjoyed the solitude and spirit in the girls' room and the beautiful, tranquil scene outside. I wanted to stay there, to look at them in their cots—so beautiful and peaceful. The whole mission home seemed unusually quiet. I reveled in the peace and the scene and the feeling and wanted to stay there.

I did stay. For a long time I sat and looked and felt. I felt to pray. I felt to bless my daughters and to pray for them. I knelt down and expressed my gratitude. The spirit of prayer came and I began to feel an increase of gratitude and of love. These feelings continued until I couldn't express them anymore. Suffice it to say that the feeling of love began to spread out from that room to everyone who lived or worked in the mission home, then to all the missionaries, then to the Saints in Ireland, and eventually to all the people of Ireland. This love seemed to comprehend everyone individually. I simply haven't words to describe it. But I loved everybody as I had never loved before, or perhaps since, and this love seemed to possess the characteristic of knowledge.

I came to feel that I was tasting a part of the kind of love that lay behind the Atonement. I felt it was charity, the pure love of Christ, and that such a supernal love was a gift of God. I felt it was in part at least an answer to my prayers for understanding of the Atonement. Moroni 7:48 became precious to me:

> Wherefore, my beloved brethren, pray unto the Father with all the energy of heart, that ye may be filled with this love, which he hath bestowed upon all who are true followers of his Son, Jesus Christ; that ye may become the sons of God; that when he shall appear we shall be like him, for we shall see him as he is; that we may have this hope; that we may be purified even as he is pure.

For many days the spirit of that experience stayed with me without any conscious effort on my part. And to this day I vividly remember the scene and the feeling. It has given to me a love standard and a realization that charity is truly a *gift* of God.

I have met people like President David O. McKay, President Spencer W. Kimball, Elder Mark E. Petersen, and Elder LeGrand Richards, who seem constantly to emanate this love. I can see why it is called the greatest thing in the world.

I have hesitated to share this experience but I now feel to do so in love and as my personal testimony of the Atonement and the power of love as life's central motivation.

Someone once remarked that it takes a lifetime to turn a Mormon into a Latter-day Saint. No amount of Church activity or meeting-going can compensate for the character growth and development required to become a Christlike person. However, if used right, that Church activity and meeting-going can be one of the primary sources of opportunity to give Christlike service and thereby to become more like him. For he is our model. The presence and nature of our Father in Heaven is our goal and destiny. His word is our map to bring us there. And only by coming unto him with full purpose of heart can we see him as he is. In his infinite mirror, too, we shall see ourselves as we are potentially and as we finally will be if we are faithful—with his image engraved on our countenances (see Alma 5:14, 19).

> Behold, what manner of love the Father hath bestowed upon us, that we should be called the sons of God: therefore the world knoweth us not, because it knew him not.
>
> Beloved, now are we the sons of God, and it doth not yet appear what we shall be: but we know that, when he shall appear, we shall be like him; for we shall see him as he is.
>
> And every man that hath this hope in him purifieth himself, even as he is pure. (1 John 3:1-3.)

(See chapter 1 for the purpose of this picture.)

The Obedience Path

Chapter 9

> *Verily, thus saith the Lord: It shall come*
> *to pass that every soul who forsaketh his sins*
> *and cometh unto me, and calleth on my*
> *name, and obeyeth my voice, and keepeth*
> *my commandments, shall see my face*
> *and know that I am. (D&C 93:1.)*

There is a common thread running through every dispensation of the gospel. It is the exhortation of God to his children to keep his commandments. In the Bible it is emphasized time and time again, either explicitly or implicitly. In the Book of Mormon it is the explicit central theme. It is taught more than any other single theme in all of holy writ, where it has been the burden of every prophet's message.

The Prophet Joseph Smith taught: "Happiness is the object and design of our existence; and will be the end thereof, if we pursue the path that leads to it; and this path is virtue, uprightness, faithfulness, holiness, and keeping all the commandments of God. But we cannot keep all the commandments without first knowing them, and we cannot expect to know all, or more than we now know, unless we comply with or keep those we have already received." (*TPJS*, pages 255-56.) At another time he said, in effect, "I follow one rule. When the Lord commands, I do it!"

In this last dispensation, every prophet has reiterated this theme again and again. As examples, at the October 1970 General Conference President Joseph Fielding Smith noted: "For more than sixty years I have preached the gospel in the stakes and missions of the Church—pleading with the Saints to keep the commandments" (*Improvement Era*, December 1970, page 2). When he died and was succeeded by President Harold B. Lee, in the first press conference after the First Presidency was reorganized, the new President was asked the question, "If you had one message to give to the world, what would it be?" President Lee answered, "Keep the commandments." His successor, President Spencer W. Kimball, gave the same kind of response in *his* first press conference.

Why keep the commandments? Why is this the undergirding, overarching theme? It is because it is at once the most universally needed yet the most individualistic instruction possible. It expresses the essence of the God-centered life. And it acknowledges God, the giver of the commandments, and the necessity for all of us, his children, to obey him.

Faith in God and obedience to God are unpopular ideas in many quarters today. To the sophisticated, materialistic, scientific world both ideas seem to demean man, to reduce his potentiality, to limit him. This is the result of the inaccurate, distorted map in the minds and hearts of men, the fruit of centuries of apostasy which the restoration of the gospel is designed to correct. Such a warped map gets just about everything wrong, including God, man, man's relationship to God, the role of Christ the Savior, and the purpose and meaning of life. Naturally, it also produces a warped understanding of what the commandments are and what obedience is.

LAW THE BASIS OF FREEDOM

R ather than restricting or binding man, as the incorrect map suggests, obeying God's commandments liberates man, releases his divine potentialities. To continue the map metaphor, the commandments represent the roads leading to the desired destination. Those roads have always been there; they were not artificially added as a contrived set of rules or procedures which people must comply with so as to give glory or aggrandizement to their Creator. Instead, they are the very laws of nature — eternal nature — which, when built into the fiber of the immortal spirit and the mortal flesh, enable the individual personality to grow and develop until eventually he can become like his Father in Heaven.

When man discovered the natural laws of gravity and electricity, he found the forces which would unleash power for man, multiply his abilities, and open up ways for him to transcend his own finite capacities to reshape his world. As a result he can communicate instantly over long distances, travel rapidly, restore and retrieve almost instantly vast amounts of information, and in a thousand ways change the nature of his daily existence — lighten his loads, develop his capacities, enlarge his understanding, and enhance his capacity for service and leisure and joy. In other words, obedience to the natural laws discovered by science enables man to save himself temporally.

Obedience to law is the principle of freedom in every field of endeavor. *Freedom is born of obedience;* the freedom to play the piano comes entirely from obedience to the laws of piano playing, from disciplined practicing, from sacrificing alternative activities to cultivate this talent. This is true in developing any talent, any skill, and virtually everyone accepts it as a fact. Why, then, is there resistance to the concept of obeying God, to keeping the commandments in the moral and spiritual realms? It comes primarily, I suggest, from a warped, distorted map.

GENERAL COMMANDMENTS, PERSONAL COMMANDMENTS

There are two kinds of commandments, the general commandments and the personal commandments. *The general commandments are given by God through prophets for the benefit of all of his children.* They are the natural laws of growth and happiness for individuals, of stability and freedom for nations. Obedience to them will increase the likelihood of receiving personal commandments. *Personal commandments are given by God through his Holy Spirit to his individual children.* They are individualized, that is, they are tailor-made to each individual in his or her particular situation. The general commandments come in the form of principles or laws which have general application to mankind or to a certain class or group of people. The personal commandments come in the form of practices or specific things to do, specific actions which are largely based upon the general commandments.

To illustrate, consider three men walking down the street on a beautiful Sunday morning. The first person is a member of the Restored Church and is feeling considerable guilt in not attending sacrament meeting. The second person is not a member of the Church and, having no baptismal covenant to renew, feels no guilt in not attending sacrament meeting, but he experiences deep guilt from neglecting his wife and children. The third person is a member of the Church and a faithful family man and is on his way to sacrament meeting. But on the way he is experiencing twinges of guilt because he isn't following the whisperings of the Spirit telling him to go and see a family he is assigned to as a home teacher, a family that desperately needs him *right now* although he isn't aware of the reason why.

The first two men illustrate two different kinds of general commandments. The Mormon had committed himself to be a faithful sacrament meeting attender. This is a general commandment which he accepted, and it has become part of his conscience or divine expectation. The non-Mormon has made no such covenant, therefore he feels no guilt whatsoever regarding sacrament meeting attendance. But he is aware of the commandments of God to properly take care of his family; his conscience has been educated to that extent, and consequently it communicates guilt to him. The third person is receiving a specific direction regarding an immediate need in his stewardship, but he is setting it aside in the process of keeping the general commandment to attend sacrament meeting. He rationalizes away his guilt in the name of sacrament meeting attendance, a meeting wherein the deeper principle is taught of magnifying one's priesthood by listening and responding to the whisperings of the Holy Spirit in doing the work of God in the world.

GUILT A DIVINE INDICATOR

Guilt *is a divine indicator of our doing wrong.* It serves to reprove man, to correct him. The opposite of guilt is a sense of divine approval or approbation, which gives a sense of peace about what one is doing. It confirms the rightness of a person's actions or thoughts. The conveying of both guilt and divine approbation are among the functions of the Holy Spirit. The nonmember of the Church has the Spirit of Jesus Christ or the divine spark within, which will guide him as to right and wrong. It speaks through his conscience, the still, small voice within. If he obeys it, it will eventually lead him to the covenant gospel.

> For the word of the Lord is truth, and whatsoever is truth is light, and whatsoever is light is Spirit, even the Spirit of Jesus Christ.
> And the Spirit giveth light to every man that cometh into the world; and the Spirit enlighteneth every man through the world, that hearkeneth to the voice of the Spirit.
> And every one that hearkeneth to the voice of the Spirit cometh unto God, even the Father.
> And the Father teacheth him of the covenant which he has renewed and confirmed upon you, which is confirmed upon you for your sakes, and not for your sakes only, but for the sake of the whole world. (D&C 84:45-48.)

Divine guilt is a blessing of God. It comes from an accurate map. Social guilt comes from an inaccurate map and therefore can distort and twist the natural growth processes. And social guilt is what many fine people are critical of when they feel that religion demeans, confines, and straightjackets man.

Consider what is implicitly contained in divine guilt: First, the obvious direction or correction which is being given. Second, the evidence of the potential for greater things, otherwise such direction would not be given. Third, love. It shows that the Lord cares. He says, "Whom I love I also chasten" (D&C 95:1). It is one of the clearest manifestations of our kinship to God that he corrects us through guilt. We don't discipline our neighbor's children, we discipline our own. This communicates that they are our children, that we love them and care for them enough to refrain from indulging them and instead to expect better from them.

PERSONAL COMMANDMENTS AND CONSCIENCE

L et's get back to the two types of commandments. One year, while studying the Book of Mormon from a behavioral vantage point, I was forcibly struck with an awareness of these two different kinds of commandments, general and personal. Again and again the Lord would say to the people, "You have not kept my commandments, therefore such-and-such has come upon you." Or, "You have kept my commandments, therefore, you have been led and protected and prospered." Yet when I examined the commandments he was speaking about, it appeared that often they were personal commandments and not general commandments at all. For instance, it didn't seem to me that in the early stages Laman and Lemuel were breaking general commandments, perhaps excepting the fifth of the Ten Commandments—about honoring father and mother—but rather personal commandments. Nephi, though, was keeping such commandments. The Lord told Nephi to go here and do this or that, and this situational directioning was called com- mandment. Yet the commandments were not for everyone.

This was a knowledge breakthrough for me, for I had always thought that the commandments of God basically involved the Ten Commandments (Exodus 20), the two general command- ments regarding love as given in the New Testament (Matthew 22:35-40), and the basic commandments explicit or implicit in a temple interview form. It was extremely enlightening to become aware of a whole new field of commandments called personal commandments, which are individualized, tailor-made to every person who has already been faithful to the general command- ments.

I was speaking on this subject once at a Ricks College devo- tional, attempting to point out the difference between general and personal commandments. Near the end of the speech, I asked the audience to be calm for a few moments and consult their consciences in relation to four different questions. The first question was, "What do I need to do to draw closer to the

It is extremely enlightening to become aware of a whole new field of commandments called personal commandments, which are individualized, tailor-made to every person who has already been faithful to the general commandments.

Lord?" I asked them to listen quietly to what their consciences said. I indicated that they would not hear it in their ears, but that they would feel or sense it inside and that it would probably be in terms of both general and personal commandments.

The second question was, "What do I need to do to be a better family member?" whether this meant being a son or daughter, brother or sister, husband or wife, father or mother. After a period of silence, I asked the third question: "What do I need to do to be a better member of the Church?" I asked the audience to think not only about their membership but also about any particular positions or responsibilities they held; and the brethren, about their priesthood activity and responsibility. After another minute of silence, I asked them the fourth question: "What should I do to be a better student here at Ricks College, to more fully take advantage of these educational opportunities afforded me?"

After another silence, I asked for a show of hands of those who were aware of things they needed to do in relation to these four questions, as prompted by their conscience. Almost everyone raised a hand. I then asked the question, "If you really did the things taught to you by your conscience, how many feel assured that pretty marvelous things would result?" Again, nearly everyone raised a hand. Then I asked the final question or questions: "What are we waiting for? Can we really receive more light and knowledge before we are true to the light and knowledge we have already been given? Would it not condemn us to receive more light and knowledge? Is it not a manifestation of the Lord's love for us that he gives us only that which we in our present capacity can understand and embrace?"

I went on to point out that we are uniquely blessed as Latter-day Saints with so much light and knowledge, all of it representing a whole new level of general revelation that pertains to those who have become covenant children of God. I added that on top of all the general commandments given to the world at large and the general commandments given to the Latter-day Saints is the privilege of receiving personal commandments or personal revelation and inspiration through the gift of the Holy Ghost.

SPIRIT'S COMMUNICATION SUPERIOR

Then I turned to some people near the front and asked, "If an angel of God were to come into this room and, standing in mid-air clothed in glory and light, should tell you the very things which your conscience told you a few moments ago, what would you think of that experience?" They responded that they would be overwhelmed by it. I asked them if each of them would record it in his journal or would begin a journal to record it. They nodded in the affirmative.

I then asked them: "Which would have been the greater revelation? the message from the angel or that from your conscience?" Sensing what I was leading up to, they opted for conscience. So I challenged them: "Do you really feel that? Look how easy it was to receive guidance from your conscience by simply consulting that conscience against gospel-oriented questions. And look how powerful and overwhelming and dramatic and awe-inspiring it would be to see an angel from the other side of the veil and have him give such a message. Now, which do you think would be the most powerful form of revelation?"

The Savior said to Thomas, "Be not faithless, but believing. . . . Because thou hast seen me, thou hast believed: blessed are they that have not seen, and yet have believed" (John 20:27, 29). Laman and Lemuel had plenty of opportunity to believe. They had an angel appear to them to shake them temporarily out of their sensate world into a consciousness of eternal realities. But they were changed neither before nor after the angel came, even though the experience temporarily stunned, subdued, and humbled them.

On the other hand, Nephi was capable of carrying on a communication through the Holy Ghost with his Father in Heaven and was so attuned to the Spirit, so sensitive, so aware, so familiar with it, that he could have a dialogue with the Lord regarding many issues he was facing in life. Consider the matter of his slaying Laban. Less sensitive, less spiritually minded persons would probably have required an angel to appear to them before following such instructions. Nephi was so spiritually minded, so sensitive, so capable of distinguishing between God's Spirit and other spirits, that he knew he was properly instructed when he was told to slay Laban. He knew it truly was better that one person perish than that a nation dwindle and perish in unbelief. (See 1 Nephi 4:10-18.)

SIMPLE PROCESS—NO DRAMATICS

After the Ricks College devotional, one young sister came up to me and said, "Brother Covey, can you tell me the difference between a heartburn and a burning in the heart?" She was really asking, "How do I know it is the Lord who is answering my prayers? How do I know that it's not just a combination of various psychological forces in myself? How can I distinguish between God's answers and other kinds of answers that come or voices I sense?" Many people ponder this question in its various guises.

I asked her in return, "When we had this little listening exercise, did you sense some things that you needed to do to improve your life?"

"Oh, yes, Brother Covey," she replied. "I know so many things I need to do under all four questions."

I said, "Well, then, Sister, just forget your question and start doing those things; and as you do, you will find that your conscience will gradually become educated. You will become more familiar with the voice that speaks to you, and that will be the answer to your question."

At this she grew rather dejected, and I said, "You didn't like that answer, did you?"

"No," she said.

"Why not?"

"Because I have no excuse anymore."

She was in effect trying to escape from the need to deal with the mundane, simple directives from her conscience by giving preference to some big academic question, some intellectual inquiry regarding how God answers prayers.

A year later I spoke at another devotional on another topic and the same girl came up to me afterwards. When she mentioned the heartburn question I immediately remembered our entire conversation, and I asked her how things were going. She said, "The greatest thing I have ever learned in my life is that all things will work together for my good if I will simply educate and obey my conscience."

I asked her to tell me more of her story. She gave me quite a long account of how she had struggled with my answer but had come to realize that she should immediately begin to do some of the things her conscience directed her to do. Then she seriously did those things. I pushed her a little and said, "Do you mind if I ask you what those things were?"

"Not at all," she said. "For instance, I began to pray meaningfully every day. I started to study the scriptures in earnest. I made reconciliation with some people I had had bad feelings about. I was more pleasant and helpful at home." She went on at length in this vein. She recounted the innumerable blessings that had come into her life because of her efforts to be obedient.

A year later I was speaking at a Know Your Religion lecture in Fresno, California, and she was there. "Would you be interested in the third installment?" she asked. She then related additional marvelous things that had taken place, glorious blessings that she had received. Not long after this she phoned me and asked me to speak at her missionary farewell. And she went on to have a glorious mission experience.

One day I was teaching this lesson to my daughter Maria. "Listen to your conscience in your prayer," I said, "then respond to what you feel or sense."

She questioned how to do this. I suggested that whenever she asked for a particular blessing, she should also ponder the law on which that blessing was predicated (D&C 130:20), and then the Lord would speak to her heart through her conscience. She now did this as she asked for a specific blessing she wanted, but then she said she had not received anything new, for "I already know what I should do."

I asked her where she obtained that knowledge. She answered, "In my Sunday School class." I pointed out that Sunday School was part of the Lord's kingdom and had the express purpose of teaching the gospel, and that the true principles she had learned there were now lodged in her heart and mind. I told her that the Holy Ghost would bring those principles to her remembrance as she needed them to meet the demands of each situation.

We studied together 2 Nephi 31:18-20 and 32:1-5 and John 14:26, and she came to understand one of the central processes of personal revelation.

She was both disappointed and elated—disappointed to have the more dramatic mystery surrounding revelation eliminated, and elated to sense that the Lord was listening and speaking to her and that the process was very simple. She also felt she was responsible for doing the thing the Lord required. She had no escape.

Many times over the years in different meetings I have asked people to be silent, to be calm, to meditate on spiritual matters and then consult their conscience regarding the things they need to do in life. Inevitably they acknowledge that they receive impressions or answers. Yet it is so easy to ignore these answers, to press other questions on the Lord beyond our present level of obedience. If we are members of the Church and have received

> **The Church primarily teaches principles rather than practices. Obedience to the principles (the general commandments) will lead people to the source of direction regarding practices (the personal commandments).**

the truth that has been given in this last dispensation, then we have received revelation. We have received that revelation through the prophets as confirmed by the Spirit. These are general revelations or commandments. If we have the gift of the Holy Ghost and we receive promptings about specific practices, things to do in life, we have received personal revelation. We don't have to look for dramatic spiritual experiences. It can take place constantly, on a daily basis. We can have the Holy Ghost as our constant companion, so that our mind views life through the frame of reference of the gospel. Then we can be guided continuously from that divine frame of reference.

PRINCIPLES AND PRACTICES

Now let's take the general and personal commandment question a step further. Some Church members would like to have an official Church position stated in any one of a number of areas, but often they cannot get a clear, definitive answer. Some do not understand and tend to get frustrated at this. The reason is simple, however. It is that the Church primarily teaches principles rather than practices. *Obedience to the principles (the general commandments) will lead people to the source of direction regarding practices (the personal commandments).* There perhaps are some who would want the practices set so that they can use them to lever themselves over others and judge others by. This is the pharisaical approach: It enables a person to follow the practices and then label himself as faithful and obedient, whereupon others who are his kind join with him to give him a sense of community and social security. Together they then label everyone else as unfaithful or liberal or unorthodox.

Grasping the concept of general and personal commandments helped me to understand something else — why the Lord could give two different individuals different answers to the same question. Probably these individuals are at different levels of faith and development, and what is applicable to one is not applicable to the other. In fact, it might even serve to tear down the other.

There are of course certain commandments with common denominators applicable to all. The Word of Wisdom is an example. For those who want to enter into the covenant gospel, this principle, as the Church teaches it, is adapted to the capacity of the weakest and therefore has general applicability. But it is wrong for someone to take upon himself the right of divine interpretation by pinpointing other possibly or probably harmful foods or drinks and making abstinence from them a general commandment. That is going beyond his stewardship. The Lord may give him personal direction and guidance on this matter, but that is not for general consumption. In fact, one of the conditions for a person's maintaining a continuous personal source of direction is to keep it personal and not presumptuously suppose that he can speak the word of the Lord to others on this matter. He can speak that word within his stewardship when so prompted by the Spirit, but not for the entire Church. The prophet and President of the Church alone has such a stewardship.

Nor is an unauthorized person to teach practices to someone else. While the Church teaches the *principles*, representing the general revelations given, one of the roles of the Holy Ghost is to teach appropriate *practices*. We might almost conclude that *one form of priestcraft takes place when a person sets himself up as a counselor and tries to usurp the role of the Holy Ghost as he teaches practices rather than correct principles.* This of course does not refer to leaders such as parents, bishops, stake presidencies, and General Authorities, whose callings and steward-ships may require that from time to time they counsel others as to practices when they perceive the need. Generally, however, leaders will teach the applicable principles.

The spirit of one practicing priestcraft as distinct from mag-nifying a priesthood calling consists in setting himself up to be a light. (See 2 Nephi 26:29.) Such self-aggrandizing attitudes motivate some people to tell other people what specific practices or actions they should take in different circumstances. For the one being advised, this being told what to do increases depen-dence upon the teacher or adviser as opposed to developing in-dependence and self-reliance. And the effect is to weaken rather than strengthen him, to retard or even reverse the process of his becoming more like his Father In Heaven.

PROMPTINGS THROUGH THE CONSCIENCE

The key to spiritual growth is to teach correct principles and then to encourage others to govern themselves according to those principles, allowing the Spirit to prompt or inspire the appropriate responses or practices. In this way a person becomes increasingly independent of things of this earth and develops appropriate dependence upon the things of heaven. Such a per-son can readily face circumstances or situations entirely different from the familiar, safe, comfortable circumstances of the past. With a frame of mind and heart based on correct principles and a life lived close to the Holy Spirit, he will receive guidance or promptings on the appropriate practices. These promptings are the equivalent of what we have been calling personal revelations or commandments.

The conscience is the divine, spiritual faculty, unique to man, through which the Holy Ghost will normally give these prompt-ings. They come when a person has properly educated his con-science, when he has learned and internalized correct principles. The Holy Ghost can go to work on that person's mind, bringing to his remembrance whatever divine principles he has learned. It is then that the upsurge of energy will take place. This energy effect is synergistic — the whole is greater than the sum of its parts. Through the Spirit's influence the person's mind and God's mind overlap; the person gains new insights, new understanding, a new synthesis, a higher wisdom; and he feels inward confirmation of its rightness. Then, when he follows the course indicated, blessings inevitably result and they bring him to a higher level of faith and practice.

AWARENESS OF PERSONAL REVELATION

Latter-day Saints often seem to be like "fish who discover water last," in that they are so immersed in the revelations of the Restoration as to be almost unaware of them. These revelations often become so much a part of the person's thinking and acting that he discounts the spiritual roots behind his frame of reference, his common sense.

A member of one of my home teaching families once remarked to me, "There are times when I find it's best to ignore my conscience and just follow my common sense." I questioned his reasoning, and he recited several experiences in which his conscience had told him one thing and his common sense another. At this he felt both confused and guilty, but on balance he concluded that reason was more to be trusted than feeling.

He gave an example: He was trained that whenever he went through a stop sign while driving, he must go several times around the block, stopping at the stop sign each time, as evidence of his repentance. This is an excellent illustration of "looking beyond the mark." The Jews spoken of in Jacob 4:14 despised the simple, plain truth and sought to mystify things. Like the blind, they stumbled, and they rejected Christ, their only safe and sure foundation.

> But behold, the Jews were a stiffnecked people; and they despised the words of plainness, and killed the prophets, and sought for things that they could not understand. Wherefore, because of their blindness, which blindness came by looking

beyond the mark, they must needs fall; for God hath taken away his plainness from them, and delivered unto them many things which they cannot understand, because they desired it. And because they desired it God hath done it, that they may stumble.

And now I, Jacob, am led on by the Spirit unto prophesying; for I perceive by the workings of the Spirit which is in me, that by the stumbling of the Jews they will reject the stone upon which they might build and have safe foundation.

But behold, according to the scriptures, this stone shall become the great, and the last, and the only sure foundation, upon which the Jews can build. (Jacob 4:14-16.)

In a fundamental sense we have two consciences, a divine one and a social one. The divine one is the true one, the Spirit of Jesus Christ, the light God has given to every person who comes into the world. The social one is also given to us, but this one comes from our human experiences—our upbringing, the culture surrounding us, made up of norms, mores, traditions, values, beliefs—and from the level of our obedience to the divine conscience. If we do not obey that conscience it is gradually subordinated, then eventually eliminated, and replaced by the social one. Whatever the focus and content of this social one is will be the center of that person's life and the primary source of his security, wisdom, guidance, and power.

REASON AND GENERAL COMMANDMENTS MAY SUFFICE

Now let's return to the situation with my friend in my home teaching family. In my opinion, what he called his conscience was his social conscience, and what he called common sense was his divine conscience, or a *frame of reference of correct principles, spiritual and temporal, which he had already received.* When he described the situational details wherein the conflict between conscience and common sense emerged, it was evident to me that his conscience had been educated by people in a Church-centered culture, which for the reasons given in earlier chapters was clearly unable to give wise guidance on the specific things he should do (practice). He had enough common sense or Spirit of Christ to sense how foolish these directions were, so he stayed with his divine conscience, a memory bank of correct principles. But he also had been victimized by wrong cultural maps, which made personal guidance and revelation mysterious, leaving him somewhat confused and guilt ridden (internal stumbling).

I encouraged him to tap divine sources to educate his conscience and assured him that in so doing he would make it stronger until he became more and more acquainted with the voice; and that as he continued to follow it he would feel his reason confirming his feeling, and vice versa, which would leave him feeling peaceful and settled inside.

I told him of an experience I had with Elder S. Dilworth Young, who was then a member of the First Council of the Seventy. He told a group of mission presidents in Scotland how a particular scripture had reconverted him to the practice of studying the scriptures.

> These words are not of men nor of man, but of me; wherefore, you shall testify they are of me and not of man;
>
> For it is my voice which speaketh them unto you; for they are given by my Spirit unto you, and by my power you can read them one to another; and save it were by my power you could not have them;
>
> Wherefore, you can testify that you have heard my voice, and know my words. (D&C 18:34-36.)

This was a revelation given to Joseph Smith the Prophet, Oliver Cowdery, and David Whitmer in June 1829. It contained instructions from the Lord to the Twelve Apostles *several years before those apostles were called*, telling them that when they had the words and read them, they could "testify that you have heard my voice, and know my words." Elder Young said that these words had greatly impressed him with the importance of the scriptures, as if in reading them he was actually hearing the voice of the Lord.

Elder Boyd K. Packer counseled:

> We are expected to use the light and knowledge we already possess to work out our lives. We should not need a revelation to instruct us to be up and about our duty, for we have been told that

> How many times have we repented by
> changing our behavior while our mind
> remains unchanged! And how quickly we
> have returned to the old behavior again! We
> repent of our sins again and again and again,
> but we don't repent of sinning.

already in the scriptures; nor expect revelation to replace the spiritual or temporal intelligence which we have already received— only to extend it. We must go about our life in an ordinary workaday way following the routines and rules and regulations that govern life.

Rules and regulations and commandments are valuable protection. Should we stand in need of revealed instruction to alter our course, it will be waiting along the way as we arrive at the point of need. The counsel to be busily engaged is wise counsel indeed. (Seminar for New Mission Presidents, June 25, 1982.)

SPIRIT OF CHRIST AND THE HOLY GHOST

On one occasion when Elder Bruce R. McConkie was teaching some seminary and institute people the difference between the Spirit of Christ and the Holy Ghost, he gave the following illustration or metaphor. The Holy Ghost is analagous to a radio transmitter; you and I may be compared to radio receivers; and the Spirit of Christ may be likened to the radio waves. He didn't say this, but I think it would be appropriate in this comparison to think of the Father and the Son as the radio announcers, since the messages originate with them. The Savior taught that the Holy Ghost will speak not of himself but what he hears, one of his functions being to bring to our remembrance what we have previously learned of Christ (see John 14:26; 16:13). In administering his affairs and in sending forth his gifts, the Holy Ghost uses the agency of the light of Christ (see Joseph Fielding Smith, *Doctrines of Salvation* [Bruce R. McConkie, compiler] Bookcraft, volume 1, pages 38-55; Moroni 10:17).

REPENTANCE INVOLVES CHANGE OF MIND

Much more could be said about the operations of the Holy Ghost in giving us personal revelation, enlightening our minds, and assisting in the education of the conscience. But this is essentially a book on behavior, not on theology. Let's consider, then, another important behavioral aspect of our subject — repentance.

"By this ye may know if a man repenteth of his sins — behold, he will confess them and forsake them" (D&C 58:43).

Confessing and forsaking sin is behavior, but repentance precedes this behavior. Confessing and forsaking are fruits of repentance. They indicate that repentance has taken place, but they are not the essence of repentance. The essence of repentance is change of mind. In Greek the word *repentance* literally means change of mind.

What does change of mind mean in relation to God/Christ-centeredness? It means to develop the mind of Christ; to see the world differently, to see ourselves differently, to have a different perception, a different frame of reference, a different paradigm, a different map, a different pair of glasses.

How many times have we repented by changing our behavior while our mind remains unchanged! And how quickly we have returned to the old behavior again! We repent of our *sins* again and again and again, but we don't repent of *sinning.* We may try to exercise great self-control so that our inward tendency is not outwardly manifested in behavior, but eventually the pressures build to the breaking point and our true self then surfaces again. This causes us social embarrassment and/or spiritual dissonance, and we resolve to repent again. So again we put brakes on our natural impulses and tendencies, and again for a period of time we seemingly repent by changing our behavior. We might even have confessed our misdeeds, but perhaps it was not done with full purpose of heart, because our mind has not yet changed. This could mean we confessed rather ritualistically; we went through the motions, as it were, to say we were sorry to the offended person or to God, and our prayers necessarily became increasingly ritualistic and hypocritical because of the degree of personal light against which we were sinning.

On the other hand, if you really confess with all your heart, then this indicates that your mind has changed or is changing. Here we speak of the heart as just another way of expressing the mind. Many of the Book of Mormon prophets referred to the heart in this connection. Paul spoke frequently of the mind — thinking of the deeper mind, the inward mind (e.g., see Ephesians 4:23; Titus 1:15). The Old Testament uses the metaphor of the heart and the mind at the same time; it speaks also about imagination, which reflects the contents of that mind or heart (1 Chronicles 28:9).

When we say we need to change the mind or heart in order to repent, does this mean that repentance does not involve change of behavior? Absolutely not. Of course it involves a change in behavior, but that new behavior is the fruit of repentance and not the repentance itself. When a person's mind is changed, his behavior will change to reflect that new mind-set.

To illustrate, on one occasion one of my sons attended a Sunday School class I taught on the general commandment of keeping the Sabbath Day holy, wherein we are instructed to worship our Heavenly Father and serve his children in the name of his Son. I used the spectacle metaphor of Sunday being the day to make certain we have his pair of glasses on and that we recommit (renew our covenants at sacrament) ourselves to that eternal perspective. After the class was over, my son told me he had greatly enjoyed the lesson and learned a lot from it.

A little later I suggested the family travel to Salt Lake City to visit the children's two grandmothers, a trip which has averaged seven to eight hours over the years, including preparation and van clean-up and put-away time. My son was upset with this suggestion. He had planned a rather leisurely afternoon, including a long, long nap and a pleasant rap session with his friends.

He and I discussed the two alternatives in light of that day's lesson on the Sabbath, and my son acknowledged that he felt inwardly torn between "doing the Lord's thing or my thing." It was an ideal teaching / learning moment for us both.

On the one hand, how easy and natural it is to both know and do appropriate things on the Sabbath when our minds are right! And on the other hand, how difficult and forced and unpleasant it is to do those same things when our minds have other priorities! This is so with any of the teachings and commandments and principles of the gospel. When the Lord comes first in our minds, proper behavior will follow. When our own pleasures and will come first, the same proper behavior is awkward and disagreeable and is easily rationalized away.

Again, the key is the priority in the mind. The behavior or works will inevitably follow. Intent or motive governs.

> For I remember the word of God which saith by their works ye shall know them; for if their works be good, then they are good also.
>
> For behold, God hath said a man being evil cannot do that which is good; for if he offereth a gift, or prayeth unto God, except he shall do it with real intent it profiteth him nothing.
>
> For behold, it is not counted unto him for righteousness.
>
> For behold, if a man being evil giveth a gift, he doeth it grudgingly; wherefore it is counted unto him the same as if he had retained the gift; wherefore he is counted evil before God.
>
> And likewise also is it counted evil unto a man, if he shall pray and not with real intent of heart; yea, and it profiteth him nothing, for God receiveth none such. (Moroni 7:5-9.)

What then is the role of self-control and self-discipline? This is the behavior that is required to change your mind and that will eventually lead to changed behavior in relation to various thoughts, words, or deeds in life. In other words, there are two kinds of behavior changes: behavior change that leads us to God / Christ-centeredness and behavior change that follows God / Christ-centeredness. To become God / Christ-centered — to develop the mind of Christ, the frame of reference, the map, the pair of glasses we have been speaking about — will call for some specific behavior changes: from routine prayer to meaningful prayer, from cursory scripture reading to concentrated, inspired study, for example. Then, as the mind or heart begins to change toward Christ, other behavior changes will be called for which will accelerate this process of change of mind and will demonstrate that it has in fact taken place.

Let me give an illustration of this process. The early Saints, we are told, polluted their inheritances by lustful and covetous desires and by contentious spirits. Consequently they were chastened, and the Lord allowed their enemies to cast them out of the lands of their inheritance. Their troubles humbled them, and they prayed to God for help and mercy. The Lord told them that he was slow to listen to their prayers because in the day of their peace they had esteemed his counsel lightly.

> Verily I say unto you, concerning your brethren who have been afflicted, and persecuted, and cast out from the land of their inheritance —
>
> I, the Lord, have suffered the affliction to come upon them, wherewith they have been afflicted, in consequence of their transgressions;
>
> Yet I will own them, and they shall be mine in that day when I shall come to make up my jewels.
>
> Therefore, they must needs be chastened and tried, even as Abraham, who was commanded to offer up his only son.
>
> For all those who will not endure chastening, but deny me, cannot be sanctified.
>
> Behold, I say unto you, there were jarrings, and contentions, and envyings, and strifes, and lustful and covetous desires among them; therefore by these things they polluted their inheritances.
>
> They were slow to hearken unto the voice of the Lord their God; therefore, the Lord their God is slow to hearken unto their prayers, to answer them in the day of their trouble.
>
> In the day of their peace they esteemed lightly my counsel; but, in the day of their trouble, of necessity they feel after me. (D&C 101:1-8.)

The Lord was counseling them to be constant in prayer, in and out of season. Regardless of external circumstances, they were always to put him first and keep his commandments. Their faithfulness toward him must be independent of circumstances.

GODLY SORROW AND WORLDLY SORROW

Paul wrote to the Corinthians about the two kinds of "repentance":

> Now I rejoice, not that ye were made sorry, but that ye sorrowed to repentance: for ye were made sorry after a godly manner, that ye might receive damage by us in nothing.
>
> For godly sorrow worketh repentance to salvation not to be repented of: but the sorrow of the world worketh death.
>
> For behold this selfsame thing, that ye sorrowed after a godly sort, what carefulness it wrought in you, yea, what clearing of yourselves, yea, what indignation, yea, what fear, yea, what vehement desire, yea, what zeal, yea, what revenge! In all things ye have approved yourselves to be clear in this matter. (2 Corinthians 7:9-11.)

The kind of repentance Paul urged upon the Corinthians was the repentance of changing their hearts through a genuinely godly sorrow rather than a superficial repentance born of social sorrow, the unhappy consequences of their sin or of the conditions of life.

In the same epistle Paul made one of the most penetrating observations of all time, a kind of summary statement reflecting God-centeredness. "If any man be in Christ, he is a new creature: old things are passed away; behold, all things are become new" (2 Corinthians 5:12).

Mormon decried the unrepentant hearts of the Nephites, who were humbled because of the disastrous circumstances they were in and who mourned and sorrowed before the Lord. In other words, their outward behavior looked right, but their hearts were wrong:

> Thus there began to be a mourning and a lamentation in all the land because of these things, and more especially among the people of Nephi.
>
> And it came to pass that when I, Mormon, saw their lamentation and their mourning and their sorrow before the Lord, my heart did begin to rejoice within me, knowing the mercies and the long-suffering of the Lord, therefore supposing that he would be

> # What I am suggesting basically is that we need to change the behavior in order to change the mind; and that once the mind or heart is thereby changed, we are capable of altogether different, higher kinds of behavior than we ever were before.

merciful unto them that they would again become a righteous people.

But behold this my joy was vain, for their sorrowing was not unto repentance, because of the goodness of God; but it was rather the sorrowing of the damned, because the Lord would not always suffer them to take happiness in sin.

And they did not come unto Jesus with broken hearts and contrite spirits, but they did curse God, and wish to die. Nevertheless they would struggle with the sword for their lives. (Mormon 2:11-14.)

A scriptural passage quoted earlier in a slightly different connection will bear repetition here. This is the Savior's oft-quoted words, "Search the scriptures; for in them ye think ye have eternal life: and they are they which testify of me" (John 5:39). They are generally quoted to indicate the importance of the behavior of studying the scriptures. Such behavior, of course, is appropriate. Far more important than the behavior of searching the scriptures, though, is *the purpose or the intent of searching the scriptures — that of coming to him;* or, to use the expression of this book, becoming God/Christ-centered. Carefully read the above scripture again, particularly reading the last phrase of verse 39 and adding verse 40.

Search the scriptures; for in them ye think ye have eternal life: and they are they which testify of me.

And ye will not come to me, that ye might have life. (John 5:39-40.)

Now, I don't wish to imply that behavior and heart are totally separate. They are definitely interlocking, interdependent.

It is almost like the proverbial chicken-and-egg question, so far as concerns which comes first. What I am suggesting basically is that we need to change the behavior in order to change the mind; and that once the mind or heart is thereby changed, we are capable of altogether different, higher kinds of behavior than we ever were before.

LOVE AND SELF-MASTERY LEAD TO CHRIST

President David O. McKay, speaking in his home one Christmastime, stressed the proper attitudes of mind a Saint of God has toward his fellowman and God. He speaks of "real intent." His highly instructive words show the close connection between intent and works, as he illustrates how the true follower of Christ finds the Savior by first practicing self-mastery and love in his relationship with his brothers.

Some men say, "We must find God before we can love our fellowmen." Is it not more nearly in keeping with the truth to say: "We shall find our God by living and loving our brethren"? I think it is.

Shall we say that a man first loves God and then spontaneously will love his neighbor? The New Testament reverses that order. "For he that loveth not his brother whom he hath seen, how can he love God whom he hath not seen?" (1 John 4:20.) Shall we say that a man first is forgiven by God and then naturally overflows into magnanimous relations with his fellows? The New Testament puts it the other way around. "But if ye forgive not men their trespasses, neither will your Father forgive your trespasses." (Matthew 6:15.) Shall we say that the worship of God comes first and love of man inevitably follows?

The New Testament states the contrary: "Therefore if thou bring thy gift to the altar, and there rememberest that thy brother hath ought against thee; leave there thy gift before the altar, and go thy way; first be reconciled to thy brother, and then come and offer thy gift." (Matthew 5:23-24.) Shall we say that a right attitude toward Christ is the precedent condition of a right attitude toward men? The New Testament says it is impossible to take a right attitude toward Christ without taking an unselfish attitude toward men. "Inasmuch as ye have done it unto one of the least of these my brethren, ye have done it unto me." (Matthew 25:40.) We may think as we please, but there is no question about what the Bible thinks. In the New Testament there is no road to the heart of God that does not lead through the heart of man. (*Living Truths from the Book of Mormon*, Deseret Sunday School Union, 1970, page 265.)

The Various Steps

Chapter 10

*And I, John, saw that he received not of the
fulness at the first, but received grace for grace;
And he received not of the fulness at first,
but continued from grace to grace, until he
received a fulness.
And thus he was called the Son of God,
because he received not of the fulness at the
first. (D&C 93:12-14.)*

How do you eat an elephant? Answer: A bite at a time.
How do you take a thousand-mile journey? Answer: A
step at a time.

How do you achieve perfection? Answer: Line upon line,
precept upon precept; here a little, there a little.

If Satan were answering for us the question, "How can I
achieve perfection?" I suppose he would give one of four
answers: First, you can't do it; it's impossible; it's futile to try.
Second, it's presumptuous to think you could do it; it's prideful,
it's the height of arrogance; man is not made for it. Third, you
can do it all at once, the whole shooting match. Fourth, you
don't have to do it; it has been done for you by Christ; just
receive him by believing in him, and that's all there is to it.

Of course, Satan is the father of lies.

In this concluding chapter we are going to explore the Lord's
plan for growth, happiness, and perfection for his children under
the following four principles: First, light precedes life — in other
words, in order to be properly motivated, we must have a
correct understanding. Second, some things must come ahead of
other things. Third, the essence of centering is to yoke up.
Fourth, we need to recognize the signs of progress so that we are
encouraged to keep going.

LIGHT PRECEDES LIFE

To take hold of any principle or concept and use it for growth and development, the first thing we always need to do is to get a vision. Without it, the writer of Proverbs teaches us (29:18), people perish. So first we need to understand the Lord and his plan so that we can relate to that plan.

The best way I know to do this is to think about or hypothesize the role of a father or a mother to their child. How do you or would you look at your little child as he is growing up? You know something of his potential, what he is capable of, but you also know he has to go through a process. You would be patient with him, you would encourage him. You would teach him correct principles to govern his life. You would not give up on him if he faltered along the way. You would not give in to him if he wanted things you knew would work against his long-term interests. You would lovingly correct him and discipline him.

I suggest this is the best frame of reference in which to understand our Heavenly Father and his plan for his children. So in order that we don't fall into the trap of Satan's answers given above, let us simply maintain the concept of a loving, wise father or mother and we will not be far wrong when we think of our Heavenly Father and his plan for us, his children.

SOME THINGS MUST PRECEDE OTHER THINGS

When we study the entire context of the scriptures and also the processes of nature, we are powerfully taught that some things come ahead of other things. This principle cannot be violated. You cannot do calculus before you understand algebra, and you cannot do algebra before you understand basic math. You cannot run before you walk, or walk before you crawl. You don't enter high school until you have completed grade school, and you don't go to college until you have completed basic high school requirements. A medical student doesn't study surgery until he has mastered fundamental physiology.

Most of the positive, encouraging comments I received on my earlier book *Spiritual Roots of Human Relations* dealt primarily with chapter 2 of that book, which was entitled "Six Days of Creation." There I drew an analogy between the six days of creation and life, pointing out, for instance, that we cannot receive the benefits of days two and three unless we live the laws of day one, and so on. I quoted extensively from the writings of President David O. McKay, who taught emphatically that a person must master his appetites before he is able to gain much control over his passions, and that he must control his passions before he will be able to perfect his desires. In another chapter named "The Three Temptations," I analyzed the three temptations of Christ, suggesting that they represented different levels of self-mastery and achievement, and that a person could not consecrate himself to the Lord's will (temptation no. 3) and purposes until he had good control over himself and was able to subordinate the body to the mind (temptation no. 1) and the mind to the spirit (temptation no. 2).

So often, so many of the gospel principles are thrown at us at the same time that we feel almost overwhelmed by them, and as a result we gradually come to believe one of Satan's messages above. We lose awareness that some things simply must come ahead of other things; that this is the way it is intended; and that therefore there is no call for discouragement that we can't learn it all at once.

EXTERNAL AND INTERNAL DISCIPLINES

The New Testament followed the Old Testament. Most of the Old Testament deals with people who were living the law of Moses, which was a lesser law. It was necessary for them to live this law before they were capable of receiving and living the higher law. The law of Moses was a set of external regulations and rules that governed every phase of life. Paul told the Galatians (3:24) that it was a schoolmaster to bring people to Christ.

It was a set of external disciplines, obedience to which gradually developed the capacity to receive and live internal disciplines. The Sermon on the Mount was the transition sermon in which the Savior related the lesser law of Moses to the higher law of love, which he was then teaching. That sermon taught that it was now time to move away from the plenitude of external disciplines and rule definitions of righteousness and instead take up the internal disciplines of discipleship and the spiritual definitions of righteousness, which have to do with the heart, with intent, with desires, rather than only with behavior.

To use the Old and New Testaments as a figure of speech exemplifying this principle of some things coming ahead of other things, what happens when a person is in the Old Testament of his life and he hears New Testament teachings but is not capable of understanding or appreciating them or of fully receiving them? He might mouth them, intellectualize about them, pretend to live them, but it is all empty, hollow, and shallow, and as soon as the first real storm descends the weaknesses will be exposed. The shallow roots will be clearly evident.

CULTIVATE FUNDAMENTAL DISCIPLINES

This principle that some things must come ahead of other things, must form a base for further growth, has led me to believe absolutely in the importance of cultivating certain basic, fundamental disciplines in life. One of these is the habit of getting up early in the morning and exercising physically and spiritually. This is what I call the daily private victory. The very process of rising early (D&C 88:124) involves mastery over self — mind over mattress, in this case.

Time and time again I have encouraged people to get up earlier, exercise, prayerfully ponder the scriptures, then plan their day in that spirit. Try doing this, and then watch what happens. I admit there are situations in which this counsel does not apply, and I need to be very careful before I teach practices. However, the principle I am trying to teach is to *get control of your own life.* Start in small ways and have small successes, and then move to larger and larger ways. I know I have had more success in teaching this principle within the context of "the big picture" than I have in teaching almost anything else.

LEARN TO USE COMMITMENTS

The bottom line is this: *Learn to make and keep a promise.* Start small, make a small promise to yourself; continue fulfilling that promise until you have a sense that you have a little more control over yourself. Now take the next level of challenge. Make yourself a promise, then keep it till you have established control at that level. Now the next level; make the promise, keep it. As you do this, little by little your sense of personal worth will increase; your sense of self-mastery will grow, and your confidence that you can master the next level will increase. Be serious and intent in the whole process, however, because if you make this commitment to yourself and then break it, your self-esteem will be weakened and your capacity to make and keep another promise will be decreased.

Making and keeping promises has both an Old Testament and a New Testament application. (I am using these two terms as a figure of speech here, as explained earlier.) The Old Testament application has to do with certain basic disciplines in life. In fact, it's a kind of straightjacket a person willingly puts upon himself in order to develop self-control, self-mastery, so that he will have the power over his body and mind to start working on New Testament challenges, namely, becoming God/Christ-centered by educating and obeying his conscience, which is merely an advancement on learning to make and keep a promise.

Now, isn't this very like the way we raise our children? You give a child small tasks or teachings within the scope of his capacities and interests, get a commitment from the child to do those things, then follow through to see that they are done. Then you gradually increase the level of those challenges and tasks. Isn't this basically the way we learn any skill, even as adults?

REALITY AND FLEXIBILITY

Timing is essential; when to do what. This involves a sense of reality, a sense of process, a sense of self.

Professionally I train managers and consult with organizations on how to strengthen the organizational culture so that it is more productive in accomplishing its purposes. The above principle applies here too. For instance, if the organization has a low-trust culture and communication processes have therefore deteriorated, there is no way you can immediately implement a compensation system based on merit. The employees will not sustain it. You must rebuild the trust before you can attempt to implement a merit compensation system. People who have intense feelings about the organization must be involved in the process of change so that they "buy into" the new system and are committed to making it succeed.

The trust must come before the change. Some things must come ahead of other things. The same principle applies in families. Once we had some friends attend our family home evening, which went unusually well that night. Our friends went home and tried to apply with their family what we had done with ours —and it was a total disaster. The groundwork we had laid was different from that which they had laid. What works for us won't necessarily work for somebody else, and vice versa. Each family situation is unique, and it takes flexibility and a sense of reality to know what will work with a particular family.

THREE BASIC CAPACITIES

Problem solving, whether specific to an individual problem or general to the improvement of one's life, requires at least three basic capacities: 1) vision, or what is desired or should be; 2) reality, or what is; 3) the ability to deal with what is in moving toward what should be. Failure results when a person is engrossed in what should be and has little sense of what is. Similarly, nothing will improve if a person has a sense of what is but has no real vision or sense of what should be. The key is to be able to discern and adapt to them both and to realize that there are principles and processes involved. You cannot successfully violate those processes; you cannot push them or shortcircuit them. The processes must be followed in sequence and with proper timing. In the temple endowment, for example, you can't move ahead in the ceremony until you have completed the earlier requirements in their proper order. Neither can a person who is telestial in spirit and character all of a sudden become totally committed to the kingdom or God without the repentance and self-mastery processes.

NEED FOR BALANCE

Someone has said there are three essential principles in missionary work: spirituality, personality, and reality. This is similar to what the previous paragraph says. We can liken these principles to the legs of a three-legged stool—if one leg were eliminated, the stool would fall over. If a person had spirituality and personality but no sense of reality, in the sense of which we speak, he would topple. Similarly if he were spiritually minded and realistic but lacked the personal skills and attitudes to be effective, he would topple. If he had such a personality and a high sense of reality but no spiritual vision or power, he would topple. Again, as we have seen in other places in this book, the key is balance. That is why looking to Christ as our model is so basic and fundamental—he embodied these three capacities marvelously on every recorded occasion.

THE ONE THING

"One thing thou lackest." This is the answer the Savior gave (Mark 10:21) to the rich young ruler who asked what he needed to do to obtain eternal life. "One thing thou lackest," the Savior said, and then he went on to say what that one thing was for that person. Since the individual was possessed by his possessions, that one thing was to sell his possessions, give the money to the poor, and come and follow Christ. To me there is a fundamental principle in this. I believe that most people, in their hearts, know what that one thing is; that if they would do that one thing, they would be enabled to come and follow Christ; and that then the other things would be opened up to them in their right sequence.

When President Harold B. Lee answered the missionary's question, "What is the most important commandment?" he said, "The most important commandment for you, Elder, is the one you are having the greatest difficulty in living right now." He was saying essentially the same thing as the Savior said to the young ruler: There is one thing that is needful at this time; if you do that you will find that increased power and capacity will be given to you to do the next one thing. Thus a person is led line upon line, precept upon precept, here a little and there a little along the path of life.

In two powerful and popular films, it seems to me, this principle was illustrated in the lives of individuals who were rather advanced in the New Testament of their lives. One character portrayed was Sir Thomas More, in the movie *A Man for All Seasons;* the other was Eric Liddell, in the movie *Chariots of Fire.* Both were historical characters, and the movies properly represented their respective challenges. The ultimate test of "the one thing" was given to them both.

As I have indicated, these were not individuals who were struggling with the "Old Testament" of their lives. They were very God-centered men, strongly directed by their consciences. They were good and noble, honest and true. But still it appears they needed one more test to show that they put God first, above everything else they prized. Both were put under tremendous pressure to give in, to capitulate, but they would not do so. Thomas More's test was to be true to his conscience rather than save his life by swearing to the parliamentary acts of Succession and Supremacy as required by King Henry VIII. To do so would have been going against his integrity and faith. Eric Liddell's test came when he discovered that his race in the Olympics was scheduled for a Sunday; and to race on Sunday would be to go against his integrity and faith.

After years of training for the great event, Eric Liddell was willing to lose the opportunity to run rather than do so on a

Sunday. The pressure included the Prince of Wales, the future King of England, asking him to make the sacrifice for the sake of the nation. He essentially answered: "God made kings. God made nations. This is too much of a sacrifice. I will not do it." Eventually they put him into a different race so that he could run on a weekday. And he won. But his running was essentially an extension of his character, and if he had violated his commitment regarding the Sabbath Day, he would have lost his motivation and competence to run.

With his life at stake, Sir Thomas More had even greater pressures. In the movie, his daughter pleaded with him to take the Oath of Succession and Supremacy, leave his prison in the Tower of London, and come home to his family. His response was essentially the same as Liddell's, that when a person is untrue to the truth within, he loses the essence of his life. He would not bow to the king's will, and he eventually was beheaded.

The point is that generally people have an internal sense of what that one thing is that they need to do, and if they will do it, everything else will begin to work together for their good. Thomas More and Eric Liddell were far ahead of most of us in the growth processes of life, and their one thing was different from our one thing, but it still was one thing. If a person is uncertain as to what his one thing is, perhaps he should ask the questions, "What would I need to do to gain a knowledge of what I need to do?" He should then sense what "that one thing" is and do it.

The one thing is usually, as President Lee said, the most difficult thing we are confronting. To Abraham, the ultimate test and the most difficult thing he could ever deal with had to do with sacrificing his child of promise, Isaac. The Lord was testing: "Are you, Abraham, going to put me first under every condition?" Once Abraham passed the test by proving his internal commitment to obey the Lord under all circumstances, the Lord knew he had the father of the faithful. And Abraham knew that he was faithful. He became the father of many nations, of an innumerable seed that extends to many millions in the modern world. It wasn't necessary that Abraham consummate the sacrifice. All that was necessary was that he was willing to do so.

As with Eric Liddell and Thomas More, so with Job of old, or Paul, or Peter, or Joseph Smith, or you, or me. I really believe that in our heart of hearts most of us know what that one thing is, and that any effort to look elsewhere or to do something else will fail. Let each of us search his heart.

KEY TO CENTERING IS TO YOKE UP

Basically, yoking up means putting on the harness of God. In other words, serving. Thinking of others rather than oneself.

Try to visualize in your mind's eye a team of horses pulling a wagon. See the cowboys harnessing these horses. Now try to visualize the Saints coming across the plains, putting the yoke around the neck and shoulders of the oxen so that they could pull the wagons. Now visualize yourself early in the morning, yoking up, putting on the harness of service in your various stewardships. See yourself taking the straps and connecting them around your shoulders and your neck so that you are prepared to do the work assigned you for that day. See yourself allowing someone else to help adjust the yoke or harness about you and your being willing to be yoked up to another brother or sister at your side, or to your wife or husband, with whom you must learn to pull.

DIVINE-CENTEREDNESS REQUIRES A LOAD

I emphasize this principle of service or yoking up to the Lord's service because I have come to believe that efforts to become God/Christ-centered without a load to carry will simply not succeed. We may attempt to do it as a kind of intellectual or spiritual exercise, but if we don't have a sense of responsibility, of service, of contribution, something we need to pull or push, it becomes a futile endeavor. The Lord had to live a totally pure and sinless life before he could have power to work out the infinite and eternal atonement, and his life certainly carried the load.

Private victories, those of the heart and mind and soul, precede public victories, but they derive their efficacy from the awareness that there is going to be a public challenge out there. For example, if your child was suddenly taken ill, was near death, and you came to realize that his life lay in your own hands, that is, in your faith, prayers, and righteousness, how motivated you would be to live righteously! How anxious you would be to be one of the living branches drawing strength from the vine, as in the Savior's metaphor!

> I am the vine, ye are the branches: He that abideth in me, and I in him, the same bringeth forth much fruit: for without me ye can do nothing.
> If ye abide in me, and my words abide in you, ye shall ask what ye will and it shall be done unto you.
> Herein is my Father glorified, that ye bear much fruit; so shall ye be my disciples. (John 15:5, 7-8.)

When I sense that there are generations that have preceded me and generations that will follow me, as well as the present generation for which I carry responsibility, and that this represents my yoke, I feel its weight. In fact, it sometimes seems so heavy that I could give up, give it all up. Then if I focus my thoughts on Christ I am strengthened, for he who is our model and who carried this weight for the whole human race said:

> Come unto me, all ye that labour and are heavy laden, and I will give you rest.
> Take my yoke upon you, and learn of me; for I am meek and lowly in heart: and ye shall find rest unto your souls.
> For my yoke is easy, and my burden is light. (Matthew 11:28-30.)

In what way is the burden light and the yoke easy? In the sense that you realize you are being used by and empowered from another source, the divine source — that you are filling your essential mission in life; that you have peace of mind and are not

> **The successful person has the habit of doing the things failures don't like to do. The successful ones don't necessarily like doing them either, but their disliking is subordinated by the strength of their purpose.**

internally buffeted by conflicting priorities, self-doubts, and fears; and that your shoulders will be made equal to the burdens placed upon them.

When your work and the Lord's work are one and the same, you will know that you are divinely centered. When you see your life as a mission and not as a career, you will know you are divinely centered. Someone said, "An obstacle is what you see when you take your eye off your goal." So let's keep our eye on the goal. The most advanced state of the soul in the New Testament of our lives is to consecrate everything we have and are or ever will be to his holy work, to the building up of his kingdom in the world, and to the establishment of Zion. When this is the consuming purpose of our lives, the Lord will use us in unimaginable ways. The powers of heaven will attend us. We won't be striving for God / Christ-centeredness, we simply will be so centered.

COMMON DENOMINATOR OF SUCCESS

In his brilliant little essay, "The Common Denominator of Success," Albert E. M. Grey summarized his entire life's work in one idea, which I paraphrase here: The successful person has the habit of doing the things failures don't like to do. The successful ones don't necessarily like doing them either, but their disliking is subordinated by the strength of their purpose.

Grey had made a lifelong study to try to find the common denominator of success — the one element or ingredient which was present in every success. He did not find it in hard work, good luck, or positive attitude. He found it in a consuming purpose. His finding is worth stating again: The successful person has the habit of doing the things failures don't like to do. The successful ones don't necessarily like doing them either, but their disliking is subordinated by the strength of their purpose.

THREE-PERSON APPROACH

In this matter of yoking up I have been powerfully influenced by a wonderful educator and stake patriarch, Walter Gong, from San Jose, California. He helped me to understand that the key in an educational setting is to turn it into a three-person situation. The first person is the teacher; the second person is the learner who "captures" from the teacher — that is, he understands what is being presented and taught, then expands upon it (adds to it from his own experience, thinking and application); he then teaches the third person or the next individual or group. When the learner becomes a teacher, he becomes the first person in a new triad and his learner becomes the second person — who then captures the learning, expands upon it, and teaches the next third person. Thus new triads are formed each time a learner becomes a teacher. "Teach ye diligently and my grace shall attend you, that you may be instructed more perfectly. . . ." (D&C 88:78.)

Most of us have learned over and over again that if you really want to learn something, you need to teach it. In fact, the moment you sense you are responsible to teach it, you simply learn it better. You feel responsible. You pay more attention, you concentrate more fully. You ask questions. You get involved. You seek clarification and illustration. And if the thing taught makes sense to you, you apply, you do, you become not just a hearer but a doer of the word. You think about it, read about it, pray about it; in other words, you expand upon it. And then you desire to share it with others. Most importantly, *the spirit of the three-person situation is the spirit of service*, of contribution, of sharing, of giving, of yoking up, of the great first and second commandments to love the Lord and our neighbor.

This yoking-up concept, this ideal of service, is well illustrated in the oft-quoted piece by Bruce Barton on the two seas.

> There are two seas in Palestine. One is fresh, and fish are in it. Splashes of green adorn its banks. Trees spread their branches over it and stretch out their thirsty roots to sip of its healing waters.

283

Along its shores the children play, as children played when He was there. He loved it. He could look across its silver surface when He spoke His parables. And on a rolling plain not far away He fed five thousand people.

The river Jordan makes this sea with sparkling water from the hills. So it laughs in the sunshine. And men build their houses near to it, and birds their nests; and every kind of life is happier because it is there.

The river Jordan flows on south into another sea.

Here is no splash of fish, no fluttering leaf, no song of birds, no children's laughter. Travelers choose another route, unless on urgent business. The air hangs heavy above its water, and neither man nor beast nor fowl will drink.

What makes this mighty difference in these neighbor seas? Not the river Jordan. It empties the same good water into both. Not the soil in which they lie, not in the country round about.

This is the difference. The Sea of Galilee receives but does not keep the Jordan. For every drop that flows into it another drop flows out. The giving and receiving go on in equal measure.

The other sea is shrewder, hoarding its income jealously. It will not be tempted into any generous impulse. Every drop it gets, it keeps.

The Sea of Galilee gives and lives. This other sea gives nothing. It is named The Dead.

There are two kinds of people in the world. There are two seas in Palestine.

When I first learned the concept of three-person teaching, along with the technology on how to do it in an educational setting, I significantly changed my approach in teaching students at Brigham Young University as well as in training managers and leaders of the various organizations I work with. Now, right at the beginning, I challenge them to get into the three-person situation and to take the responsibility to share with others that which they are about to capture and expand upon.

To emphasize how immediately motivating the three-person challenge is, I often ask a student or learner, "If you knew you were responsible to share with another group of people tomorrow what I'm going to share with you today, would that have any impact on your learning today?" Everyone answers in the same vein: "Absolutely," "Yes," "Definitely." The basic concept really is a spiritual one: we receive in order to give.

In the book *Gospel Doctrine* (page 262) President Joseph F. Smith attributes to Thomas Gibbons the following graphic verse:

> That man may last, but never lives,
> Who much receives, but nothing gives;
> Whom none can love, whom none can thank,
> Creation's blot, creation's blank.

EUSTRESS — THE GOOD STRESS

When people start living selfishly, narcissistically, interpreting everything in terms of its effect upon themselves, they lose the spirit of giving and sharing, contributing, helping, serving, and they begin to die. In his book *Stress Without Distress*, Dr. Hans Seyle, the international expert on stress from Montreal, Canada, presents considerable evidence to show that when people lose a sense of contribution, a sense of meaningful projects in their life (which he calls eustress) the degenerative processes of the body are accelerated, the immune system tends to break down, and people literally die earlier than they otherwise would have. Eustress is good, constructive, and healthy. It keeps us alive; it strengthens the immune system and slows down the degenerative processes. These physical benefits are shared by those who have a desire to share, to give, to contribute, to build, to do something in helping other people and in making the world better. This was also the central message of Dr. Viktor Frankl, the Austrian psychiatrist who was imprisoned in the death camps in Nazi Germany. He learned that as long as an inmate had some purpose, something out there to live for, some project, some goal, someone to touch, to bless, to help, then life would be meaningful and the chances of survival in those conditions of great deprivation were greatly increased.

Of course, the three-person approach is used to its greatest advantage at the celestial level, in doing the work of the Lord— helping to bring to pass the immortality and eternal life of man.

RECOGNIZING THE SIGNS OF PROGRESS

A re there any immediately detectable signs of progress in the effort to be God/Christ-centered? How do you see your own efforts?

It is important to first understand that we are not dealing with an either/or situation but rather with a continuum. It is a matter of degrees. From study and observation and from my own strivings, I have isolated eight discernible characteristics or signs of progress, signs that arise naturally out of the dimensions of security, guidance, wisdom, and power of a divinely centered life and are therefore evident in the lives of those who are making the strong attempt:

1. They genuinely love to pray and to study the scriptures.
2. They are service oriented.
3. They are continually learning and growing.
4. They radiate positive energy and regularly sidestep negative energy.
5. They believe in other people, in the unseen potential and good in them.
6. They lead balanced lives, combining idealism with realism.
7. They see life as an adventure.
8. They are synergistic or creatively productive.

The above list is incomplete. It really could almost go on endlessly, describing the beautiful characteristics of divinely centered people. But these eight seem to be obvious and clearly indicative of such people. Let's briefly discuss each one in turn. (Some of these concepts have been mentioned previously, but the following will serve as review and summary and also as a "how-to" on this intensely practical matter.)

1. THEY LOVE TO PRAY AND STUDY SCRIPTURES

Their model, their mentor, is Jesus Christ. They have drunk deeply from the sweet waters of the gospel until they have become acquainted with the divine voice and the feelings and gifts of the Holy Spirit. It has nurtured them, nourished them, enabled them to grow and develop, giving them comfort, insight, inspiration, guidance, protection, direction, answers to prayers, peace of mind. They look forward to returning to these eternal springs. They know for themselves the meaning of the scripture that

> the doctrine of the priesthood shall distil upon thy soul as the dews from heaven. The Holy Ghost shall be thy constant companion, and thy scepter an unchanging scepter of righteousness and truth; and thy dominion shall be an everlasting dominion, and without compulsory means it shall flow unto thee forever and ever. (D&C 121:45-46.)

To go for any length of time—even a few hours—and not seek this refreshment would cause them genuine withdrawal pains, similar in the physical sense to going without food and water. These people know who does the watering and the fertilizing and the weeding in perfect and gentle yet necessary ways. They also have a sense of being a vehicle or a vessel to serve divine purposes.

2. THEY ARE SERVICE ORIENTED

I sought my God, and my God I could not see;
I sought my soul and my soul eluded me;
I sought to serve my brother in his need and found all three:
My God, my soul, and thee.

Those striving to be divinely centered see life as a mission in the Lord's cause. Their nurturing sources have armed and prepared them for his service, to do his work with his other children. Elder Neal A. Maxwell wrote, "Indeed our lives could not truly be Christ-centered if we shunned the chores of the kingdom." ("The Christ-centered Life," *Ensign,* August 1981, page 13.)

Note the Savior's words to the three Nephite disciples who desired to remain on the earth until the Second Coming.

> And again, ye shall not have pain while ye shall dwell in the flesh, neither sorrow save it be for the sins of the world; and all this will I do because of the thing which ye have desired of me, for ye have desired that ye might bring the souls of men unto me, while the world shall stand.

Those who are divinely centered are not naive; they are aware of weakness and evil. But they realize that behavior and potential are two different things. Since they believe in the unseen Christ, they also believe in the unseen Christlike potential of all our Heavenly Father's children.

And for this cause ye shall have fulness of joy; and ye shall sit down in the kingdom of my Father; yea, your joy shall be full, even as the Father hath given me fulness of joy; and ye shall be even as I am, and I am even as the Father; and the Father and I are one. (3 Nephi 28:9-10.)

3. THEY ARE CONTINUALLY LEARNING AND GROWING

The divinely centered are constantly educated by their experiences. They read, they seek training, they take classes, they listen to others, they learn through both their ears and their eyes. They are curious, always asking questions. They continually expand their competence, their ability to do things. They develop new skills, new interests. They literally discover that the more they know, the more they realize they don't know; that as their circle of knowledge grows, so does its outside edge of ignorance. Most of this learning and growth energy is self-initiated and feeds upon itself.

4. THEY RADIATE POSITIVE ENERGY

The countenances of God/Christ-centered people are cheerful, pleasant, happy. Their attitude is optimistic, positive, upbeat. Their spirit is enthusiastic, hopeful, and believing. They "believe all things, [they] hope all things, [they] have endured many things, and hope to be able to endure all things. If there is anything virtuous, lovely, or of good report or praiseworthy, [they] seek after these things." (Thirteenth article of faith.)

This positive energy is like an energy field or an aura that surrounds them and that similarly charges or changes weaker, negative energy fields around them. They also attract and magnify smaller positive energy fields. When they come into contact with strong, negative energy sources they tend to either neutralize or sidestep this negative energy. Sometimes they will simply leave it, walking away from its poisonous orbit. Wisdom gives them a sense of how strong it is and a sense of humor and of timing in dealing with it.

This one characteristic is a good measuring rod and a continuous sign of your own growth. Be aware of the effect of your own energy and understand how you radiate and direct it. And in the middle of confusion or contention or negative energy, strive to be a peacemaker, a harmonizer, to undo or reverse destructive energy. You will discover what a self-fulfilling prophecy positive energy is when combined with the next characteristic.

5. THEY BELIEVE IN OTHER PEOPLE

Ponder the words of the Savior: "Judge not, and ye shall not be judged: condemn not, and ye shall not be condemned: forgive, and ye shall be forgiven." (Luke 6:37.)

Divinely centered people don't overly react to negative behaviors, criticism, or human weaknesses. They don't feel built up when they discover the weaknesses of others. Charity seeks no evil. They are not naive; they are aware of weakness and evil. But they realize that *behavior and potential are two different things.* Since they believe in the unseen Christ, they also believe in the unseen Christlike potential of all our Heavenly Father's children. They feel humbly grateful for their own blessings of mercy and forgiveness and feel naturally to compassionately forgive and forget the offenses of others. They don't carry grudges. They refuse to label other people, to stereotype, categorize, and prejudge. Rather, they seek to have the mind of God, who sees his children in an entirely different light. They see the oak tree in the acorn and understand the process of which they can be a part in helping this acorn become a great oak.

The Prophet Joseph Smith told the Saints of his day:

If you do not accuse each other, God will not accuse you. If you have no accuser you will enter heaven, and if you will follow the revelations and instructions which God gives you through me, I will take you into heaven as my back load. If you will not accuse me, I will not accuse you. If you will throw a cloak of charity over my sins, I will over yours—for charity covereth a multitude of sins. (*TPJS*, page 193.)

I have known individuals who have earnestly sought to understand God's views of their own children in order either to break an overreactive behavior pattern toward annoying behavior or to gain a fresh new map of the child's innate potential. One person had a dream wherein she saw herself and her daughter, with whom she had had a running ego battle for some time, as best friends in the premortal life. Awakening, she felt totally different, saw her daughter in a new light, and entirely lost the desire to remake her personality.

I have seen others given new maps through deep sustained prayer, through patriarchal blessing experiences, through ordinances, through the eyes of others who "see and believe," through seeing their children in entirely new settings (mission field, school, work, athletics) in which they were significantly achieving and highly respected.

Once my wife and I, though behaviorally confirmed in a label (map) we had on one of our sons, felt spiritually very uneasy about it. Through prayer and visualization we gradually came to see him differently. When we believed in the unseen potential, the old label naturally vanished and we were at peace and stopped trying to push natural processes. We simply knew that his talent and potential would come forth in its own time. And it did, to the astonishment, frankly, of others, including other family members. We were not surprised because we knew who he was. Truly, believing is seeing.

For we must seek to believe in the unseen. This creates a *climate for growth and opportunity.* Self-centered people believe that the key lies in them, in their techniques, in doing "their thing" to others. This works only temporarily. If you believe it's "in" them, not "in" you, you relax, accept, affirm, and let it happen. Either way, it is a self-fulfilling prophecy.

The Prophet Joseph Smith taught, "All the minds and spirits that God ever sent into the world are susceptible of enlargement" (*TPJS*, page 354).

6. THEY LEAD BALANCED LIVES

For the God/Christ-centered, religion is both vertical and horizontal: man's relationship both to God and to man. Both dimensions are important. To suppose that we feel the pulse of God while we lack effective contact with his other children is an illusion. Similarly it is an illusion to think that we feel the pulse of his other children if we do not feel the pulse of God. We really won't understand who we are unless we understand who he is. The whole concept of the brotherhood of man is based on the concept of the fatherhood of God.

In my opinion, balanced people read the wholesome literature and magazines which the world produces and they keep up with current affairs and events. They are active socially, having many friends and a few confidants. They are active intellectually, having many interests. They read, watch, observe, and learn. Within the limits of age and health they are active physically, athletically. They have a lot of fun. They enjoy themselves. They have a healthy sense of humor, particularly laughing at themselves and not at others' expense. You can sense they have a healthy regard for and honesty about themselves. They can feel their own worth, which is manifest by their courage and integrity and by the absence of a need to brag, to drop names, to borrow strength from possessions or credentials or titles or past achievements. They are open in their communication, simple, direct, nonmanipulative. They also have a sense of what is appropriate, and they would sooner err on the side of understatement than on the side of exaggeration.

They are not extremists—they do not make everything all or nothing. They are not dichotomizers—that is, they do not divide everything into two parts, seeing everything as good or bad, as either/or. They think in terms of continuums, priorities, hierarchies. They have the power to discriminate, to sense the uniquenesses, similarities, and differences in each situation. This does not mean they are relativists, seeing everything in terms of situational ethics. They fully recognize absolutes and courageously condemn the bad and the evil and praise the good and the righteous.

I'm talking primarily about their reactions, their attitudes. These reactions and attitudes are proportionate to the situation —balanced, temperate, moderate, wise. For instance, they're not work-aholics, religious zealots, political fanatics, diet crashers, food bingers, pleasure addicts, fasting martyrs. They're not slavishly chained to their plans and schedules. They don't condemn themselves for every foolish mistake or social blunder. They don't brood about yesterday or daydream about tomorrow. They live sensibly in the present, carefully plan the future, and flexibly adapt to changing circumstances. Their self-honesty is revealed by their sense of humor, their willingness to admit then forget mistakes, and to cheerfully do the things ahead which lie within their power.

They have no need to manipulate through either intimidating anger or self-pitying martyrdom. They are genuinely happy for others' successes and do not feel in any sense that these take anything from them. They take both praise and blame proportionately without head trips or overreactions. They see success on the far side of failure. The only real failure for them is the experiences not learned from.

7. THEY SEE LIFE AS AN ADVENTURE

Divinely centered people savor life. Because their security comes from within instead of from without, they have no need to categorize and stereotype everything and everybody in life to give them a sense of certainty and predictability. They see old faces freshly, old scenes as for the first time. They are like courageous explorers going on a Lewis and Clark type of expedi-

Divinely centered people savor life. Because their security comes from within instead of from without, they have no need to categorize and stereotype everything and everybody in life to give them a sense of certainty and predictability.

tion "into the northwest territories"; they are really not sure what is going to happen, but they are confident it will be exciting and growth-producing and that they will discover new territory and make new contributions. Their security lies in their initiative, resourcefulness, willpower, courage, stamina, and native intelligence rather than in the safety, protection, and abundance of their home camps, of their comfort zones.

They rediscover people each time they meet them. They are interested in them. They ask questions and get involved. They are completely present when they listen. They learn from them. They don't label them from past successes or failures. They see no one bigger than life. They are not overawed by General Authorities, top government figures, or celebrities. They resist becoming anyone's disciple. They are basically unflappable and capable of adapting to virtually anything that comes along. One of their fixed principles is flexibility. They truly lead the abundant life.

President David O. McKay taught, "Spirituality impels one to conquer difficulties, a leaning into life not away from it." (*Treasures of Life*, Deseret Book Co., 1962, page 447.) After all, for our dispensation it all began with a courageous boy in a quiet grove of trees.

8. THEY ARE SYNERGISTIC

We have mentioned synergy previously — the state in which the whole is more than the sum of the parts. Divinely centered people are synergistic. They are change catalysts. They improve almost any situation they get into. They work as smart as they work hard. They are amazingly productive, but in new and creative ways.

In team endeavors they build on their strengths and strive to complement their weaknesses with the strengths of others. Delegation for results is easy and natural to them, since they believe in others' strengths and capacities and, not being threatened by the fact that others are better in some ways, feel no need to hoveringly supervise.

When the divinely centered negotiate and communicate with others in seemingly adversarial situations, they don't see it this way. They learn to separate the people from the problem being discussed. They focus on people's interests and concerns rather than fight over positions. Gradually others discover their sincerity and become part of a creative problem-solving process, and the solutions which come out of these interactions are usually far better than either of the originally proposed solutions. They are not compromise solutions wherein both parties give a little and take a little, but they are synergistic solutions wherein they arrive at a solution far better for both parties than either had thought of initially.

Again, the Savior is their model, because wherever there are yielding, believing hearts he produces synergistic solutions to problems. And of course, when we consider the great infinite atoning sacrifice, the eternal synergy flowing from that for every human soul that ever lived is beyond compare. It guarantees immortality for all and eternal life for the obedient.

> Look unto me in every thought; doubt not, fear not.
> Behold the wounds which pierced my side, and also the prints of the nails in my hands and feet; be faithful, keep my commandments, and ye shall inherit the kingdom of heaven. (D&C 6:36-37.)

BASIC EXERCISES FOR SELF-RENEWAL

Finally, I strongly urge the development of one basic habit. In my opinion, it is the single most beneficial discipline or habit in life. It is the habit of regularly exercising the four dimensions of the human personality: physical, mental, emotional, and spiritual.

Physical exercise essentially means exactly that—some kind of balanced, moderate, systematic, regular program of aerobic exercise, meaning cardiovascular exercise (using large leg muscles) so that the heart and lungs are stressed sufficiently to improve the capacity of our bodies and brains to utilize oxygen. This gives endurance along with many other physical and mental benefits. Also valuable are stretching exercises for flexibility and resistance exercises for strength and muscle tone. It is important, of course, that before you embark on such a program you check with your doctor.

For the other three kinds of exercising, there is no need to check with anyone. We exercise our minds through reading, creative problem-solving, writing, and visualizing. Emotionally, we exercise ourselves through learning to be patient, to listen to others with genuine empathy, and to accept responsibility for our own lives and decisions and reactions, and by giving unconditional love to others. Spiritually, we focus on the four classical descriptions spoken about a great deal throughout this book: prayer, scripture study, meditation, and fasting.

My experience and conviction is that if a person will spend a minimum of one hour a day in total on these basic exercises, it will improve the quality, the productivity, and the satisfaction of every other hour of the day, including the depth and restfulness of sleep. Some of these things are done in the normal course of activities throughout the day and take no additional time whatsoever. The others will take time initially but in the long run will save time—a great deal of time. We must never get too busy sawing to take time to sharpen the saw, too busy driving to take time to get gas.

It is constantly instructive, almost amazing to me, to see the results coming from people who take a balanced, systematic, regular approach to sharpening the saw, that is, exercising these four dimensions of the human personality. If a person, particularly one filled with self-doubts and loaded with problems, will commit to do this on a regular basis and keep that one commitment, the impact for good on his life will in my opinion be greater than that of any one other beginning thing he could do.

For myself, I enjoy running or bicycling, then making a prayerful, meditative study of the scriptures, then carefully planning, visualizing, spiritually creating the day under the influence of that spirit. I find that if I do this regularly early in the morning, it is like a private victory and just about guarantees public victories throughout the day. If I take the course of least resistance and neglect all or part of this program, I have lost that private victory and find myself uprooted under the pressures and stresses in the public arena throughout that day. I don't think morning time is sacred in this respect, however, and I don't think all these exercises necessarily need to be done together. Basically, I am trying to teach a principle rather than a practice, the principle being the habit of self-renewal combined with the habit of making and keeping a promise. It is clear to me that gradually, little by little, under the influence of the Spirit, this will produce a strong and healthy divinely centered character with a powerfully disciplined, service-focused will.

A PERSONAL NOTE

I feel that at the conclusion to this book I should add a personal note, more or less to set the record straight. A natural question in the reader's mind might be, "Does he do what he is telling us we ought to do? Does he practice what he preaches?" It is a fair question, and I will answer it honestly.

This book has been difficult to write because of the personal spiritual challenge it represents. Do I do all these things I recommend? I answer honestly that often I do not. But I also must honestly respond that I try, I continually strive to do so. Should we allow personal inadequacies and faults to prevent us from passing on learnings and convictions we have been blessed with? On that point I was encouraged by the statement Elder Spencer W. Kimball (then a member of the Council of the Twelve) wrote in the preface to his book *The Miracle of Forgiveness:*

Likewise in writing about sin and repentance, no intent is implied that either the writer or any of those quoted, except the Lord himself, is without fault. But we would not have much motivation to righteousness if all speakers and writers postponed discussing and warning until they themselves were perfected!

On this basis I decided to write the book.

As I review my life, I conclude that at one time or another I have experienced just about every center described in this book. Much of my life I have been either Church- or family-centered, and I have experienced many of the consequences of that centering described in these pages. I also have had some powerful and sacred experiences that have helped and inspired me to be more God/Christ-centered, thus enabling me to be more effective in my family and Church stewardships and in everything else in life.

Nevertheless, I want to acknowledge that living the gospel is for me a constant struggle. And frankly that very struggle is the main source of my most valuable learnings. As I "look in" on myself in the middle of life's processes I discover common chords that resonate with those of others. I believe there is a most provocative insight in the statement, "That which is most personal is most general." "Keep thy heart with all diligence," said the writer of Proverbs, "for out of it are the issues of life." (Proverbs 4:23.) For all of us, I feel, the struggle is eminently worthwhile, for we are told, "The best gifts . . . are given for the benefit of those who love me and keep all my commandments, *and him that seeketh so to do.*" (D&C 46:9; italics added.)

I am sobered and challenged also by this magnificent insight:

> Moral truth can be conceived in thought. One can have feelings about it. One can will to live it. But moral truth may have been penetrated and possessed in all these ways, and escape us still. Deeper even than consciousness there is our being itself—our very substance, our nature. Only those truths which have entered into this last region, which have become ourselves, become spontaneous and involuntary as well as voluntary, unconscious as well as conscious, are really our life—that is to say, something more than property. So long as we are able to distinguish any space whatever between Truth and us we remain outside it. The thought, the

feeling, the desire or the consciousness of life may not be quite life. To become divine is then the aim of life. Then only can truth be said to be ours beyond the possibility of loss. It is no longer outside us, nor in a sense even in us, but we are it, and it is we. (From Amiel's Journal, as quoted by Lewis Dunnighton, *Keys to Richer Living*, Macmillan Company, New York, 1952, page 131.)

I am deeply grateful for the principle of repentance, for the opportunity to partake of the sacrament every week, to pray every day and to renew my covenants frequently, to apologize to those I have offended, and to study the scriptures so as to regain a vision and sense of what life is about and who I really am and who my Heavenly Father is and who his beloved Son, my Savior, is. As trite as the expression is, words are completely inadequate to express the depth and extent of my feelings on this matter.

I have been blessed to be surrounded with good influences. Outside of my wife and children, my parents and my three sisters and brother, the individuals who have most influenced my life for good are Presidents David O. McKay, Spencer W. Kimball, Stephen L Richards, and N. Eldon Tanner, Elder Mark E. Petersen, and my mission president, A. Hamer Reiser. The most powerful scriptures in my life have been the Gospel of John, the epistles of Paul and Peter, the Book of Mormon, and the Doctrine and Covenants.

I testify that I know that God lives, that Jesus is the Christ, that Joseph Smith was the restoring prophet, that The Church of Jesus Christ of Latter-day Saints is God's kingdom on earth. And I testify that the divinely centered life is the only abundant one and is the life God would have us live.

Index